Children with Disabilities
in America

Recent Titles in
Children and Youth: History and Culture
Miriam Forman-Brunell, Series Editor

Children and Youth in Sickness and in Health: A Historical Handbook and Guide
Janet Golden, Richard A. Meckel, and Heather Munro Prescott

Asian American Children: A Historical Handbook and Guide
Benson Tong, editor

Children and Youth in Adoption, Orphanages, and Foster Care: A Historical Handbook and Guide
Lori Askeland, editor

Children with Disabilities in America

A Historical Handbook and Guide

Edited by Philip L. Safford and
Elizabeth J. Safford

Children and Youth: History and Culture
Miriam Forman-Brunell, Series Editor

GREENWOOD PRESS
Westport, Connecticut • London

KH

Library of Congress Cataloging-in-Publication Data

Children with disabilities in America : a historical handbook and guide / edited by
Philip L. Safford and Elizabeth J. Safford.
     p. cm.—(Children and youth: history and culture, ISSN 1546–6752)
   Includes bibliographical references and index.
   ISBN 0–313–33146–4 (alk. paper)
   1. Children with disabilities—United States—History. 2. Children with disabilities—
United States—Education—History. 3. Children with disabilities—United States—
Handbooks, manuals, etc. I. Safford, Philip L. II. Safford, Elizabeth J., 1958– III.
Series: Children and youth (Westport, Conn.)
HV888.5.D57 2006
362.4083'0973—dc22   2005025480

British Library Cataloguing in Publication Data is available.

Library of Congress Catalog Card Number: 2005025480
ISBN: 0–313–33146–4
ISSN: 1546–6752

First published in 2006

Greenwood Press, 88 Post Road West, Westport, CT 06881
An imprint of Greenwood Publishing Group, Inc.
www.greenwood.com

Printed in the United States of America

The paper used in this book complies with the
Permanent Paper Standard issued by the National
Information Standards Organization (Z39.48–1984).

10 9 8 7 6 5 4 3 2 1

3\16\07

Contents

Series Foreword

Pocahontas, a legendary figure in American history, was just a preadolescent when she challenged two cultures at odds to cooperate instead of to compete. While Pocahontas forged peace, many more now forgotten Native American, Anglo-American, African American, and other children contributed to their families' survival, communities' development, and America's history in just as legitimate, though perhaps less legendary ways. Contracts and correspondence from colonial Chesapeake reveal that even seventeenth-century toddlers labored. But the historical agency of the vast majority of children and adolescents has been undervalued and overlooked in dominant historical narratives. Instead, generations of Americans have credited fathers and other hoary leaders for their actions and achievements, all the while disregarding pivotal boyhood experiences that shaped skills and ideals. Reflecting these androcentric, Eurocentric, and age-based biases that have framed the nation's history, American history texts have reinforced the historical invisibility of girls and boys for centuries. For students searching libraries for scholarly sources and primary documents about children and adolescents in various historical contexts, this near absence of information in master narratives has vexed their research.

The absence of children in standard history books has not only obscured children's history but also the work of scholars who have been investigating youth's histories and interrogating their cultures since the turn of the last century. A new curiosity about children in times past was generated by the progressive era agenda which sought to educate, acculturate, and elevate American children through child study and child welfare. In *Child Life in Colonial Days* (1899), "amateur historian" Alice Morse Earl drew upon archival sources and material culture in order to examine the social history of Puritan girls and boys. Children were also included in Arthur W. Calhoun's *A Social History of the American Family* (1917) and in Edmund S. Morgan's *The Puritan Family: Religion and Domestic Relations in Seventeenth Century New England* (1944), but few other professional historians within the male-dominated profession considered children worthy of study. Those children who made appearances in historical accounts were typically the privileged daughters and sons of white men of means and might.

In the 1960s, larger social, cultural, and political transformations refocused scholarly attention. The influence of sixties' youth culture and second wave feminism and renewed interest in the agency of "ordinary people," youth in particular, laid the foundation for a "new" social history. The confluence of a renewed interest in youth and the development of new methodological approaches led French demographer and social historian Philippe Ariès to study a nation's youngest population. Challenging a dominant assumption that childhood was transhistorical in *Centuries of Childhood: A Social History of Family Life* (1962), Ariès argued that over time, changing cultures and societies redefined notions of childhood and transformed children's experiences. Ariès' work on European children was soon followed by Bernard Wishy's *The Child and the Republic: The Dawn of American Child Nurture* (1968), which explored the changing nature of child rearing advice in the United States.

Despite important inroads made by these and other scholars (e.g., Robert Bremner), the history of childhood became embedded within historical sub fields during the 1970s. The history of childhood was briefly associated with psychohistory due to the controversial work of Lloyd deMause, who founded *The History of Childhood Quarterly*. It was largely historians of the family (e.g., John Demos, Philip Greven Jr.) and those in the history of education (who refocused attention away from the school and onto the student) who broke new ground. Essays appeared in scholarly journals in the 1970s but were not reprinted until the following decade when *Growing Up in America: Children in Historical Perspective* (1985) brought new visibility to the "vitality and scope of this emerging field" (preface). That important collection edited by historians Joseph M. Hawes and N. Ray Hiner, along with their *American Childhood: A Research Guide and Historical Handbook* (1985), served to promote research among an up-and-coming generation of historians whose work would be included in another path-breaking anthology. By placing children at the center of historical inquiry, privileging gender as a critical factor in childhood socialization, and expanding social history to include cultural history, historians in *Small Worlds: Children and Adolescents in America, 1850–1950* (1992) demonstrated that the relationships between childhood and adulthood and kids and culture were historically significant. By privileging previously overlooked and disregarded historical sources, "reading" material culture artifacts as historical texts, and applying gender, race, and class analyses to an age-based one, these historians continued to the mapping of childhood's terrain. Creatively and methodically, they traced childhood ideals and children's experiences within cultures and over centuries.

In the early to mid 1990s, those in the fields of psychology and education initiated a scholarly debate about the dangers that popular culture posed to the healthy development of female adolescents in contemporary America. Those scholars influenced by a different scholarly trajectory—cultural studies and feminist theory—saw agency instead, illuminating the many ways in which girls and female adolescents (as other youth) resist, contest, subvert, and reappropriate dominant cultural forms. Moreover, scholars such as Kimberly Roberts brought to light the discursive nature of the contemporary "girl crisis" debate just as others have uncovered numerous other discourses that create, reflect, and reinforce the cultural norms of girlhood, boyhood, female and male adolescence. Trained in fields other than history (e.g., American Studies, communications studies, English, Rhetoric and Composition), the latest generation of scholars has blurred the boundaries and forged new fields. Informed by the work of cultural studies scholar Angela McRobbie, "girls' culture" aimed to balance the boy-centered biases of the older "youth studies." Nevertheless, such late-twentieth-century anthologies as *The Children's Culture Reader* (1998), *Delinquents & Debutantes: Twentieth-Century American Girls' Cultures* (1998) and *Generations of Youth: Youth Cultures and History in Twentieth-Century America* (1998) reflect a new multi- and inter-disciplinarity in the study of children and youth that utilizes textual and representational analyses (as opposed to social history) to study the subcultures that children and youth have constructed within larger historical contexts. By developing new methods of inquiry and widening subjects of study, scholars have been able to examine "lived experiences" and "subjectivities," though most of the recent work focuses on teenagers in the twentieth century.

Today, there is an abundance of scholarly works (e.g., monographs, anthologies, and encyclopedias), book series on children (e.g., The Girls' History & Culture Series), national, regional, and local conferences, major academic journals, and in 2000 the Society for the History of Children and Youth was finally founded by two of the field's pioneers, Joseph M. Hawes and N. Ray Hiner. That professional organization draws together the many college and university professors who teach courses on the history of children and youth, girlhood and female adolescence regularly offered in schools of education, departments of history, psychology, political science, sociology, and in programs on Women's Studies, Media/Communications Studies, and American Studies. But the history of children and adolescents has an even broader audience as media attention on bad boys and mean girls (e.g., "Queenbees") generates new questions and a search for answers in historical antecedents.

To meet the research needs of students of all ages, this accessibly written work—as the others in the series—surveys and synthesizes a century of scholarship on children and adolescents of different classes, races, genders, regions, religions, sexualities, and abilities. Some topics in the series have a gendered, racial, or regional focus while others (e.g., sickness and health, work and play, etc.) utilize a larger multicultural perspective. Whichever their focus, every book is organized into three equal parts to provide researchers with immediate access to historical overviews, primary source documents, and scholarly sources. Part I consists of synthetic essays written by experts in the field whose surveys are chronological and contextual. Part II provides access to hard-to-find primary source documents, in part or whole. Explanatory head notes illuminate themes, generate further understanding, and expedite inquiry. Part III is an extensive up-to-date bibliography of cited sources as well as those critical for further research.

The goal of the Children and Youth: History and Culture reference book series is not simply a utilitarian one but also to ultimately situate girls and boys of all ages more centrally in dominant historical narratives.

Miriam Forman-Brunell, Series Editor
University of Missouri, Kansas City

Preface

For persons with differences associated with disabilities, and also for children, history has not followed a uniformly positive trajectory, despite the many quite apparent evidences of progress. Childhood diseases that once caused permanent deafness, blindness, other physical impairment, or mental impairment have been virtually conquered, at least in the United States and other industrialized nations. Yet, there is presently national concern about, and frantic effort to understand, the current "epidemic" of a condition until recently unknown to most people, and formerly believed to be quite rare: autism spectrum disorder. Children in the United States are no longer routinely exposed to maiming or toxic conditions in mines, mills, and the marketplace. Yet, American children regularly incur permanent physical, mental, and emotional crippling as a result of being shaken, sexually brutalized, or exposed to prenatal toxic influences in the form of drugs or alcohol, or to developmental toxic influences in the form of exposure to violence.

African American and other minority children with sensory impairment are no longer purposefully schooled, if at all, under separate and manifestly unequal conditions. Yet, African American, Hispanic, and Native American students continue to be disproportionately labeled as cognitively or emotionally "special" and educated in separate sites. Children and youth who in earlier times would have been considered unable to learn are now provided an individualized free, appropriate, public education, including a Transition Plan for entry into adult life, and are protected from discrimination based on their disability. Yet, a greater proportion of students with disabilities than of students without leave school before completion, only to join the ranks of the underemployed or unemployed.

In one significant respect, however, recent decades have brought major positive changes for children and adults, with disabilities: through the disability rights movement, they have a voice. Evidence that that voice is heard, and the agency of persons with disabilities is a reality, has been present in a succession of federal and state laws; leadership in successful school inclusion efforts; and the success of the "Deaf President Now!" protest by Gallaudet University students and faculty, which resonated throughout the Deaf community and throughout the world.

Like much other historical inquiry, this book was undertaken in part to consider what the lessons of history might teach as families, service providers, policy makers, and most especially individuals with disabilities meet present challenges and plan for the future. Also, consistent with the series of which the book is a part, its additional purpose is to model and motivate historical inquiry on the part of students concerning American childhood and children—in this case, children who have experienced disabilities.

Toward that end, it is intended to inform and provide resources for readers—whether students, practicing professionals, scholars, or interested laypersons—concerning a promising yet neglected focus of inquiry: the intersection of the fields of childhood studies and disability studies. Accordingly, the book is intended to synthesize current knowledge about children's experience of physical, cognitive, and social-emotional impairments over the course of American history; examine the social constructions of both disability and childhood as they have changed over time; and stimulate and support inquiry concerning children's experience of, and societal response to, differences associated with disability.

To address these aims, this book, like others in the Children and Youth: History and Culture series, is divided into three sections. Part I comprises essays pursuing unique histories associated, respectively, with deafness and with visual, neuromotor or orthopedic, cognitive, and social-emotional disability. Part II comprises selected, representative primary source documents or other materials, such as interview transcripts. Part III is intended to serve as a comprehensive, topically organized bibliography to assist with historical inquiry in this field, complemented by electronic media access information.

Each of the five essays in Part I reflects use of a variety of methods of inquiry consistent with the goal of accessing experiences of children and youth with disabilities as expressed through their own voices. However, while the historical record is replete with annual reports by school directors, speeches by officials and advocates, and texts and journal articles by experts, it is not as easy to hear the voices of children themselves. The essayists have confronted this challenge in a variety of ways, such as locating "insiders'" accounts wherever possible, asking living adolescents and adults to recall their childhood experiences, and considering images present in literature and other media.

Robertta Thoryk, Angela Battistone-Potosky, and Fred Palchik invoke the voices of African American, Native American, Hispanic, and Asian children who are deaf to illustrate a key point: to posit a unified "d/Deaf Experience" is to indulge in a myth. (As they explain, the lower case/upper case construction is employed to distinguish the physical condition of hearing loss from membership in a distinct cultural group, unified by a distinctive history and a common language, which in North America is American Sign Language.) As they describe, that myth is compounded by another: that the events and issues that have impinged upon the lives of all children in America at any particular historical moment have not also affected the lives of d/Deaf children. An especially striking instance of the latter that they describe was the eugenics movement, which in the United States emphasized "negative eugenics," in combination with a xenophobic attack on "differentness," including that of a linguistic minority—the signing community. While education of d/Deaf children has undergone many changes, the authors show that these—from day classes to the current Inclusion movement—have not necessarily affected d/Deaf children positively.

The essay by Carol Linsenmeier and Jeff Moyer similarly invokes the voices of African American and Native American children, while also raising the spectre of a return to the "negative eugenics" era. In the course of their inquiry, the authors obtained oral histories that tended to confirm much of what the historical record had suggested about children's experiences associated with visual disability over time. Moreover, the voices of persons they interviewed consistently evidenced the universality of issues associated with the work of growing up, rather than the "otherness" of difference.

Brad Byrom's essay locates a critical turning point in the history of children (and also adults) who were called "crippled" at a time in American history coterminous with an extraordinarily significant, and arguably uniquely American, movement: Progressivism. The author's intent was to understand why progressives became so concerned about physical disability in the early twentieth century and how the progressive values of science, efficiency, and expertise influenced their proactive, yet ambivalent, response.

Elizabeth Brennan's essay reminds readers in a host of ways of three crucial points: First, the experiences of children who have had—or have been considered to have—significant cognitive disabilities occur in family, social, and educational contexts. Second, these children are, first of all, children. And third, like other children, they do not remain so, but instead hopefully find, and follow, "the road to self-determination" as fulfilled and productive adults. While the voices of children with cognitive disability express hope, a look at history reveals that the range of obstacles with which they and their families have been faced has included social isolation, forced segregation, exclusion, and deprivation of opportunity to learn, and—once again—"negative eugenics," operationalized by the 1930s in the form of mandatory sterilization laws in nearly all states.

The chapter on children considered "different, difficult, or disturbed," by Philip Safford and Elizabeth Safford, is intended as an essay about "blaming the victim" and the social construction of behavioral deviance. It is a revealing historical curiosity that the first special classes in America's public schools were created for students who "didn't fit" and were labeled "unruly." That is revealing because throughout the nation's history, policies concerning and provisions for a significant number of American children reflect the dual aim of protecting society while ostensibly providing "special" help for the child. On the other hand, Beech Brook's story reveals continuity of a basic, child-serving mission in the face of transition from orphanage to treatment facility. As a variety of "new" disabilities are increasingly understood not to be caused by contrariness or bad parenting, and found amenable to positive intervention, "troubled and troubling" children will hopefully be understood rather than blamed, helped rather than punished, and included rather than stigmatized.

The documents, transcripts, and other items selected for inclusion in Part II are intended to be representative of the sources available for historical inquiry. In light of the overall intent for this book, two other criteria were applied in selecting items to be included: (1) specific relevance to the history of children with disabilities in America, and (2) insofar as possible, information and insight concerning how children experienced disability.

The same criteria were applied in selecting the bibliographic and electronic media resources for inclusion in Part III, which appropriately begins with selected citations of works of autobiograpy, biography, fiction, and drama addressing the experience of disability. Also, many biographical accounts of nondisabled educators, physicians, and reformers provide essential information and insight concerning the history of children with disabilities in America.

While regrettably little attention has until recently been explicitly focused on this area, a vast array of sources are available that bear on one's understanding of the history of American childhood and disability. Accordingly, a section of the bibliography consists of texts, key articles or papers, or other writing addressing disabilities through the admittedly arbitrary device of "classification" or "category" subsections. These are preceded by a subsection comprising sources that address key issues that have affected children with disabilities, such as "negative eugenics," labeling, families, early intervention, organization of special education, and inclusion. Finally, a listing of web addresses is provided to guide the reader in accessing informational resources concerning disability studies, children's literature and disability, and organizations and agencies important to persons with disabilities and their families and advocates, as well as students.

ACKNOWLEDGMENTS

The essays and documents in this book concern a very diverse group of children and youth, a "group" having in common only their differentness—differentness, that is, from whatever a particular society might consider normative at any particular time. Each contributing author or authorial team has undertaken the daunting task of tracing over time the experiences of children identified by a common "difference," yet who are themselves as diverse as any sample drawn at random from the pool represented by four centuries of American childhood. Moreover, each essay represents a sincere attempt to provide a medium for the expression of those experiences by the children and youth themselves, a task made especially formidable by the fact that those voices have not often been heard. We thank, and honor, our colleagues for responding to this dual challenge with sensitivity, conscientiousness, and creativity.

The contributors, including ourselves, also express gratitude to those who helped them with their inquiry, whether through suggesting sources of information, permitting access to archives and providing guidance in their use, locating and forwarding documents, or recounting personal narratives. While those who deserve thanks are too numerous to mention, persons who provided especially invaluable assistance with specific essays and resource documents are acknowledged in the respective chapters.

We, as editors of this volume, also extend our particular gratitude for the guidance and encouragement provided by Professor Miriam Forman-Brunell, editor of the Children and Youth: History and Culture series of which this book is a part, and to Marie Ellen Larcada, Senior Acquisitions Editor for Greenwood Press.

Finally, we can with confidence speak for our fellow contributors in expressing our admiration for our fellow Americans whose childhood was experienced with the added challenge of being—or being considered—"different."

Philip L. Safford, Cleveland, Ohio
Elizabeth J. Safford, Stoneham, Massachusetts

I Essays

1 Multilingual, Multicultural, Multitalented: The History of a Diverse People

Robertta Thoryk, Angela Battistone-Potosky, and Fred Palchik

INTRODUCTION: *WHOSE* d/DEAF EXPERIENCE?

The charge to this book's contributing authors was to describe the experience, over time, of American children and youth with "conditions" associated with exceptionality. The actual task, however, was less straightforward: to represent the "d/Deaf experience"[1] in a single chapter. How can one chapter reflect the experience of culturally Deaf and audiologically deaf children; mildly hearing-impaired versus profoundly deaf or later-deafened versus born-deaf children; Alaskan and New York d/Deaf children; Native American, African American, Asian and Pacific Rim American, Latino/a, and European American d/Deaf children; dual-diagnosed and multiply-disabled d/Deaf children; male and female d/Deaf children; signing versus oral Deaf children; day-class versus residential school versus inclusion/mainstreamed d/Deaf children; children with cochlear implants? Educators often employ the term "hearing-impaired," a term many d/Deaf people dislike. While the authors recognize that diverse labels reflect various preferences, the term "d/Deaf" will generally be used here.

The three authors themselves, while all d/Deaf, reflect considerable diversity. Two are female; one is male. One is a first and one a second generation American; both sets of parents spoke languages other than English. One attended a regional, oral day program and transferred to a state res-

The authors wish to thank Gary E. Wait, Archivist, American School for the Deaf, Mary Guyette and Donna Meehan, Clarke School for the Deaf, and John Curtis Bechnold, Jr.

1. Individuals who identify themselves with a culture, defined by valuing American Sign Language and visual experience, tend to represent themselves by an uppercase "D," while audiological deafness is referenced with a lowercase "d."

idential program that used American Sign Language (ASL) prior to attending Gallaudet University, the world's only liberal arts university for d/Deaf students, where all classes are taught in sign. Another was enrolled in public, regional, oral day programs before attending the National Technical Institute for the Deaf at Rochester Institute of Technology, then transferring to a community college. The third began signing in her parochial elementary school, attended public high school, and graduated from college, ultimately earning a Ph.D. Two of the authors attended middle and high school *after* the Education for the Handicapped Act (EHA) was enacted in 1975; the other *graduated* in 1975. We therefore make no claim to represent THE singular d/Deaf experience.

Besides the challenge of attempting to trace a mythical, composite history, the authors were challenged by another myth—that there is a separate "d/Deaf" educational history. The history of education itself is inseparable from that of the society that generates educational policies, and equally the history of "d/Deaf" education is inseparable from that of non-deaf children and of the majority culture. When schools have been faced with staff shortages, funding problems, or such philosophical conflicts as assimilation versus individuality or allegations of a "hidden curriculum," the education of d/Deaf children has felt the impact of those same issues, sometimes more strongly. Similarly, when schools have been affected by changes in the employment market, violence in the community, or terrorism on the news, the education of d/Deaf children has also been impacted. African American d/Deaf children after the Civil War, d/Deaf descendents of Asian ancestors during World War II, and d/Deaf females have experienced *at least* the same biases and prejudice as their h/Hearing counterparts, and d/Deaf children died from influenza epidemics and caught polio just like those who could hear. The history of d/Deaf children, then, is inseparable from the history of America.

EARLY AMERICA

While loss of hearing acuity, in colonial times as now, was associated with aging, there were certainly children whose deafness was recognized as one of the frailties to which human beings were subject, or whose deafness was mistaken for dullness or contrariness. However, early accounts of "the d/Deaf experience" are generally accounts of the work of their teachers. Thus, the historical record provides little information about American children's experience of deafness until the point at which the story of American d/Deaf education conventionally begins: early in the nineteenth century, with British Isles descendants on the east coast. At the same time those children were being educated, there were Native American deaf children whose deafness was often a result of the introduction of European illnesses, for Europeans not only brought d/Deaf education to American, they also brought deafness, or rather surely increased its prevalence in the New World. Their history was never recorded.

The earliest accounts of European deaf children are also accounts of the attempt to teach them, and specifically to teach them to use speech, long assumed to be essential to educability. This project had its origins in the reported success of a sixteenth-century Spanish Benedictine monk, one Pedro Ponce de Leon, in teaching "children of great nobles . . . to speak, to read, to write, and to keep accounts" so they would be eligible to inherit and manage family estates (De Carlo 1964, p. 12). What methods he employed to accomplish this "amazing feat" remained a mystery, although he may have been familiar with an account by a fifteenth-century humanistic educator, Rodolphus Agricola, of a congenitally deaf man who had reportedly learned to read and write expertly, previously thought to be impossible. It was a successful young deaf courtier named Luis, also taught by a Benedectine, who indirectly influenced the spread of "oral education" of the deaf to the British Isles in the seventeenth century, when a visiting dignitary, Sir Kenelm Digby, conveyed Luis' story to fascinated countrymen (Bender 1970). And it was to the oral schools of Great Britain, founded by Thomas Braidwood and by then world famous, that a well-to-do American family with English roots would turn more than a century later for help for their deaf children.

THE NINETEENTH CENTURY: THE GOLDEN AGE

The century did not begin as a "Golden Age" for d/Deaf children. As for most Americans, life was hard and, for most children, dangerous, especially with the threat of often fatal infection, exacerbated by lack of sanitation and by poor personal hygiene (O'Rourke 1994). Many children who survived childhood carried sequelae of scarlet fever and other infectious diseases, which often included deafness. While adults who became deaf after establishing a trade might retain their clients, the fate of children who became deaf early in life was heavily influenced by economic status. Children—usually sons—of wealthy families might be sent to the Braidwood School in England or to schools in Spain or, later, Germany to be educated; those less fortunate were part of "a dependent class . . . that included . . . orphans, widows, aged, blind, infirm, and insane" (Valentine 1993, p. 69).

Preaching to the "unfortunates" in a New York City almshouse in 1811, the Reverend John Standford was frustrated by his inability, lacking a shared system of communication, to give religious training to several deaf children. His solution was to give each child a slate to write the names of objects, probably the first attempt in America to teach a group of deaf children. Similarly inspired by a growing concern for the religious education of deaf individuals, a survey in Connecticut in 1812 revealed that there were 84 deaf persons in the state, none of whom had received any education (ASD 1938). The following year, Colonel William Bolling of Virginia, whose family had a history of congenital deafness, arranged for his three deaf children to sail for England, where he had enrolled them in the Braidwood School. Later, pleased with their success, the Bolling family hired John Braidwood, brother of the school's director, to establish a private school in Virginia using the oral approach. The project was soon abandoned, as were subsequent efforts, owing to Braidwood's mismanagement (Gannon 1981).

The American School for the Deaf

After these abortive attempts, in 1815 a group of nine men led by Dr. Mason Fitch Cogswell, whose young daughter, Alice, was deaf following spinal meningitis, met in Hartford, Connecticut, to plan an actual school. To this end, they raised funds to send seminarian and Yale graduate Thomas Hopkins Gallaudet to England to study the Braidwood method. However, frustrated by the Braidwood family's secrecy and demands for money, Gallaudet went instead to study at the famed school in France founded in 1789 by Charles Michel, l'abbe de l'Epee. There he met Laurent Clerc, a Deaf teacher (and former student) in the Paris school, who agreed both to teach Gallaudet the "methodological system" of French signs (based on French syntax, a separate sign used for each word) and to accompany Gallaudet back to America (Lane 1984).

Upon their return, the Connecticut Asylum at Hartford for the Instruction of Deaf and Dumb Persons was incorporated in May, 1816, the nation's first permanent school for d/Deaf students. With the Connecticut General Assembly's appropriation of $5,000 for construction—the first instance of state aid for special education in the United States—the Connecticut Asylum opened in 1817 in Bennett's City Hotel, on Main Street in Hartford, with Alice Cogswell its first student, Gallaudet its first principal, and Clerc its first teacher. By the end of the year enrollment had reached thirty-three, and five years later the school relocated to a new building on Asylum Hill where it remained for a century. In 1922 "The Old Hartford School" moved to West Hartford, its present location; housing both a lower and upper school in eight main buildings, it is known as The American School for the Deaf (ASD 1938; History through Deaf Eyes).

Religious Ties

The American School for the Deaf (ASD) was established as a Congregationalist school, with students expected to stay for a period of five years (Groce 1985). Instruction was originally in sign, but eventually three forms of communication were used: American Sign Language (ASL), written English, and fingerspelling (Lane 1984). From the beginning its two main goals were to teach *language*, as distinct from speech, to enable access to general learning, and religious values and concepts to provide both a means to salvation and a foundation for appropriate behavior. Laurent Clerc (in Lane 1984, p. 229) recalled, "The one subject that was not neglected was religion." Chapel attendance twice each weekday was required, as was catechism instruction on Saturdays and two services on Sunday (Valentine 1993).

In keeping with classical educational theories that viewed teaching as a matter of pouring information into receptive minds, submissive, unquestioning behavior was expected of students. Rather than physical punishment for misbehavior, "only moral suasion . . . submission to the will of authority gained through the affection of a child for his guardian . . . [was used to] produce happy, productive, and controlled students" (Valentine 1993, p. 62). Although such discipline might have been successful with younger students, many of the students who were first admitted were much older, rendering "moral suasion" less effective: in 1822, Gallaudet was alerted that several "boys" between ages 16 and 25 "were surreptitiously leaving school at night and returning intoxicated." When, despite Gallaudet's efforts, the offenses continued, several were expelled (Valentine 1993, p. 63).

ASD was not the only religiously-based school established in the nineteenth century. In 1838, two Sisters of Saint Joseph founded the nation's first Catholic school for the deaf, the Maria Concillia Deaf Mute Institution in St. Louis. In 1859, the same order founded St. Mary's School for the Deaf in Buffalo. St. Joseph's School opened in New York City in 1869, and St. John's School opened near Milwaukee in 1876, followed shortly by six other Catholic schools for the deaf. Among Protestant denominations, the Lutheran Church of the Missouri Synod in 1874 converted its orphanage in Detroit into the German Evangelical Lutheran Deaf Mute Institution (Gannon 1981).

Religious connections continued well into the twentieth century, as at the Indiana School for the Deaf, where during the 1930s Monday morning chapel was compulsory (Reis 1993), although religiously based discipline seemed no more effective than in Gallaudet's time. Mary Herring Wright (1999, p. 118), a student at the North Carolina School for Black Deaf and Blind Children during the 1930s recalled, "Miss Laws proved to be a very nice teacher. She was also a missionary for her church. Most of the time, instead of punishing the children, she tried to tell them of Jesus to get them to behave. . . . They tolerated her and watched her sign without any comment or expression, then went right back to whatever they had been doing."

Growth During the 1800s and a Changing Student Population

The American School for the Deaf set four important precedents that influenced the course set by facilities established in the decades that followed. It was a residential school that drew from a large area; received private, state, and federal funding; employed sign language as the main communication method; and had many d/Deaf instructors (Van Cleve & Crouch 1989). As was the case with schools that were established subsequently, the ages of ASD's early students, nearly all of whom had hearing parents, ranged from ten to fifty, with most in their twenties (Lane 1984). Originally intended to serve all the eastern states, ASD by 1819 had students from ten states from Maine to Georgia, although New York had opened its own school in 1818 with four students in the almshouse where Standford had preached. However, the greatest sources of early ASD students were Martha's Vineyard and Maine's Sandy River area, the latter heavily populated by families with patterns of hereditary deafness who had emigrated from Martha's Vineyard (Groce 1985).

Many ASD graduates traveled to new territories in the opening West, establishing schools and founding Deaf publications and organizations, creating "a true society of the deaf . . . with a single language" and causing the early to mid nineteenth century to be called the "Golden Age" (Lane 1984, p. 238). As the nation moved westward, so did the establishment of schools for the d/Deaf. A school opened in Pennsylvania in 1820, another in Danville, Kentucky, in 1823, the latter initially serving all southern states except Florida and territories as far west as Montana, a mission proving as impracticable as had that envisioned for ASD. With funding provided by the legislature, the Kentucky Asylum for the Tuition of the Deaf and Dumb became the first state-supported school for the d/Deaf. Tuition support was originally limited to twenty-five students, for a stay limited to three years, but by 1854 all students thirteen or younger were supported until they reached age twenty-one (Rich History 1998).

While the Pennsylvania and Kentucky schools were being established, a private school for the d/Deaf opened in Tallmadge, Ohio, succeeded in 1829 by the Ohio School for the Deaf in Columbus. With no reliance on private tuition, this was the first school to affirm the state's responsibility to fund the entire cost of education for deaf students—and the first instance of Free Appropriate Public Education as set forth in 1975 in the EHA (reauthorized in 1990 as the Individuals with Disabilities Education Act). The Ohio school subsequently produced principals and teachers for schools in Indiana, Illinois, and Tennessee.

In 1836, the Georgia School for the Deaf, Dumb, and Indigent was established; Georgia by 1842 was no longer compelled to send students out of state (Childers 2003). The Texas Deaf and Dumb Asylum in Austin opened with three students in a two-room cottage, three log cabins, and an old smokehouse in 1856, while the twenty-three ladies of the Society for the Instruction and Maintenance of the Indigent Deaf and Dumb and Blind opened the California Institution for the Deaf and Blind in San Francisco in 1860, with three students in a rented home (Norton 2000). In the late

1850s, Amos Kendall founded the Columbia Institution for the Instruction of the Deaf and Dumb and the Blind, in Washington, D.C., for twelve deaf and six blind students. It became the first to be able to confer college degrees in 1864, when Abraham Lincoln signed the charter for what would become Gallaudet University (History of Kendall Demonstration Elementary School).

By the 1850s, there were twenty schools for d/Deaf students in the United States; by 1900, after Lars M. Larson and his wife, Isabelle Porter, both of whom were d/Deaf, opened the New Mexico School for the Deaf in Santa Fe (Paris & Wood 2002), there were fifty. By this time, many changes were already occurring, both in student demographics and in the viewpoints of some administrators. At ASD during Gallaudet's tenure, social difference had not been an issue: the 1817 and 1818 classes were filled with students whose parents could afford hefty annual tuition fees of $200.00 plus traveling expenses. Charity students were not a majority until after 1828, when the New England states agreed to provide public support. A change in the social mix occurred between 1817, when genteel children socialized with Gallaudet, and 1854, when Superintendent Turner, testifying in an 1853 court trial, stated that deaf pupils needed special guidance because of their feelings of inferiority and lack of enlightenment (Valentine 1993).

Another change was also in the air—a change in perspective as to the goals of deaf education and the role of language.

THE GREAT DEBATE AND THE "HUNDRED-YEARS WAR"

If throughout the "Golden Age" sign language was almost universally considered "indispensable" (Baynton 1993, p. 93), why did "oralism"—the exclusive use of the majority spoken language in instruction—reemerge as the new century approached? The so-called Hundred-Years War in the field of d/Deaf education was about more than teaching methodology; it was about culture, and for more than a century, in fact, many d/D persons have waged a quiet struggle against the suppression of their language and cultural identity. According to one account (in Paris & Wood 2002, p. 211), teachers at the New Mexico School "claimed to be practicing 'oralists' . . . and denied any use of sign whatsoever. Yet . . . a deaf principal, remembers with a grin that, behind the classroom doors, many of the so-called oralists used 'bootleg' sign language." In most oral schools, however, the matter was not treated lightly.

Increasing Dissension and the Emergence of Oral Schools

The Bolling family's hiring of John Braidwood had introduced the oralist movement to America, where it lay dormant for decades. However, even during the "Golden Age" educators disagreed about the *type* of sign to be used, one camp advocating use of "Natural Signs," which became American Sign Language (ASL), the other favoring "Methodological Signs," which used signed hand shapes to encode English, following English grammar rules, with a separate sign for each English word (Walworth, Moores, & O'Rourke 1992). ASL has its own syntactic and morphological rules that result in word formation, word order, and word modification that differ from English. In ASL, such linguistic concepts as pronominalization, verb tense, and modification involve facial expression, head position, direction of sign movement, eye gaze, and body position, rather than relying only on hand shape.

It was in this already divided setting that "a new generation campaigned to replace the use of sign language with the exclusive use of lipreading and speech" (Baynton 1993, p. 93). The New York Institution for the Improved Instruction of Deaf Mutes opened in 1867 as a purely oral school, using methods recently pioneered in Germany. The previous year, Harriet B. Rogers and Gardiner Greene Hubbard, president of what would become the Bell Telephone Company, founded the Chelmsford School in Massachusetts, whose five deaf pupils were taught via oral methods. The students' performance so impressed the Massachusetts Legislature that in 1867 the Clarke School for the Deaf in Northampton was chartered as the first permanent oral school in the United States (Clarke School—Historical Information). From that time on, oral instruction was the rule, as "Oralists charged that the use of sign language damaged the minds of deaf people, interfered with the ability of deaf children to learn English, and reduced the motivation of deaf students to undertake the . . . task of learning to communicate orally" (Baynton 1993, pp. 93–94).

Lane (1984) ascribes oralism's ascendancy to trends in the general society: the popularization of evolutionary theory; religious notions regarding expression of feelings and sensory experience; economics, since women teachers earned lower salaries; the rise of nationalism and need to define group membership through a national language; and parents' desire to have their children communicate in the parents' language. Publication of Darwin's *Origin of Species* in 1859 fanned the flame of the oralist movement by identifying spoken language with evolutionary advancement, and considering sign language inferior to even primitive spoken language systems (Baynton 1993).

Alexander Graham Bell, Evolutionary Theory, and Nationalism

The perception of sign as inferior fit well with growing feelings of nationalism and the felt need for a national language, and Alexander Graham Bell, who would later become even more famous as an inventor than as the leader of the oralist movement in d/Deaf education, stood firmly for both. He was convinced that Americans must have a common language "for the preservation of our national existence," (Burch 2002, p. 13). Similarly, "Bell's belief in evolutionary science and a hierarchy of evolutionary superiority . . . led to his supporting immigration restrictions, and restrictions on marriage and reproduction" (Lane 1984, p. 356). Like others who carried the banner of eugenics, he saw his mission as stopping, or at least slowing, the transmission of bad "germ plasm" responsible for problems like deafness, as well as insanity, retardation, pauperism, and criminality.

Bell's quest to strengthen the human race led him to study the inordinately high concentrations of deafness in areas of Martha's Vineyard, and in families of former Vineyarders, seemingly clear evidence of hereditary patterns. However, he could not account for the puzzling fact that the parents of children who had been born deaf were not usually deaf themselves; this would continue to puzzle hereditarians like Bell until Gregor Mendel's research explained recessive hereditary patterns. Notwithstanding his inability to find an explanation, Bell published articles, gave testimony, and in 1883 published his controversial *Memoir upon the Formation of a Deaf Variety of the Human Race.* Although his findings had shown that hearing parents may have deaf children and vice versa, he nevertheless warned that intramarriage would inevitably result in "a whole race or 'variety' of congenitally deaf people. . . . Eugenicists . . . relied heavily on Bell's data to persuade many deaf individuals in the United States not to marry. A number were sterilized, often against their knowledge or will" (Groce 1985, pp. 47–48).

Bell was also convinced that sign language was a major factor in intramarriage among deaf people, as well as a barrier to assimilation in the majority society; hence, he was outspoken in opposing the residential schools which had permitted and even encouraged signing (Bragg 2001). By the late 1800s, in no small measure due to Bell's influential voice, "focused attacks on deafness and Deaf culture intensified, nurtured by broader trends in America, including . . . eugenics and the Progressive movement," the latter with respect to its Social Darwinist assumptions (Burch 2002, p. 3). However, the attempt to assimilate deaf children with hearing peers was likely to result in humiliation. In 1877, Fredrick Knapp enrolled several deaf students in his Baltimore private school, an early instance of mainstreaming. Sign was forbidden, and students who appeared to be using their hands to sign were made to wear gloves as punishment (Gannon 1981). The conflict was heating up, but it was a conference an ocean away that set off "the hundred-years war of methods."

The 1880 Conference of Milan and the Spread of Oralism

Heated debated about oral versus manual methodology had occurred in previous conferences, but the issue was brought to a head at an interna-

tional conference in 1880 in Milan, Italy. In the context of growing nationalism, conflicts within and between emerging nations, evolutionary
theory, and eugenics, the Milan conference was the first to be "conceived
and conducted as a brief rally by and for opponents of manual language.
. . . The officers . . . location, organizers, exhibitions, and membership were
chosen to ensure the oralist outcome" (Lane 1984, p. 387). The sole d/
Deaf delegate, James Denison, was powerless to oppose the resolution that
was passed "disbarring the sign language of whatever the nation" (p. 394).
Effectively barred from the proceedings, d/D people from more than
twenty states met that year in Cincinnati in protest and to express support
for use of a "combined method." Although their opinions were disregarded, as education of American deaf students "entered into a dark age
that was to last for the better part of a century" (Walworth, Moores, &
O'Rourke 1992, p. xi), the meeting led to the formation of a major self-
advocacy force, the National Association of the Deaf.

As a result of the Milan Conference, male d/Deaf instructors virtually
vanished from schools within seven years, replaced by female teachers, a
markedly cheaper work force. Students' age at school entrance dropped,
since oral methods were felt to be more successful if begun as early as
possible. Because parents were less willing to be separated from these
younger children, day schools gained popularity, and by the end of the
1800s, even the annual reports of residential schools listed "the number of
students who were being taught to talk" (Gannon 1981, p.15). Eventually,
"all schools for deaf children were oral-only, at least up to twelve years of
age. After that, some schools tracked children considered 'oral failures'
into manual classes" (Gannon 1981, p. xi). For example, at the Kentucky
School for the Deaf, after 1884 "students were first placed in the oral department, and kept there if they made good progress. If they failed, . . .
they were transferred to the manual department" (Rich History, p. 24).

In 1889, the Clarke School inaugurated a program to train teachers in
oral methods (Clarke School—Historical Information). In the same year,
the Albany Home School for the Oral Instruction of the Deaf opened in
New York, and three years later The Home for the Training in Speech of
Deaf Children before They Are of School Age was formed in Philadelphia.
In 1942, the John Tracy Clinic in Los Angeles, soon famous for its correspondence course, was founded with the goal of training parents so oral
language instruction could begin as early as possible. As Lane (1984,
p. 339) summarized, "by the early 1900's there were 70 day oral school
programs, 12 oral residential schools, and most teachers of the deaf were
speech teachers," while Baynton (1993, p. 94) noted, "[B]y 1900, nearly 40
percent of American deaf students sat in classrooms from which sign language had been entirely banned. . . . By the end of World War I, nearly 80
percent of deaf students were taught entirely without sign language."

As the oralist hegemony grew, so did the pervasiveness of medical, rather than cultural, perspectives on deafness and the education of d/Deaf children and youth. A key instance was the founding in St. Louis in 1914 of the Central Institute for the Deaf by Max Goldstein, an otologist. From its modest beginning in two rooms above his medical office, the facility grew to become a major center for research and teacher training (Gannon 1981). Over a span of 100 years, d/Deaf education had gone from being sign-based, cultural, and religious, to oral, medical, and prescriptive, with minimal involvement of d/Deaf people in decision making.

PROBLEMS IN CONTEXT

The role of the zeitgeist in fanning the fires of latent oralism illustrates how d/Deaf education has been affected by broader societal issues. Throughout the history of the larger American community myriad events have impacted the marginalized d/Deaf community, but while African American historical figures are often discussed only during Black History Month, "general history and general education texts almost never discuss deaf people" (List 1993, p. 115). Conversely, "Any historical inquiry relating to deaf people . . . must encompass more than just a concentration on the history of deaf society as an isolated or autonomous historical phenomenon (p. 115)." Natural disasters, epidemics, industrialization, and wars affected d/Deaf students as well as hearing, illustrated in this account of the San Francisco earthquake of 1906 in the history of the California School for the Deaf: "The first sharp jolt at 5:13 a.m. awakened and frightened everyone. The second, more severe, shock caused quite some damage. . . . For the two days following the first shocks classes were held out-of-doors. . . . a few children were removed from school to flee the state with their terrified families" (Norton 2000, p. 35).

Impact of Epidemics on d/Deaf Children in Residential Schools

While infectious disease had been a major cause of deafness, and also blindness, in children throughout the nineteenth century, it had also been a major factor in child mortality. Deaf children and others housed in congregate facilities, such as orphanages, were at particular risk, for as epidemics regularly swept the nation, residential schools, which brought students together within contained settings, provided excellent places for illnesses to be transmitted. Cholera epidemics in the 1830s and 1840s had forced the Kentucky School for the Deaf to close, sending students who lived nearby home and temporarily placing others with farmers (Rich History 1998). The California School for the Deaf recorded the impact of a succession of diptheria and smallpox epidemics in the last decades of the century, in the first of which three of its students were among the thousand children in the San Francisco area who died (Norton 2000, pp. 28–35). Even with major public health efforts instituted early in the twentieth century, during the 1929–1939 decade alone, the Indiana school's records reported epidemics of, and deaths resulting from, diphtheria, spinal meningitis, pneumonia, measles, and scarlet fever (Reis 1993).

Mary Herring Wright (1999), an African American deaf woman, described how yearly bouts of illness affected life in the North Carolina residential school she had attended in the 1930s: "Every year . . . girls got the flu or measles. . . . The nurse visited them each day, bringing doses of castor oil and a bitter-tasting cold remedy. . . . Not all the patients had flu; some just wanted to play hooky and get lots of cornflakes from the kitchen. That was standard fare for all sick people, no matter what the ailment. That was the only time we got cornflakes" (p. 171).

Impact of Industrialization and the Manual Training Movement

The nation's change from a rural to an urban-industrial economy also impacted d/Deaf students. Many of the first students at the American School in Hartford were adults who already practiced various trades, and they were allowed to continue to ply their skills. As other students became interested in the businesses being conducted, ASD in 1825 instituted training in "the mechanic trades" (Lane 1984). By 1830, ASD students were spending three to four hours per day in vocational instruction, and as industrialization progressed over the next two decades, more than half of the nineteen residential schools provided vocational training (Leakey 1993). Such training not only served to supply the students with some salable, albeit limiting, skills; it also provided needed services for the schools. At the Indiana School for the Deaf, for example, male students did maintenance and repair work; printed the school newspaper, the *Silent Hoosier/ Hoosier*, as well as stationery and school forms; and grew flowers in the greenhouse to landscape the campus. Girls were responsible for preparing the athletic and other banquets and weekly faculty luncheons, as well as mending clothing and linen (Reis 1993).

However, vocational training failed to "train deaf Americans . . . to participate in the country's larger political, social, and economic spheres. . . . Deaf people and African Americans were denied access to positions of significant power in American society since their education channeled them into manual trades" (Leakey 1993, p. 76). These constraints led to the emergence of institutions of higher education for d/Deaf students, most notably the National Deaf-Mute College, founded in 1864 at the Kendall School for the Deaf, which later became Gallaudet University. Similarly, Congress established the National Technical Institute for the Deaf (NTID) in response to the need for workers with technological skills and English language facility in the manufacturing workplace and in emerging service industry jobs (Frisina 2001).

War and Race: Impact of Fear, Discrimination, and Patriotic Fervor

While d/Deaf educators were debating whether to use "Natural" or "Methodological" signs, and hearing educators were beginning to advocate for oral methods, the nation as a whole was enduring a much more significant rift: the Civil War. Prior to the Civil War, hearing and d/Deaf African slaves were denied a formal education, although they could supply the labor needed at southern residential schools. At the Kentucky School, "black slaves did most of the manual labor. . . . Some of the parents of students felt that it would be a degradation for their children to perform manual labor of any kind. Several girls were taken out of school because their parents didn't want them doing 'servile' work like making their own beds, washing dishes, or assisting with other household tasks" (Rich History 1998, p. 20).

War became a subject for discussion not only in hearing classrooms, but also for d/Deaf students. For example, in 1865 Ira H. Derby wrote about conditions in Libby Prison, in Richmond, Virginia, and Olive A. Derby wrote about Lincoln's assassination and the wounding of Secretary Seward. As war broke out in 1861, students at the Tennessee School for the Deaf were sent home two weeks early and the school closed. It was then taken over by the state to serve as a Confederate hospital until the Union army assumed control in 1863, and not returned to control by its trustees until 1865. The Mississippi school was burned down (Rich History 1998); the Louisiana State School for the Deaf at Baton Rouge was mistaken for Confederate headquarters, fired upon, and eventually occupied and used as a hospital (Gannon 1981). The Kentucky school remained open but, "in Perryville, only 9 miles away . . . one of the bloodiest battles of the war was fought. Wandering bands of guerrillas engaged in robbery and murder. Knowing that one such band was approaching Danville, students helped to hide the school's horses and cows in the hills near the Dix River" (Rich History 1998, p. 22).

Schools that did not close had little money for expenses, and food was scarce. Teachers and students at the Texas Deaf and Dumb Asylum supported themselves by farming, raising sheep, and selling woolen clothes (Texas School for the Deaf). Despite their deprivations, students and teachers contributed to their sides' war efforts. For example, "students at the Illinois School for the Deaf organized the Deaf Student Military Company which was appointed by Governor Richard Yates to be the Home Guard for the city of Jacksonville . . . [and] the print shop at the North Carolina Institution for the Deaf and Dumb and Blind in Raleigh printed currency for the state of North Carolina" (Gannon 1981, p. 8).

Reconstruction did not bring quick relief to the South or to the d/Deaf residential schools. Demands for the southern states to educate African American d/Deaf children usually resulted in segregated facilities; in 1868, North Carolina's "Colored Department" became the first institution for

African American d/Deaf students. In 1872, the South Carolina School for the Deaf and Blind prepared a separate building for African American students; however, the Board of Commissioners ordered the school not only to accept but actively encourage applications from African American students, who were to live and learn in the same rooms, taught by the same teachers, as white students. In response, the superintendent, school officers, and all the teachers resigned, thus closing the school for another four years. It reopened in 1876 when permission was granted to establish separate departments (Gannon 1981, pp. 13–14).

The Kentucky School for the Deaf (KSD) accepted applications but declined registration of African American students. In 1884, KSD purchased a homestead across the street from its facilities and finally opened its "Colored Department," which was one-tenth the size of the "White Department" and which received only a fraction of its budget (Rich History 1998, p. 18). "In most southern states, deaf African Americans attended inferior segregated facilities—if schooling was available to them at all" (Buchanan 1999, p. 7). As late as the 1930s, Wright (1999, pp. 179–180) and her African American schoolmates were left "depressed and angry" by the "unbelievable" differences between the institutional nature of their school and the attractive, homelike atmosphere of the "white" school (for blind children) they had visited.

As in general education, segregation died slowly in the d/Deaf schools of the south. In 1952, parents won a court ruling that Kendall School must accept d/Deaf African American students, who were provided a separate building until classes were integrated two years later with the *Brown vs. Board of Education* Supreme Court ruling. However, although the ruling established that segregation by race was unconstitutional, no deadline was set for compliance (Hairston & Smith 1983). The Kentucky school did not desegregate until 1963 (Rich History 1998, p. 18).

The successive World Wars affected d/Deaf students just as they did hearing children in public schools, although the residential schools, unlike individual families, had to address such issues as rationing on an institutional basis. Staff shortages occurred, and students were involved in supporting war efforts. At the Kentucky school during World War I, although "lack of appropriations forced KSD to open late and close early. . . . Everyone participated in Liberty Bonds, fundraising drives, and the restrictions on the consumption of sugar and other conservables" (Rich History 1998, p. 24). Similarly, at the Clarke School, students supported the Red Cross's efforts by having the girls knit and sew items for shipment overseas, while the boys made packing cases. The students also collected more than 150 books for the War Library and sold $35,000 worth of bonds for the Second Liberty Loan Campaign (Yale 1918, pp. 43–44).

World War II brought the same issues of rationing and staff shortages, along with declining enrollment as older students left school to work in the war industry and in jobs vacated by hearing workers. The December 7, 1941, attack on Pearl Harbor, however, gave new dimensions to students' concerns, as Gannon's (1981, pp. 219–220) account of one child's experience illustrates. Eight-year-old Bill Sugiyama and his schoolmates at the Diamond Head School for the Deaf, ten miles from Pearl Harbor, finally understood what was causing the vibrations they felt when a stray shell exploded nearby. Older students were directed to construct makeshift bomb shelters from heavy tables and mattresses until underground shelters could be dug. Thereafter, "windows were covered completely and lights were turned out before outside doors were opened. Food was rationed, drinking water was boiled, and everyone was required to carry a gas mask wherever they went. Children slept with their clothes on. . . . School remained unofficially closed until February. . . . Those children who lived on other islands stayed at school."

But, as for other American children, school "kept" for d/Deaf children, unless their families happened to be Japanese Americans. The Oregon School for the Deaf, among others, denied admission to d/Deaf students of Japanese descent, and with President Franklin D. Roosevelt's signing of Executive Order 9066, d/Deaf children, as well as hearing children, of Japanese American families living in western states went with their families to internment camps.

At her school in Raleigh, North Carolina, Mary Herring Wright (1999, pp. 262–263) was experiencing the shock of the war news in a more typical manner, typical, that is, for a child separated from her family: "If I had to get bombed, I wanted to be with those I loved best. When I told Miss Watford and Mr. Mash . . . they both assured me I wasn't about to be bombed, and that the president was sending planes and men over there to fight them. . . . I couldn't rest until I wrote Mama about my fears, but she told me the same things."

At the California School for the Deaf, windows were blacked out with paint, and wire netting was nailed over them so that students could study during blackouts. Cabinet shop students built models of warplanes for the U.S. government to use in military training (Norton 2000). Students at the Virginia School for the Deaf and Blind sold $3,217.00 worth of stamps and bonds and collected over 10,000 pounds of paper and scrap metal (Gannon 1981). Students at ASD used school land to supply the schools with food in response to shortages and rationing (*American Era* 1943a). The school newspaper also reported, "The Junior Class began selling War Stamps and Bonds as a patriotic and mathematical project. . . . No prizes were offered because pride in helping our country win the war is incentive enough" (*American Era* 1943b). Clarke School girls established the Red Cross Knitting Army and a Red Cross Surgical Dressing Unit (Coolidge 1943; 1944).

d/Deaf schools' involvement in war-related issues continued through the Vietnam era. During the radical period of the 1960s, the California School

for the Deaf was only a few blocks away from the University of California–
Berkley, where armed police quelled rioters with rifle butts and tear gas.
Winds blew the tear gas onto the CSD campus, where students were confined for their safety, and also to prevent their participation. (Norton
2000).

Complex Meanings of Minority Status, Gender, and Deafness

While d/Deaf persons have always been affected by more general social
attitudes, deafness itself often elicits reactions based on stereotyped images
and lack of experience. Those reactions can become even more significant
when the person who is deaf is also a member of another marginalized
group, such as an African American student in the Jim Crow era, or a
student during World War II of Asian or Pacific Rim heritage. Reactions
based on erroneous, stereotyped images also occur *within* the Deaf community itself, making these individuals marginalized members within an
already marginalized group.

For d/Deaf women, this has often meant traditional roles in male-female
interactions, and an education that has not only been inferior to that of
their hearing counterparts, but also to that of d/Deaf males. "Like their
counterparts in public schools, most educators of deaf students assumed
that women graduates would get married and likely not enter the paid
workforce" (Buchanan 1999, p. 7). Other reasons given for providing inadequate education to d/Deaf females, in addition to the excuse of lack
of appropriate housing, included beliefs that they were "lazy, needing much
help, . . . dependent and could not endure" (Jankowsi 2001, p. 285). Fifty
years after American colleges began enrolling women students, six women
were finally admitted to Gallaudet in 1887 on a two-year trial basis; one of
them, Alto Lowman, became Gallaudet's first female graduate in 1892 (Jankowski 2001).

Native American d/Deaf people also have been doubly marginalized,
often leading them to question their own identity and self-worth: years
later, a man recalled that he had first become aware that some of his
schoolmates at the Oklahoma School for the Deaf in the 1930s were Indian.
When his mother told him, at age nine, that he too was part Indian, he
"burst into tears," having absorbed the negative stereotypes portrayed in
the movies he had seen (Paris & Wood 2002, p. 53). A 1951 graduate of
the Arkansas School for the Deaf, curious about both his Indian background and his d/D grandparents, who had attended the same school, was
discouraged from asking about his family history. "It was almost as if the
family did not want to discuss it" (Paris & Wood, p. 11). Dixie Vetterneck
Baker, whose Chippewa father had lost his hearing as a boy and subsequently fathered several d/Deaf children, recalled that when her school-

mates at the Oregon School for the Deaf learned she was half Chippewa, she was shunned and called "dirty savage" (Paris & Wood 2002, pp. 224–225).

This dual discrimination—both within the marginalized group and also within the larger, dominant group—often led to the feeling there is no place where one can belong: like Dixie, Eugene, whose parents were Athabascan Indian, was picked on by schoolmates at the Washington State School for the Deaf, where he was placed at age five. However, although in time he adjusted to the games of Cowboys and Indians, the latter invariably the "bad guys," and learned sign, visits home were painful due to communication barriers (Paris & Wood 2002, pp. 93–94). Isolated from his family by hearing and language differences, from his Athabascan culture by his "western" schooling, and from other d/Deaf children by the color of his skin and the stereotyped images of the media, where do children like Eugene fit?

PROBLEMS IN ISOLATION

Although simultaneous membership in another marginalized group adds to the complexity, being deaf alone has provided its own challenges for children navigating the American educational system. Although educators were daunted by the challenge of assimilating waves of non-English-speaking immigrants during the late 1800s and early 1900s, those hearing children came with an understanding of *some* language, while "deaf children entering school frequently do not have ASL as a native language, or any language for that matter" (Supalla 1992, p. 171).

Lacking an established language has also made them objects of curiosity. Deaf students had often been taken to perform before legislators to demonstrate their acquired skills. The newly opened Kentucky School for the Deaf "became something of a popular attraction. Visitors popped in to 'marvel at the spectacle of' imparting useful knowledge to persons deaf and dumb" (Rich History 1998, p. 14). In the 1920s, "groups from the University of California and elsewhere were paying visits to the California School for the Deaf or requesting demonstrations" (Norton 2000, p. 39).

Difficulties in deciding how to communicate with and teach d/Deaf children often meant multiple school transfers, disrupting the continuity of instruction for students. Although Michelle had been deaf since infancy, her parents enrolled her in regular schools. Finally, her high school principal, noting her reports of feeling "dumb" and concerned about her academic work, encouraged her to transfer to the New Mexico School for the Deaf (Paris & Wood 2002, p. 122). Judy Cummings Stout recalled finally entering the Eastern School for the Deaf in North Carolina at age eleven after years of unaddressed communication needs in the reservation schools, unable to read or write or count beyond ten, and being placed in the second grade (pp. 77–78).

Not understanding how to react to a child's deafness has also at times made deaf children vulnerable to becoming victims of hearing people's "kindness." As Mary Herring Wright (1999, pp. 75–76) recalled, after losing her hearing, "School that I once loved so well was a nightmare. When the other children learned that I was losing my hearing, I was either shunned or pitied" and humiliated when patronized and given unneeded help.

The "uniqueness" of being deaf, given its low frequency of occurrence, has made it difficult for deaf students not educated in a residential setting to find a peer or cohort group. The disappearance of d/Deaf teachers added the difficulty of finding successful adult d/Deaf role models. Stout (p. 78) described the importance of this when she was a student at the Eastern School for the Deaf: "I was thrilled. . . . We had many deaf staff and teachers . . . who were excellent role models for us. We were able to communicate daily in the dorm as well as in the classroom." As Wright (1999, p. 198) recalled, "Children felt a kinship for each other because of their deafness [and] . . . looked forward to school opening so they could be with people who understood them."

But such benefits might be counterbalanced by the weakening of ties within their hearing families, already impacted by communication challenges, as it was for Eugene. Another man, recalling his student days in the 1930s, observed, "When I came home, communication with my family was very limited. . . . I was withdrawn, sitting at the table with my family and eating quietly, not talking with anyone because no one signed" (in Paris & Wood 2002, p. 195).

Problems with social interactions have not been limited to d/Deaf children who use sign. Henry Kisor (1990), who became deaf at three and a half and attended regular schools with oral support services in Illinois during the 1950s, recalled his mainstream junior high classmates snickering at the way he talked: "When called upon in class, I'd simply shrug and say, 'I dunno'. . . . On days when I had to deliver an oral report in class, I'd stay home sick" (p. 71). In addition to the social difficulties, Kisor vividly describes the practical difficulties a d/Deaf student faces in a mainstream school situation: "Hearing students can relax and listen passively. . . . Lip readers . . . must [be] . . . actively hunting for clues to what is being said. . . . If the teacher suddenly goes off on a tangent, we may flounder helplessly, searching for familiar words to help us get on track" (p. 75).

Problems with communication and social acceptance, multiple program transfers, difficulties finding a support network of peers and adult role models who share the same experiences, challenges in maintaining bonds with a hearing family, and the developmentally unusual experience of being used as an object for demonstration and research have historically been the burden of deaf students. These issues also persist into the present.

MODERN TIMES: CONFLICTS CONTINUE

In 1869, the Western Pennsylvania School for the Deaf opened the nation's first day school for d/Deaf students. Although it closed seven years later, it was followed in 1892 by the Cleveland Day School and in 1895 the Minneapolis Day School for the Deaf. By the mid-1940s, "there were 119 public day schools . . . [and] not one had a deaf teacher" (Gannon 1981, p. 227). The intent, as Lane (1992, p. 133) explained, was for "deaf children [to] live at home in a majority-language environment," to be taught in, and use, spoken English rather than sign, and ultimately, not marry other deaf persons.

Other societal changes were occurring that affected services for d/Deaf students. The end of World War II saw numerous servicemen returning with injuries, including hearing loss. Aural rehabilitation programs began to expand and develop in hospital and university settings. These, combined with educators from oral schools, and with university-based speech-and-hearing scientists, to produce the new fields of audiology and speech pathology, which further supported the medicalization of d/Deaf education.

Simultaneously, the field of electronics was evolving, with the invention of the transistor and printed circuits, semiconductors and digital processing (Frisina 2001). The explosion in technology not only yielded TTYs and TDDs (Telecommunication Devices for the Deaf), video recorders, the Internet, and e-mail, all of which have impacted d/Deaf education but also freed d/Deaf students to become more mobile, as bulky earphones tied into a table unit by a cable gave way to body aids and, eventually, to behind-the-ear hearing aids (BTEs). With greater mobility, d/Deaf students could more easily move out of the residential school and the specialized day program and into classrooms within their local schools.

The d/Deaf student population also changed. Prior to the 1960s one-third of deafness was due to high-fever diseases such as meningitis, which tend to yield profound deafness, but at a later age of onset. However, as antibiotics and other medical advances emerged, many of the diseases that had once caused deafness began to be reduced or eliminated. At the same time, medical advances enabled neonates who in the past would have died to remain viable, often yielding deaf children with multiple disabilities. Additionally, an epidemic of maternal rubella swelled the number of children who were born deaf.

The frequency of deafness crested and waned, sometimes in opposition to trends in the general population. Space in local public schools, which had been expanded to accommodate the post-war baby boom, was underutilized in the 1960s due to enrollment declines. However, the 1964–1965 rubella epidemic resulted in many deaf preschool-age children needing to be housed. An economic solution emerged to address this "one-time-only" problem. Thus, by 1975 most of the increased numbers of deaf students were served in local programs, while residential school enrollment had declined significantly (Moores 1992); the movement into now-available classrooms was supported on economic grounds as well as passage in 1975 of the Education of the Handicapped Act (EHA), Public Law 94-142, renamed in 1990 the Individuals with Disabilities Educational Act (IDEA). The law mandated that all children with disabilities are entitled to a *free, appropriate public education* in the *least restrictive environment* (LRE) to "the maximum extent appropriate." It did not address the beliefs and characteristics of the teachers and administrators—the hidden curriculum. Moreover, "neither the law nor the courts have defined LRE or 'to the maximum extent appropriate' in operational terms, leaving those decisions primarily in the hands of nondisabled individuals" (Schildroth & Hotto 1994).

The movement now called *inclusion* began with Bell's fear regarding the creation of a deaf race, was supported by economic factors, and played to the emotions of hearing parents, without ensuring or adequately funding qualitative changes needed in educational contexts. Using available space in local schools represented a cost savings and, as LRE decisions led to declining numbers at residential schools, state legislatures began to cut their budgets, sometimes threatening closure (Burch 2002; Lane 1992; North Carolina 1993). Decisions, made largely by adults without disabilities, failed to consider that "least restrictive" might be defined differently by people with disabilities (Supalla 1992; Thoryk 1999).

Inclusion for d/Deaf children presents a number of problems. The mainstream settings may be required to "include" d/Deaf children, but rarely extend inclusion to faculty, resulting in few d/Deaf adults to serve as role models. Communication with classmates and teachers may rely on an intermediary interpreter, often with questionable skills, leaving the student poorly educated and socially isolated (Lane 1992). While critical mass theory suggests there must be a sufficient number of similar students to support learning and social interaction, a d/Deaf student may be the only one in a school. Thirteen years after the EHA was enacted, the Commission on the Education of the Deaf concluded that "the [law's] emphasis on mainstreaming . . . has been more detrimental than beneficial to many deaf children" (Supalla 1992, p. 171).

A graduate (Levesque 2001, p. 40) recalled that as a mainstreamed high school student he tried to "bluff" his way through to be accepted socially by his hearing classmates: "My mother wrote down the words of popular songs so I could 'be cool' and know what was going on. I faked knowing the words to songs like I faked knowing what was going on in class. One day, I got sick of being a fake. I wanted to be just me. Plain, old, deaf me."

Alphabet Soup: A Modern Tower of Babel

Recent decades have seen a resurgence of debate regarding communication systems to be used in teaching d/Deaf students. In the nineteenth century, Dorothy Shifflett devised a system combining "speech, speechreading, [and] auditory training [with] fingerspelling and signs"; in the 1960s, her "Total Approach" became known as Total Communication (Gannon 1981, pp. 368–369). Multiple manual codes for English were devised, including The Barry Five Slate System; Wang's Symbols; The Fitzgerald Key; Signing Essential English (SEE); Linguistics of Visual English (LOVE); Signing Exact English (SEE II); and Cued Speech (Gannon 1981). However, the "attempt to unify the two methods (oral and manual) . . . confuses children [with] manually coded English systems." (Bahan 1989, p. 118).

These systems appealed to hearing teachers who knew English but had a poor grasp of the syntax of American Sign Language (ASL). Many tried to implement the "Total Approach" by attempting to speak in English and sign at the same time, a method known as "SimCom" or Simultaneous Communication. However, trying to speak in English while signing in ASL is similar to trying to speak English while writing Mandarin Chinese, providing the child a poor model of either language (Barks 2001). As Lane (1992, pp. 134–135) objected, "It is simply impossible to use two languages simultaneously, so the hearing teacher subordinates the manual language to the spoken one, omitting the rich morphology of the signed language and scrambling the sign order, thus rendering the manual message ungrammatical and nearly unintelligible."

This implies an ethical question: If deaf children enter school without a first language, should their model of ASL be hearing teachers and interpreters, for whom ASL is a second language? An alternative is teaming Deaf and hearing teachers to teach English and ASL along with hearing and Deaf cultural behaviors and mores. This "bilingual/bicultural" model emerged after the 1960s when William Stokoe, a linguist at Gallaudet, demonstrated "that ASL was a language in its own right, with its own lexical and syntactical system" (Barks 2001, pp. 213–214).

The "Bi-Bi" model, in which English is taught as a second language, supported by ASL as the primary language, was pioneered in the 1980s by Marie Philip at the Learning Center for Deaf Children in Framingham, Massachusetts, Marlon Kuntz at the California School for the Deaf at Fremont, and Dave Reynolds and Ann Titus at the Indiana School for the Deaf (Walworth, Moores, & O'Rourke 1992; Philip 2004). In 1993, the Metro Deaf School (MDS) opened in St. Paul, Minnesota as the nation's first charter bicultural-bilingual school. (A charter school is a "district-sponsored semi-autonomous school with ownership by parents, the community, and teachers, and is publicly funded" [Moers 1998].) "A majority of the teachers at MDS are Deaf, and all are fluent in ASL and English"

(Barks 2001, p. 212). Two more Bi-Bi magnet charter schools subsequently opened: The Laurent Clerc Elementary School in Tucson, Arizona, and the Magnet School for the Deaf, in Lakewood, Colorado (Colorado's First Deaf Charter School Signs On 1998; Cummins 1998; Wolf 1998).

"Deaf President Now!"

Along with P.L. 94-142 and Stokoe's validation of ASL, the third greatest factor influencing d/Deaf education during the latter half of the twentieth century occurred in March 1988, when Gallaudet University staged a protest that was carried by international news media since it interfered with the daily commute and life in the nation's capital. Gallaudet's President, Jerry C. Lee, had announced his plans to leave the university; a search committee identified three candidates to succeed him, two of whom were deaf. Rallies were held urging the trustees to select a "Deaf President Now!" However, on March 6, the board announced the selection of Elizabeth Ann Zinser, a hearing woman who knew no ASL. The campus erupted with demonstrations; alumni, staff, faculty, and students blocked entrances to the campus and marched to Capitol Hill during rush hour. Four days later, Zinser resigned, and I. King Jordan became the first deaf president in Gallaudet's 124-year history.

Besides providing a rallying motto, "Deaf people can do anything but hear," the protest sparked a surge of pride and self-advocacy among d/Deaf people that reverberated around the nation. Deaf alumni associations and Deaf clubs banded together to protest proposed closings of residential schools, and states passed legislation supporting ASL as a legitimate language, making it eligible to be offered for high school and college credit. Basically, "The Deaf President Now Movement . . . challenged the prevailing relationship of deaf dependency on hearing persons" (List 1993, p. 115), thus beginning to reverse the pattern that began in 1854 when Turner stood in a courtroom and asserted that deaf people, represented by his indigent deaf pupils, felt inferior and needed supervision.

New Challenges

Education, for d/Deaf or for hearing students, continues to face new challenges. Schildroth and Hotto (1994, p. 17) noted that, "between 1976 and 1993 the number of Deaf and Hard of Hearing students representing Asian/Pacific Rim groups increased by 320% (from 435 to 1825). . . . The total number of Deaf/HOH Hispanic students increased by 114% . . . (an increase of 4,077 students)." By the 1990s, the Pennsylvania School for the Deaf reported that 50 percent of their total student body, 80 percent of whom qualified for reduced or free lunches, was African American, with 15 percent Hispanic (Walworth, Moores, & O'Rourke 1992). Thus, one of the main twenty-first-century challenges is to meet the needs of children with multiple cultural memberships and multiple language issues. A child's needs in ASL, English *and* Spanish or perhaps Vietnamese must be addressed, as educators also attempt to work in partnership with families across boundaries of languages, culture, and perspectives regarding education and disability.

The experiences of these children are illustrative (Paris & Wood 2002): Monica, a thirteen-year-old Navajo girl, uses English when communicating with hearing people and ASL with her friends at the New Mexico School for the Deaf (p. 3). Another child whose first language was Mexican Sign Language (LSM) learned first to sign in English word order, then in ASL (pp. 74–75). Another young person states, "I consider myself to be involved in several cultures. The first is Indian culture, because of my bloodlines. . . . The second is Deaf culture. . . . The third culture is the hearing culture" (p. 218). Since in Navajo culture pointing at another is considered insulting, among other cultural differences such as the use of eating utensils, flush toilets, and electricity, six-year-old Karen at first had difficulty adjusting to life at the New Mexico School for the Deaf (pp. 124–127).

Advances in technology also pose new challenges with respect to cultural identity. Many deaf children, including infants, are now receiving cochlear implants, which the Deaf community has traditionally not accepted. In consequence, school programs will not only need to address new communication issues, but also questions related to identity, body image, and group acceptance or rejection.

Multicultural memberships, family economic factors, and technological advances join with the problems of school funding and accountability measurement to add new issues to the challenges d/Deaf education faces in the future. These new challenges emerge while historical issues affecting d/Deaf children—communication mode, instructional technique, educator training, and educational setting—remain unresolved.

The cochlear implant, and the intense feelings it inspires (both in hearing supporters and Deaf critics), brings us full circle to the issues of heterogeneity within the Deaf community and membership of d/Deaf persons in the global arenas of American society and American history. The d/Deaf community *is* diverse in its members' experiences. Despite their differences, however, they are similar in also being an integral part of the holistic history of the United States. Nor is there a singular history of d/Deaf education in America, any more than there is a singular history of the education of white males or of immigrants in America. Deaf education had a pioneer role in such fields as vocational education, early childhood education, and federally- and state-funded education, all of which have impacted far more than d/Deaf children alone. Whether recorded or not— or recognized or not—d/Deaf people will continue to be an active force in American life in the twenty-first century, as in the past.

REFERENCES

American Era[a]. (1943). 30(8) (May/June). West Hartford, CT: American School for the Deaf.

American Era[b]. (1943). 30(1) (October). West Hartford, CT: American School for the Deaf.

American School for the Deaf: A Brief History of ASD. http://www.asd-1817. org/hist/histb.htm.

American School for the Deaf: A Brief History of Deaf Education in America. http://www.asd-1817.org/hist/histed.htm.

American School for the Deaf. (1865). Annual Report. West Hartford, CT: ASD.

American School for the Deaf. (1938). Biennial Report. West Hartford, CT: ASD.

American School for the Deaf. (1961). Annual Report. West Hartford, CT: ASD.

Bahan, B. (1989). Total Communication: A Total Farce. In S. Wilcox, ed., *American Deaf Culture: An Anthology*. Burtonsville, MD: Linstok Press.

Barks, C. (2001). Deaf-centric Teaching: A Case Study in ASL-English Bilingualism. In L. Bragg, ed., *Deaf World: A Historical Reader and Primary Sourcebook* (pp. 211–233). New York: New York University Press.

Baynton, D. (1993). "Savages and Deaf-Mutes": Evolutionary Theory and the Campaign Against Sign Language in the Nineteenth Century. In J. V. Van Cleve, ed., *Deaf History Unveiled: Interpretations from the New Scholarship* (pp. 92–112). Washington, DC: Gallaudet University Press.

Bender, R. (1970). *The Conquest of Deafness*. Cleveland, OH: Case Western Reserve University Press.

Bragg, L., ed. (2001). *Deaf World: A Historical Reader and Primary Sourcebook*. New York: New York University Press.

Buchanan, R. (1999). *Illusions of Equality: Deaf Americans in School and Factory 1850–1950*. Washington, DC: Gallaudet University Press.

Burch, S. (2002). *Signs of Resistance: American Deaf Cultural History, 1900 to 1942*. New York: New York University Press.

Childers, D. (2003). Treatment of Deaf Citizens in Antebellum America: From Benevolent Paternalism to Forced Assimilation. http://www.arches.uga. edu/~mgagnon/students/Childers.htm.

Clarke School—Historical Information. http://www.clarkeschool.org/school.html.

Colorado's First Deaf Charter School Signs On. (1998). *Deaf Life* 10(7), 11–12.

Coolidge, G. (1943). Report of the Corporation, Seventy-sixth Annual Report, Clarke School for the Deaf.

————. (1944). Report of the Corporation, Seventy-seventh Annual Report, Clarke School for the Deaf.

Cummins, C. (1998). Magnet School for the Deaf Opens Doors in Jeffco. *Deaf Life* 10(7), 12–14.

De Carlo, L. M. (1964). *The Deaf*. Englewood Cliffs, NJ: Prentice-Hall.

Frisina, D. (2001). Past, Present, and Future of Education for Deaf and Hard of Hearing Persons. Keynote address, Conference of Educational Administrators Serving the Deaf, Rochester, NY.

Gannon, J. (1981). *Deaf Heritage: A Narrative History of Deaf America.* Silver Spring, MD: National Association of the Deaf.

Groce, N. (1985). *Everyone Here Spoke Sign Language: Hereditary Deafness in Martha's Vineyard.* Cambridge, MA: Harvard University Press.

Hairston, E., & Smith, L. (1983). *Black and Deaf in America: Are We That Different?* Silver Springs, MD: TJ Publishers.

History of Kendal Demonstration Elementary School/Laurent Clerc National Deaf Education Center, Gallaudet University. http://www.Clerccenter.gallaudet.edu/k.des/history.html.

History through Deaf Eyes: Traveling Social History Exhibition. http://depts.gallaudet.edu/deafeyes/about.html

Jankowski, K. (2001). 'Til All Barriers Crumble and Fall: Agatha Tiegel's Presentation Day Speech in April 1893. In L. Bragg, ed., *Deaf World: A Historical Reader and Primary Sourcebook* (pp. 284–295). New York: New York University Press.

Kentucky School for the Deaf. http://www.ksd.k12ky.us/.

Kisor, H. (1990). *What's That Pig Outdoors? A Memoir of Deafness.* New York: Penguin Books.

Lane, H. (1984). *When the Mind Hears: A History of the Deaf.* New York: Random House.

———. (1992). *The Mask of Benevolence: Disabling the Deaf Community.* New York: Alfred A. Knopf.

Leakey, T. (1993). Vocational Education in the Deaf American and African-American Communities. In J. V. Van Cleve, ed., *Deaf History Unveiled: Interpretations from the New Scholarship* (pp. 74–91). Washington, DC: Gallaudet University Press.

Levesque, J. (2001). CBS Hurt Deaf Children With "Caitlin's Story." In L. Bragg, ed., *Deaf World: A Historical Reader and Primary Sourcebook* (pp. 40–42). New York: New York University Press.

List, G. (1993). Deaf History: A Suppressed Part of General History. In J. V. Van Cleve, ed., *Deaf History Unveiled: Interpretations from the New Scholarship.* Washington, DC: Gallaudet University Press.

Lucas, C., & Valli, C. What Happens When Languages Come in Contact. In L. Bragg, ed., *Deaf World: A Historical Reader and Primary Sourcebook* (pp. 118–122). New York: New York University Press.

Mini-interview with Clifford Moers, Director of the Magnet School. (1998). *Deaf Life* 10(7), 21–24.

Moores, D. (1992). What Do We Know and When Did We Know It? In M. Walworth, D. Moores, & T. O'Rourke, eds., *A Free Hand: Enfranchising the Education of Deaf Children* (pp. 67–88). Silver Springs, MD: TJ Publishers.

North Carolina: Is Time Running Out for Deaf Schools? (1993). *Deaf Life* 5:9, 1–5.

Norton, K. (2000). *The Eagle Soars to Enlightenment.* Fremont, CA: The Donald Parodi Memorial Charitable Trust.

O'Rourke, P. (1994). *All the Trouble in the World.* New York: The Atlantic Monthly Press.

Paris, D. G., & Wood, S. K., eds. (2002). *Step into the Circle: The Heartbeat of American Indian, Alaska Native, and First Nations Deaf Communities.* Salem, OR: Ago Publications.

Philip, M. (2004). Personal communication.

Reis, M. (1993). Student Life at the Indiana School for the Deaf During the Depression Years. In J. V. Van Cleve, ed., *Deaf History Unveiled: Interpretations from the New Scholarship.* Washington, DC: Gallaudet University Press.

Report of the Committee of the Connecticut Asylum for the Education and Instruction of Deaf and Dumb Persons. June 1, 1817. Hartford, CT: Hudson and Company Printers.

A Rich History, Fond Memories, and a Bright Future: KSD Celebrates Its 175th. (1998). *Deaf Life* 10(11), 10–27.

Schildroth, A., and Hotto, S. (1994). Deaf Students and Full Inclusion: Who Wants to Be Excluded. In R. C. Johnson & O. P. Cohen, eds., *Implications and Complications for Deaf Students of the Full Inclusion Movement: A Joint Publication by the Conference of Educational Administrators Serving the Deaf, and the Gallaudet Research Institute.* GRI Occasional Paper 94-2, pp. 7–30. Washington, DC: Gallaudet University.

Supalla, S. (1992). Equality in Educational Opportunities: The Deaf Version. In M. Waleworth, D. Moores, & T. O'Rourke, eds., *A Free Hand: Enfranchising the Education of Deaf Children* (pp. 170–181). Silver Springs, MD: TJ Publishers.

Tennessee School for the Deaf. 100th Anniversary of the Tennessee School for the Deaf, 1845–1945: A History of the School. http://www.knoxcotn.org/schools/tsd/schoolhistory.htm.

Texas School for the Deaf. http://www.tsd.state.tx.us/.

Thoryk, R. 1999. The Power to Define, Legitimizing Viewpoint, Disablement and Difference: A Study of the Relations Between a Dominant Group and a Nondominant Group. Unpublished dissertation. Kent, OH: Kent State University.

Valentine, P. (1993). Thomas Hopkins Gallaudet: Benevolent Paternalism and the Origins of the American Asylum. In J. V. Van Cleve, ed., *Deaf History Unveiled: Interpretations from the New Scholarship.* Washington, DC: Gallaudet University Press.

Van Cleve, J., & Crouch, B. (1989). *A Place of Their Own.* Washington, DC: Gallaudet University Press.

Walworth, M., Moores, D., & O'Rourke, T., eds. (1992). *A Free Hand: Enfranchising the Education of Deaf Children.* Silver Spring, MD: TJ Publishers.

Wolf, M. (1998). Signing On: ASL Is the Primary Language at Jeffco Magnet School for the Deaf. *Deaf Life* 10(7), 14–20.

Wright, M. (1999). *Sounds Like Home: Growing Up Black and Deaf in the South.* Washington, DC: Gallaudet University Press.

Yale, C. (1918). Principal's Report: Fifty-First Annual Report, Clarke School for the Deaf, 1918.

2 Reaching Across the Divide: Visual Disability, Childhood, and American History

Carol Linsenmeier and Jeff Moyer

What has it been like to be a child in America without the sense of sight, or with vision so impaired that experiencing the world in the same manner as other children is not possible? We had hoped in writing this essay to tell the story of the lives of children with visual disabilities, over time, through the lens of their own personal accounts. However, diaries, letters, autobiographies, and other first-person writings of "typical" children with visual disabilities proved to be nearly nonexistent; those we found—memoirs written by adults—began to appear in the nineteenth century, were largely drawn from the realm of celebrity, and may or may not have represented the life experience of everyday children. To address this gap, we necessarily referred to the scholarly record, much of which revolves around education. But much of that record tells the stories of educators, rather than of the children they taught; nor can a scholarly recitation of research and theoretical writings connect with the everyday life experience of children living with vision loss.

To address this need we turned to the method of oral histories with a broad sample of interviewees. Accordingly, we asked fifteen individuals who were born between 1943 and 1984 and who attended public school, or schools for the blind, or both, to tell us about their life experiences, and particularly about what it was like growing up with a visual disability. Our informants, whose names have been changed to protect their privacy, had a range of vision loss as children including total blindness from birth, loss

The authors gratefully acknowledge the assistance of Wendy Charny, Cleveland Sight Center Librarian, and Jan Seymour-Ford, Research Librarian at the Perkins School for the Blind.

of vision in early childhood, low vision, low vision until total sight loss as teenagers, and normal vision with severe partial loss as a teenager. They lived in urban, suburban, and rural settings and varied widely in family structure and other occurrence of blindness within the family. We have interspersed extractions from our oral histories into the review of the historical record in an attempt to make such constructs as life in residential schools, training in handicrafts, and sight-saving classes come alive. We have chosen to use the term "visual disability" to denote the full range of those with vision loss, ranging from partial sight to total blindness. When the term "blind" is used, it is understood that we are referring to all those with visual disabilities.

CONTINUITY IN THE FACE OF CHANGE

Without question, a twentieth-century childhood was very different from a childhood in early America, when an almshouse was the home of many children with visual disabilities. It was also different from experiences of children with visual disabilities in the nineteenth century when residential schools, the predominant means of educating persons with visual disabilities for the next century and a half, were created specifically for them. Throughout the twentieth century, but especially since the 1970s, major changes in education law, emergence of the disability rights movement and self-advocacy, advances in technology, and refinement in the interventions for development of compensatory skill areas have created new opportunities and presented new challenges for today's children with visual disabilities and their families. Yet, to our surprise, the life experiences of our interviewees seemed in many ways to mirror both contemporary and historic attitudes, beliefs, and patterns of educational practice, and seemed to suggest a commonality of experience that, despite cataclysmic change, transcends time.

The Colonial Period: Accepting the Will of God

Berthold Lowenfeld (1956; 1975) identified three stages of societal attitudes toward persons with blindness, calling the first the Primitive Stage, defined as the level of societal attitude that allowed for the killing or abandonment of children who were blind. Although this stage and the two that followed were proposed as a chronological sequence, there is evidence that all three levels of societal attitudes toward individuals with visual disabilities have intermittently been, and continue to be, present in American society. We read with horror that the ancient Spartans threw infants with birth defects into rivers, and that the ancient Roman law of paterfamilias gave a father the right to kill his children if they were born imperfect. Later, and more humanely, unwanted Roman babies could be abandoned at the base of Columna Lactaria and left to be raised by the state or adopted by early Christians (Winzer 1997).

In colonial America, religious tenets precluded such practices, as had been true in Europe since the Middle Ages, when hospices had been established in France specifically for persons who were blind (French 1932). The "Primitive Period" described by Lowenfeld was presumably long over when colonies were established in the New World. Yet, a remnant of the attitudes and beliefs that make the killing of "imperfect" newborns seem reasonable can be discerned in *Daniel*'s remembrance: "When I lost my sight at age sixteen it devastated my family. It really hit my Mom. I learned years later that Mom considered killing the family and committing suicide. You would have to know my Mom to know what a drastic thing it was to her."

Nor is there evidence that parents in the American colonies would consider simply abandoning an infant, either to die or to be left to the "kindness of strangers," as continued to be practiced in Europe long after the Roman era (Boswell 1988). While religious teachings would similarly condemn such practices and enjoin colonial parents to accept the will of Divine Providence, accusations of witchcraft—as was the case in sixteenth- and seventeenth-century Europe—might follow the birth of an imperfect newborn, or indeed the onset of impairment in a child or adult who was previously healthy (Mintz 2004). In any case, to abandon a child, on account of a perceived imperfection or for any other reason, was to thwart the will of God.

Yet, centuries later, *Debby*'s account of her childhood in a foster home paints a picture of the psychological impact of "abandonment" in some respects similar to experiences to which children with visual or other disabilities had been subjected in antiquity: "Being a foster child you never felt like you belonged anywhere, because you knew you had parents, but where were they? Why did they give you away? And hoping someday they would knock on the door. But as I got older I got used to it . . ." Listening to her account, *Dick* observed, "Debby was one of the luckier ones. There were others who were just bouncing around from one foster home to another." *Mary* added, "We had a couple my age that were in orphanages. One girl that I went to school with. It was kind of tough for her."

While colonial America, despite hardships and primitive conditions, did not experience a Primitive Period with respect to attitudes toward, or treatment of, children with visual disabilities, that does not necessarily mean that the "Primitive Period" had ended. It has been proposed (Black 2003) that the modern eugenics movement reflects similar societal attitudes that could result in killing of unwanted infants. The eugenicists of the early twentieth century sought to prevent the birth of persons who would not be productive citizens due to disability or an "innate tendency" to crime, which was imputed to epilepsy, mental retardation, and "pauperism." The model sterilization law drawn up by Harry Laughlin in 1922 included persons who were blind or visually impaired in the list of those who should be sterilized involuntarily (Pfeiffer 1993). By 1938, thirty-three states had passed sterilization laws based on Laughlin's model. Despite the horrified reaction to eugenics that occurred when it was discovered that Hitler used American eugenics laws as the model for his "Master Race" strategy (Black 2003), there continues to be an active eugenics movement in the United States that advocates sterilization control (Miller 1997).

In our own day, some argue that decisions pursuant to genetic counseling may similarly imply such "primitive" attitudes. While at the present time the only condition that causes blindness that can be diagnosed in utero is Tay-Sachs disease (Beers & Berkow 2004), some see in genetic counseling a new form of "negative" eugenics (Berson & Cruz 2001; Dorsey 2002). A recent study of American women who had learned through genetic counseling that the fetus they carried would have a disability found that the majority stated they would have an abortion (Roberts, Stough, & Parrish 2002). The attitudes that led these women to choose abortions are indicative that, at some level, the belief continues to exist in American society that it is not desirable for infants with disabilities to be allowed to live.

"The Light of Intellect Extinguished": Blind Children in Almshouses

Lowenfeld called his second level of historical progress the Humanitarian Stage. Moral attitudes in this stage precluded the killing of children, so the child with visual disability may have been kept at home, if possible, but was not educated. In seventeenth- and eighteenth-century America, many children with visual disability were kept by their families as long as possible and then, if representing a financial liability, sent to almshouses. This practice continued well into the latter nineteenth century, even as schools for blind students became more numerous; Annie Sullivan, who would later become Helen Keller's famous "Teacher," temporarily blinded by trachoma, was sent to the Tewksbury almshouse after her mother died and her father was unable to provide for her or her siblings. She finally entered the Perkins Institution for the Blind in 1880, at age 14, "rescued" from the almshouse by the chairman of the State Board of Charities, Frank B. Sanborn (Lash 1980).

It is likely that in some families, as with other physical or with cognitive impairments, a child's blindness was a source of shame resulting in neglect, but whether that became less likely over time seems doubtful. One still hears media accounts of a child tragically "kept in a closet." *John*, who was both one of our interviewees about his own experience and who described the life experience of others with whom he worked as a social worker, reported: "I once worked with a teenage Mexican-American lad named

Luis. His family felt terrible shame about his blindness, feeling that it was a sign of God's displeasure. Luis had been hidden away and kept out of school until discovered by a neighbor when he was eleven."

Historical records generally do not address the role of parental beliefs and expectations in the lives of children with visual disabilities prior to the 1960s and 1970s, when parents began to fight for education of their children with disabilities through the courts (Thomas & Russo 1995). However, there is abundant evidence that the leaders of residential schools, once these were established, made assumptions about parental overprotectiveness. Since most students did not enter the Perkins Institution until around age fourteen, Samuel Gridley Howe, in his "Counsels to Parents of Blind Children," encouraged mothers to teach independence: "Do not prevent your blind child from developing, as he grows up, courage, self-reliance, generosity, and manliness of character, by excessive indulgence" (in Ross 1951, p. 150). Decades later, an administrator warned, "A mother is the blind baby's worst enemy. Filled with the horror of the fact that her baby is blind, she devotes her life to waiting on it, doing anything to hush or quiet the peculiar wail of the little soul that has brains, but not sight" (quoted in Lowenfeld 1975, p. 99).

While visual disability is by no means most often hereditary, several of our informants, as it happens, had parents who were blind, and one family spanned four generations of individuals with visual disabilities. In these cases, children derived a twofold benefit. First, parents who themselves had visual disabilities both understood the loss and, contrary to the protective tendencies Howe and other educators were concerned about, held their children to normalized expectations of accomplishment and developmental roles. *Mary*, who describes herself as "partially sighted" and whose mother was totally blind, recalls that in her family, "We all had chores—dishes, house cleaning, and laundry. My mother was very strict about the quality of your work. She saw blindness as normalcy. Now as a mother, I have the same expectations of my sighted and visually impaired children." Also, children saw parents as role models and were able to aspire to goals directed by parental or other relatives' capabilities, as *Bob*'s story suggests: "My father learned piano technician skills at the school for the blind and he taught me. . . . The neighborhood kids loved my father. He was a nice guy and he showed people things, a born teacher. Ham radio . . . got me in touch with all sorts of grownups, and my father helped me with the Morse code. My father's blind school friends were known to me and they all had stories."

The obvious differences between this situation and what would have been likely in the early nineteenth century are that this twentieth-century father is an educated man who possesses not only technical skills but also the ability and desire to teach, and who is apparently comfortable both in

"sighted society" and with his blind friends. He perhaps represents the realization of the vision that most early-nineteenth-century Americans believed "wild" and "Utopian" (Anagnos 1882).

Until the establishment of specialized schools in the 1830s, children with
visual disabilities, although allowed to live, had been marginalized—considered, and often resented, as dependents or as beggars, and expected to
deteriorate into indolence, weakness, and stupidity, if not worse. Samuel
Gridley Howe, who would be America's preeminent leader in the field of
education for persons with visual disabilities, gave this dire warning of the
consequences if their need for education was neglected: "Hence, we see so
many of the blind, who were comparatively intelligent and active in childhood, gradually drooping through youth into premature old age; becoming
first, inactive, then stupid, then idiotic, and finally going down to an early
grave with the light of intellect completely extinguished, and enveloped in
both physical and intellectual darkness" (Howe 1833, p. 5). Howe worked
tirelessly, and effectively, to prevent this tragic fate.

In his early treatises about the education of "the blind," Howe observed
that American society, like European society, had failed to enable persons
with visual disabilities to live without charity, a situation he was committed
to, and extraordinarily effective in, changing. Yet, it must be added that,
until the adoption of regulations for Section 504 of P.L. 93-112, the Vocational Rehabilitation Act, in 1977 and passage of P.L. 94-142, the Education
of the Handicapped Act, in 1975, it was legally possible for American children who were blind to be refused education. Children with visual disabilities could be denied education even by state schools for the blind, as *Dick*
recalled: "In our day, if a student were too slow, they would be sent home
or to a state institution for people with retardation." Lowenfeld's "Modern
Period"—the era of education for persons with visual disabilities—reached
America in the early nineteenth century. However, a century and a half
later, it was yet emerging.

EDUCATIONAL EXPECTATIONS: BEGINNINGS OF THE
MODERN PERIOD

The Modern Period is marked by the discovery that children with visual
disabilities were educable. While there had been isolated accounts since
antiquity, the beginning of the Modern Period did not occur in Europe
until late in the eighteenth century, a product of the Enlightenment, when
schools were established, as in the case of deafness, first in France, then in
Great Britain and Germany. The establishment of the first schools for the
blind in the United States is an indication of this level of attitude among
philanthropists and educators in the new nation. In 1831, the same year
the New England Asylum for the Blind, later renamed the Perkins Institution and Massachusetts Asylum for the Blind, was incorporated, the New

York Institution for the Blind was also established, inspired by the discovery of blind children in almshouses (Allen 1911; Best 1934). The third member of what came to be called "The Great Triumvirate," the Pennsylvania Institution for the Instruction of the Blind, later called Overbrook when it moved to that location, was incorporated in Philadelphia by Quakers in 1833 (Best 1934; Ross 1950).

The development of educational programs for children with visual disabilities in the United States actually began in 1826, when John Dix Fischer returned from Europe, where he had been impressed by the accomplishments of students in the specialized schools he visited (Best 1934). In 1827, Fischer and other reform-minded Bostonians began to raise funds to start such a school, and in February 1829 organized a meeting of these colleagues at the Exchange Coffee House, proposing that a school for children with visual disabilities be founded in Boston (Anagnos 1882). In 1830 the Massachusetts Legislature was asked for, and allocated, funds for the school, which eventually became known as The Perkins Institution and Massachusetts State School for the Blind (Best 1934). In 1831, Samuel Gridley Howe was asked to be this school's first director and was sent to Europe to study such specialized schools there (Allen 1911; Freeberg 2001; Gitter 2001). In 1832, Howe returned from Europe, bringing a teacher from the Paris school and another from the Edinburgh school, and began teaching a few students at his father's house in Boston until construction was completed and the school could be opened (Anagnos 1882).

Howe was determined to make American schools for children with visual disabilities superior to the European schools he had visited, which he criticized for their lack of a systematic approach to instruction, the lack of individualization of instruction to suit each student's capabilities, and the focus on handicrafts that were not appropriate for all persons who were blind (Howe 1833). While Howe felt that the exhibitions these schools produced of their students' achievements had become a driving force in curriculum decisions, exploiting the students to gain public support for the enterprise, he came to use the strategy in his appeals to state legislatures to good effect (Anagnos 1882). Indeed, this was a practice that continued well into the twentieth century. Two interviewees, both graduates of a state school for the blind, described such demonstrations. *Jayne*, who participated in many athletic and musical activities in school, recalled that she also "went on demonstrations to present programs for people in the general public." *Paula* added, "Your talents would be used to the fullest. They said I was a good singer, and we would go on demonstrations to educate the sighted world about the blind school."

Howe's stated goal for the education of the blind was to prepare them for "some constant occupation, which shall ensure them a competent livelihood" (Howe 1833). He decried the fact that most of the graduates of the European schools he had seen were not able to earn a living when they graduated and vowed that that would not be the case in the United States. However, it is estimated today that adults with visual disabilities experience an unemployment rate of 70 percent. *Bob*, blind from birth and whose father was blind, talked about an essay he had written as a student, titled, "Reduced Expectations," in which he had noted, "In my father's generation a lot of those guys had to be content with some pretty low level stuff. . . . One guy worked for Caterpillar Tractor and just reamed nozzle hoses all day. But it seemed to me that at least they were working and that was good enough for us."

The curriculum Howe designed included instruction for all students in English grammar, arithmetic, geography, history, and music (Anagnos 1882; Howe 1837). Students who were more academically inclined studied higher mathematics, astronomy, French, and natural and moral philosophy, while there was less emphasis on academics for students likely to make a living from handcrafts, although all spent about four hours per day on academic studies. However, because Howe felt that all students should be able to earn a livelihood after graduation, all were instructed in music and handicrafts, such as basket- and mattress-making (Armstrong et al. 1834; Howe 1841). Religious training was also considered important at Perkins; the Bible was read to students, and they recited the Lord's Prayer on a daily basis and attended services at the church of their choice on a weekly basis (Howe 1843).

In 1847, Howe's most famous pupil, seventeen-year-old Laura Bridgman, who was the first child who was both deaf and blind to be educated, described her day:

> At 8 my very favorite teacher read to me about the king and his rule of Scotland. . . . At 10 she taught me a lesson from the N. T. and then the N. Philosophy. At 12 she read to me from Geography. I had a very delightful morning. In the P.M. I determined to work on a basket with my wounded thumb with pleasure. I was not successful and then Miss Wight proposed to read to me for 3 quarters of an hour. I went to take a walk with Wightie . . . I met with many more pleasant incidents. (Laura Bridgman, Diary, October 25, 1847)

The mix of adaptive skill development, academics, and skill areas that were thought to be vocationally useful continued to be a dynamic area in curricula within state schools well into the twentieth century. This is evidenced by reflections of several respondents. *Dick* recalled that piano tuning was taught as a shop class, along with basketry, broom making, and chair caning, all taught by the same instructor. "I took tuning when I was in school and I pretty well figured out early on that I could not make that my life's work, but it was a really neat thing to know. It has served me well. I kept a hammer and fork, and some wedges, and once in a while I could pick up some extra money or help a friend."

As with the manual training movement in residential schools for deaf students, however, emphasis on handcraft training to the neglect of academic subjects, which continued through the 1970s, was highly limiting and also lent itself to stereotypes. As *Mary* noted somewhat wistfully, "I always thought that eliminating the craft classes was somewhat sad, too, not that I think that all blind people should only do chair caning and broom making, but it is something nice to have on the side and the demand is great, and for some of the caning jobs you can earn a lot of money doing that. There were no comparable vocational classes for girls." *Jayne* added that weaving "was about the only class that could have been considered vocational, although I don't know any girls who became weavers."

In 1837, soon after the founding of Perkins, the New York Institution for the Blind, and the Philadelphia Institution for the Blind (led by Julius Friedlander from Germany) the Ohio State School for the Blind became the first to be totally funded through state appropriation (Best 1934). Other state-supported residential schools followed. Schools frequently admitted students from other states, as did Perkins, at which in 1841 fifteen of the sixty-seven students came from states other than Massachusetts (Anagnos 1882). Visual disability being a low-incidence condition, this practice continued—and continues today. *Bob*'s family, who lived in Nevada, which had no state school, "In desperation . . . kept [him] in kindergarten another year because there was no place for me to go. All blind kids were shipped to the Utah School for the Blind." The significance of this from the standpoint of the children involved is that it meant extended separations from their families, perhaps the major reason most were not enrolled in the residential schools until their early teens.

Howe frequently took selected students on tour and did exhibitions with them to promote the founding of schools in other states, particularly Ohio, Virginia, Kentucky, and South Carolina, a practice which, as we noted, continued well into the twentieth century. By 1875, twenty-nine states had State Schools for the Blind. In most states, schools for the deaf were founded first (Best 1934), and in some states, such as Virginia, combined schools for children who were deaf and blind were formed (Anagnos 1882). The practice of housing schools for children with visual and hearing disabilities on the same campus or within adjacent classrooms has continued to this day, but it is generally not considered ideal for either group of students. The difficulties are evident in *Matthew*'s reflection concerning shared transportation: "I went to a school of all blind children in Los Angeles, and in Chicago the school had low vision, blind, and deaf children all in one three story building. The deaf kids seemed pretty scary to us, they would grab you to guide you and they were loud and would slam the windows open on the bus."

Although many less-than-optimal practices continued in the interest of efficiency, throughout the nineteenth century more scientific methods of educating children with visual disabilities were being developed (Quimby 1940). In 1880 Michael Anagnos, Howe's son-in-law and successor, added a kindergarten program, as did the Pennsylvania school in 1884, in order to serve younger children, most of whom lived at home. Curricula were being reevaluated in light of the employment patterns of graduates, which led to the introduction of new subject areas such as typewriting. Since their inception, state schools for students with visual disabilities have generally continued to keep pace with technology as access to computers and other assistive technologies replaced typewriting as a strong curricular focus. *Jimmy*, who had attended both public school day classes and a state residential school, felt "lucky" to complete his education and graduate from the latter: "The state school had a really good technology program. In public school, they had computers, but none of the teachers knew much about speech or Braille with them."

In 1870, Howe had begun housing students in a "family-cottage" system, with the goal of creating a less institutional, more family-like environment (Gitter 2001), and the practice soon became widespread in schools for the blind (Quimby 1940). All of our interviewees who attended state schools experienced the cottage model, not always positively. *Paula* recalled the kind of housework children living at home were often expected to do, although perhaps not on so large a scale: "Like one week you might have to clean the bathrooms, wash the sinks, wipe the shelves off. . . . Or you might have to empty the wastebaskets, or sweep the porch. I hated that job." *Joan*'s recollections are not unlike those of women who had attended any sort of residential school in their teens: "We had social hour in the cottages where you could sit on a sofa and talk to your boyfriend, and talk to other couples. At the end of social hour, there was "the five minutes," where the lights were turned off and you could kiss your boyfriend goodnight. And then we had what was called 'going walking.' We could walk for an hour. We were pretty restricted." *Cindy* added, "There was no privacy in the cottages. You could never get away by yourself." At *Jayne*'s school, "There were two, three, or four in a bedroom. You had no choice. Your room mates were assigned." And the living arrangements, she added, were racially segregated, still common in the mid-twentieth century.

SEPARATE AND NOT EQUAL: AFRICAN AMERICAN STUDENTS WITH VISUAL DISABILITIES

A significant development in the education of children with visual disabilities in the latter nineteenth century was the formation of segregated schools for African American children and youth. Before these schools were established, African American children who were blind were not educated at all (Jones & Morrison 1885), although the prevalence of visual disability was proportionately greater than among white children, as it is today (Roberts 1986). Between 1869 and 1929, fifteen segregated schools for students with visual disabilities were started (Building a Future 2003). In 1869, the North Carolina School for the Blind admitted two African American students, forming a "Colored Department" in 1872 (Buell 1945). Segregated residential school programs for students with visual disabilities were subsequently established in Alabama (1891), Alabama (at Piney Woods Country Life School in 1929), Arkansas (1889), Florida (1895), Georgia (1882), Kentucky (1884), Louisiana (1920), Maryland (1872), Texas (1887), Virginia (1909), and West Virginia (1919). In 1934, a sight-saving class specifically for African American students with low vision was begun in the Washington, D.C., public schools (Buell 1945). The first Braille program for African American children was begun in Washington, D.C., in 1945.

The rationale for establishing these programs was that African American children with visual disabilities were being excluded from public schools, while state policy had provided for "equal education" for all (Carroll 1913) (Separate but equal education was ruled to be legal by the U.S. Supreme Court in 1899 in *Cumming v. Richmond Board of Education.*) Exclusion of African American children from schools for the blind was the result of public objection to educating African Americans in schools with white students (Morris 1893).

Nine of the fifteen schools established for African American students with visual disabilities were dual schools in which students who were deaf were in the majority (Bischoff 1943; Buell 1945). Often the expectations for the children who were blind were lower than those for children who were deaf, as was the case in the Colored Department of the Maryland School for the Blind (Bledsoe 1907). The curricula of segregated schools for the blind followed the pattern of white schools, but were often not fully implemented (Buell 1945). Segregated schools for African American students with visual disabilities were not equipped with the laboratories and equipment needed to teach science. Some courses were not taught due to the lack of a qualified instructor (Bonner 1982). Not only were segregated schools supplied with hand-me-down texts and furniture, policy decisions were often made without input from the superintendent of the segregated school.

There is compelling evidence that by no means were all African American children who were blind provided schooling even after the formation of the segregated schools. Superintendents had a great deal of difficulty in recruiting students—recruitment often requiring an African American superintendent to travel in the Jim Crow South, where access to lodging as well as to public records might be limited (Bonner 1982). Students were occasionally referred by eye specialists, nurses, and social workers (Bischoff 1943), but it was often difficult to persuade parents to let their children attend, despite compulsory attendance laws (Bledsoe 1907). The ruling of the U.S. Supreme Court in *Brown v. Board of Education* in 1954, and the passage of the Civil Rights Act of 1964, put these schools on shaky ground legally (Brasington 2000), and between 1954 and 1978 all were integrated into the white schools for the blind (Building a Future 2003).

THE SAGA OF THE TRACHOMA EPIDEMIC IN RESERVATION SCHOOLS

As part of its program to force Native Americans to assimilate into American society, the U.S. government began an aggressive policy at the end of the nineteenth century to enroll Native American children into government-run boarding schools. For example, in 1890, government agents would enter Hopi settlements, forcibly remove children from their homes, and take them off to one of those boarding schools—often very far away (Breunig 1973). Once at the schools, children wore European-style uniforms, and boys were forced to cut their hair (Adams 1995). Children were given European names and taught how to read, speak, and write English as well as other subjects that were characteristic of curricula of that time. In 1897 a drive by the U.S. government to fill reservation schools led to the enrollment of sick children with healthy ones (Child 1998). In 1903, Indian service physicians identified trachoma as a serious health threat among Native American children, second only to tuberculosis. By 1912, the trachoma infection rates at reservation schools ranged between 10.5 percent and 92.1 percent (Allen & Semba 2002). Of the 16,470 students in Native American reservation schools in 1913, 4,916 or 29.8 percent were found to have trachoma.

Trachoma is an infection of the conjunctiva caused by chlamydia trachomatis that has three stages of infection (Markel 2000). Initially there is tearing of the eye and inflammation of the inner eyelid. As the infection progresses, granulation tissue develops on the inner eyelids, which eventually causes ulceration and scarring of the eyeball. In about 10 percent of cases, blindness results from the damage to the eye and eyelids. Trachoma is spread by contact, and the overcrowded living conditions and the mixture of healthy and sick children in reservation schools created an environment that fostered its spread (Allen & Semba 2002). In reservation schools, children shared beds, wash water, soap, towels, and school equipment, causing the disease to spread quickly (Child 1998). When the children returned home, they spread trachoma to their parents and other adults.

From 1924 to 1927, the Office of Indian Affairs administered a trachoma eradication campaign. At the time, there were three treatment options available to control the trachoma epidemic: (1) improving sanitation at schools; (2) treatments with silver nitrate, copper sulfate, alum, or bichloride of mercury; or (3) eye surgery (Benson 2001). Two types of eye surgery were used to treat trachoma. Grattage involved scraping the eyeball and the inner eyelid to remove infected tissue. Tarsectomy was the removal of the tarsal plate, a procedure that could cause the eyelashes to turn in, further damaging the eye and making it impossible to close the lids. If trachoma returned after surgery was performed, there was no way to cure it. Although the American Medical Association recommended improving sanitation to control the epidemic, the Office of Indian Affairs (OIA) chose eye surgery as the preferred method of treatment for trachoma by its physicians. Despite the level of surgical skill needed to successfully perform these procedures, the OIA hastily trained its physicians (Benson 2001) and left the post-surgical care of Native American patients to matrons or older children at reservation schools (Child 1998). By 1927, 5,978 tarsectomies and 22,773 grattages had been performed on Native Americans, with at least 3,000 of them becoming blind as a result of the surgery (Benson 2001).

In 1927, the *Journal of the American Medical Association* (*JAMA*) published an investigation of the treatment of Native Americans for trachoma. Decrying the surgery as terrible disfigurement, the *JAMA* report found that the reservation schools were a major source of the trachoma epidemic because of the admission policies and the low level of hygiene maintained at the schools. Benson, in his 2001 analysis of the OIA's trachoma policies, concludes that surgery was chosen as the preferred treatment plan because of racial prejudice. Policy makers of the OIA saw Native American traditional homes as squalid and believed that Native Americans were more susceptible to the disease than other "races." These policy makers believed that the OIA's hospitals did not need to maintain the same standards as hospitals for whites because Native Americans were considered "primitive." Native American customs were viewed as an obstacle to effective treatment. In 1927, after the *JAMA* article and months of public pressure, the OIA ended its trachoma eradication campaign. In 1957, the organism that caused trachoma was identified and found to be susceptible to sulfanilamide. By the 1970s trachoma was rare among Native Americans.

Today's Native American children with visual disabilities face an array of circumstances that impact the quality of childhood and specialized education. Poverty, population density, and the national shortage of specialists present daunting problems. However, *Tom*, who is an adult Native American with visual disability, believes the traditional cultural norms of the tribe worked to shape attitudes of normalcy, positive self-esteem, and personal ability in the face of adversity: "I would say that being Native American had a strong positive impact on my perception of dealing with vision loss. Some of our cultural values were as basic as, you did what you could do, you did it to the best of your ability, and anything that presented itself as a challenge, you were to overcome it. It wasn't talked about much, it has just always been that way."

NEW CHALLENGES AND OPPORTUNITIES IN THE TWENTIETH CENTURY

The early twentieth century brought significant changes to educational programs for children with visual disabilities. In 1917, after years of fierce debate, Braille was accepted by teachers of the blind as the best form of literacy for persons with significant visual disabilities (Lowenfeld 1981; Quimby 1940). What followed tended to be a doctrinaire, bifurcated decision as to whether a student should be taught via print or Braille, which belies the reality that most children with visual disabilities have residual sight.

Comments of our interviewees illustrate the struggle many students with visual disabilities have experienced. *Cindy* recalls that, "At the state school we were only taught Braille. When I would go home, I had two sighted friends, and they taught me to read and write in order to play school. But Braille was cool. We read in the cottages after lights out." *Matt* had a different kind of experience struggling with the "two worlds" of print and punctiform: "They had me in the class for kids with partial sight and I really struggled. I couldn't read words, only a few letters at a time. After a couple of years, they got the idea, and I was moved to the class for blind kids. Braille was a relief and I really took to it." *Dick* described the frustrations his son experiences. The young man who, like both his parents, has a vision disability, although stabilized by laser surgery "got caught in the middle, not sighted, not totally blind . . . neither fish nor fowl. He's working at one quarter the speed. He's had a hard time with large print books. They weigh a ton. Looking back, he might have done better if he had learned Braille. . . . going with print was our idea to help him to fit into sighted society as much as possible. The whole world is based on vision and print."

In 1908 the national Athletic Association of Schools for the Blind was formed in response to the growing role that sports began to play in residential schools (Quimby 1940). *Jimmy*, a recent graduate of a state school, fondly remembers his involvement with competition between state schools for the blind: "I ran track and did swimming and forensics. We would travel to different blind schools across the country to compete, and there would be at least four other blind schools there as well. And when we had the conference tournament, the last tournament of the season, there would be twelve blind schools competing." *John* recalls the exclusion he experienced in not having such opportunity to participate in sports in his "mainstream" school: "I could never see the ball in any game or sport. I tried to play, but always with miserable results. Only in college did I discover cross country, gymnastics, and scuba diving. It was great to finally feel like I could be successful in athletic activities."

In 1911, the first Sight-Saving class was started in the Cleveland, Ohio, public schools by Robert B. Irwin (Ross 1950), soon to be followed by similar classes in the public schools in Chicago, Cincinnati, Milwaukee, Racine, Boston, New York City, and Newark (Abel 1958). Memories of sight-saving classes among our informants varied, but a common thread is tension and frustration. *Matt* "couldn't see the board" in the Sight-Saving classroom in which he was initially placed so was finally transferred to a setting in which he could learn Braille. As a sixth-grade student, *John* had to arrive at his Sight-Saving class in a rural school late and leave late, due to the schedule of the bus for special education students, in which he had to ride alone. "And then twice a day I trudged down the hall to the resource room. I didn't feel at home in my neighborhood, in my classroom, or in the resource room. I hated it. I was given Braille and typing lessons, and large print books. I refused to touch the Braille, struggling to read it with my weak and damaged eyes instead. Oh, if only there had been some counseling."

Sight-saving classes were structured on the belief that to use low vision was to risk its loss. Only within the last decades of the twentieth century did educators come to believe that students with limited vision should use their remaining or residual vision as a sensory modality for learning. Today, education of students with low vision employs use of such means as high-contrast materials.

By the 1950s two models of public school day programs had emerged. In integrated programs, students began in the regular education room and were pulled out for specialized instruction. In cooperative programs, the self-contained special education room was the student's primary placement, with the student being mainstreamed into some classes (Abel 1958). *Matt* remembers being "a little shy" when he was mainstreamed in the fifth and sixth grades: "I was mainly just listening to what the girls sounded like, but a couple of my friends really were serious students and I was very proud of them when they would give a report. . . . we didn't necessarily know anybody and they would assign kids to sit with us or we would sit in among them. . . . We wouldn't necessarily talk to them through the fence that separated our playgrounds. We were visitors." *Bob* recalled, "In blind school, we'd have "partials" [students with partial sight] ship us around and all that. But by the time I was eight or nine, I discovered the difference between me and sighted kids. . . . The mainstream programs didn't quite know how to handle the differences between sighted and blind kids. There was a prevailing feeling, you just take this chimpanzee and raise him with the sighted kids, and see how he does."

After PL 94-142, now known as the Individuals with Disabilities Education Act, was enacted in 1975, typical educational placements for students with visual disabilities began to shift from self-contained classrooms to inclusive classrooms, and the presence of more programs in public schools caused a change in the role of the residential schools in the education of children with visual disabilities. In addition, medical advances that enabled the survival of premature infants, and social ills that resulted in "crack babies" (children who had experienced intrauterine exposure to crack cocaine) and increase in fetal alcohol syndrome have caused a major increase in the prevalence of children with visual impairment combined with other disabilities. *Barb*, a 1990s graduate from a state school, recalls the internal social structure that developed: "There were cool groups and not so cool groups. There was ridicule and sometimes violence, like boys fighting over a girl. And there was physical violence and ridicule against some kids with multiple disabilities. I guess it was normal teenage group stuff."

While throughout history blindness had been most frequently—though certainly with many exceptions—a single impairment, in 1994, McMahon surveyed thirty-three State Schools for the Blind and found that 54.8 percent of their students had visual disabilities coupled with other disabilities. Nearly one-third of the students attending these schools did not reside on campus. Instruction in most was offered in Braille, and curricula typically included vocational and life skills, training in use of access technology, and typing, as well as academic subjects, music, and art. About half provided mainstreaming opportunities for students in local public schools, most frequently for high school students. *Barb* recalls spending part of her senior year in classes at the residential school she attended and part at a vocational school for training to become a nurse's aide. Some of *Jimmy*'s classes were at the local public high school, "but I didn't really have many friends there, in fact my whole social life was at the school for the blind." *Paula* added, "There were social and recreational activities at the school that weren't available in public schools at the time. We would have been excluded from similar activities." However, according to *John*, "It should be noted that there are lots of changes recently within the state schools for the blind. Some are responding to the changing needs of children and families."

The concept of state schools as centers of specialized education can be seen in today's progressive state schools, such as the one in Texas. State school personnel acting as consultants to local school districts, short-term summer and weekend courses, and movement for prolonged periods between the state school, to learn compensatory skills, and back to the local school district are model practices being offered through some state programs.

One of the goals of inclusive education is the increased socialization of children with disabilities into American society. For students with visual disabilities, this goal may not always be met. A study by Sacks, Tierney, and Wolfe in 1998 found that students with visual disabilities who attended high schools were isolated from their peers by the need to spend large amounts of time being tutored in schoolwork by teachers rather than studying with friends. Another factor that caused students with visual disabilities to be isolated from their peers was the lack of independent transportation available to students who could not drive. Students with visual impairments were found to spend less time socializing with their sighted peers. The majority of the sighted students (90 percent) used a computer to do homework, but only 6 percent of students with visual impairment had access to adaptive technology that would enable them to use a computer (Sacks, Tierney, & Wolfe 1998). As *John* noted, "It took time to learn Braille and typing, and to get the special instruction you needed just to keep up and that time came from music and art class, recess and extra time at lunch, and the time when you got to know other kids and really develop friendships."

SUMMARY

Throughout American history, the life experience of children with visual disabilities has mirrored the cultural and social norms of the historical period and has been impacted by the beliefs, myths, and projections of educators, families, and policy makers. The long and slowly evolving movement toward a non-biased treatment of children with visual disabilities as unique individuals has been shaped by empirical science, advocates, adults who themselves have visual disabilities, and certainly the inexorable movement in American history toward realization of civil rights. Technology, public resources, the evolving understanding of compensatory skills required to successfully accommodate vision loss, and the research and educational acumen brought to bear over the decades have also provided both tools and methodology that have shaped personal experience. When taking the long view, however, it is striking to see how historical beliefs and constructs, assumptions and biases are mirrored in the life experience of persons with visual disabilities living today.

REFERENCES

Abel, G. L. (1958). The Education of Blind Children. In W. G. Cruickshank & O. Johnson, eds., *Education of Exceptional Children and Youth*. Englewood Cliffs, NJ: Prentice-Hall.

Adams, D. W. (1995). *Education for Extinction: American Indians and the Boarding School Experience, 1875–1928*. Lawrence: University Press of Kansas.

Allen, E. E. (1911). *Eightieth Annual Report of the Trustees*. Watertown, MA: Perkins Institution and Massachusetts School for the Blind.

Allen, S. K., & Semba, R. D. (2002). The Trachoma "Menace" in the United States, 1897–1960. *Survey of Ophthalmology* 47(5), 500–509.

Anagnos, M. (1882). *Education of the Blind: Historical Sketch of Its Origin, Rise and Progress*. Boston, MA: Rand, Avery & Co.

Armstrong, S. T., Brooks, E., Fisher, J. D., Homans, J., Mason, W. P., May, S., & Prescott, W. H. (1834). Annual Report of the Trustees of the New England Institution for the Education of the Blind. Boston, MA: New England Institution for the Education of the Blind.

Beers, M. H., & Berkow, R., eds. (2004). *The Merck Manual of Diagnosis and Therapy.* Merck. Retrieved 10/18/2004, from http://www.merck.com/mrkshared.

Benson, T. (2001). Blinded with Science: American Indians, the Office of Indian Affairs, and the Federal Campaign against Trachoma, 1924–1927. In C. E. Trafzer & D. Weiner, eds., *Medicine Ways: Disease, Health, and Survival Among Native Americans* (pp. 52–75). Walnut Creek, CA: Altamira Press.

Berson, M. J., & Cruz, B. (2001). Eugenics Past and Present. *Social Education* 65(5), 300ff.

Best, H. (1934). *Blindness and the Blind in the United States.* New York: Macmillan.

Bischoff, D. A. (1943). *Education of the Negro Deaf and Blind in the United States.* Boston, MA: Perkins Institution.

Black, E. (2003). *War Against the Weak: Eugenics and America's Campaign to Create a Master Race.* New York: Thunder's Mouth Press.

Bledsoe, J. F. (1907). Biennial Report (Thirty-third and Thirty-fourth Annual Reports) of the Department for Colored Blind and Deaf of the Maryland School for the Blind. Parkville: Maryland School for the Blind.

Bonner, C. L. (1982). *A Black Principal's Struggle to Survive.* New York: Vantage Press.

Boswell, J. (1988). *The Kindness of Strangers: The Abandonment of Children in Western Europe from Late Antiquity to the Renaissance.* New York: Pantheon Books.

Brasington, J. M. (2000). *The South Carolina School for the Deaf and Blind: 1849–1999.* Cedar Spring: South Carolina School for the Deaf and Blind.

Breunig, R. G. (1973). Schools and the Hopi Self. *Proceedings of the American Ethnological Society* 48, 51–58.

Buell, C. F. (1945). *The Education of the Negro Blind in the United States.* Unpublished master's thesis, University of Michigan–Ann Arbor.

Building a Future: U.S. Residential Schools for Blind and Visually Impaired Students (2003). American Printing House for the Blind. Retrieved 10/18/2004, from http://www.aph.org/museum/index.html.

Carroll, J. J. (1913). Biennial Report (Thirty-ninth and Fortieth Annual Reports) of the Department for Colored Blind and Deaf of the Maryland School for the Blind. Overlea: Maryland School for the Blind.

Child, B. J. (1998). *Boarding School Seasons: American Indian Families, 1900–1940.* Lincoln: University of Nebraska.

Dorsey, M. (2002). The New Eugenics: It Used to Be Forced Sterilization, and the Experiments of Dr. Mengele. Now It's Genetic Technology and the Free Market. The People Who Dream of Creating a Superior Race Are Back. *World Watch* 15(4), 21ff.

Freeberg, E. (2001). *The Education of Laura Bridgman: The First Deaf and Blind Person to Learn Language.* Cambridge, MA: Harvard University Press.

French, R. S. (1932). *From Homer to Helen Keller: A Social and Educational Study of the Blind.* New York: American Foundation for the Blind.

Gitter, E. (2001). *The Imprisoned Guest: Samuel Howe and Laura Bridgman, the Original Deaf-blind Girl.* New York: Picador USA.

Howe, S. G. (1833). *Education of the Blind.* Boston, MA: Charles Bowen.

————. (1833?). Education of the Blind (Reprint from *The New-England Magazine* ed., 11pp.).

————. (1837). Lecture I: On the Education of the Blind (26pp.). Boston, MA: American Stationer's Co.

————. (1841). Ninth Annual Report of the Trustees of the Perkins Institution and Massachusetts Asylum for the Blind (42pp.). Boston, MA: John H. Eastburn, Printer.

————. (1843). Eleventh Annual Report of the Trustees of the Perkins Institution and Massachusetts Asylum for the Blind (22pp.). Boston, MA: John H. Eastburn, Printer.

Jones, I. D., & Morrison, F. D. (1885). Twelfth Annual Report of the Maryland School for the Colored Blind and Deaf-Mutes. Baltimore: Maryland School for the Colored Blind and Deaf-Mutes.

Lash, J. P. (1980). *Helen and Teacher: The Story of Helen Keller and Anne Sullivan Macy.* New York: Addison Wesley.

Lowenfeld, B. (1956). History and Development of Specialized Education for the Blind. American Association of Workers for the Blind: Annual Report (pp. 15–21). New York: AAWB.

————. (1975). *The Changing Status of the Blind: From Separation to Integration.* Springfield, IL: Charles C. Thomas.

————. (1981). *Berthold Lowenfeld on Blindness and Blind People.* New York: American Foundation for the Blind.

Markel, H. (2000). "The Eyes Have It": Trachoma, the Perception of Disease, the United States Public Health Service, and the American Jewish Immigration Experience, 1897–1924. *Bulletin of the History of Medicine* 74(3), 525–560.

McMahon, E. (1994). The Role of Residential Schools for the Blind in 1990. *RE:view* 25(4), 163–172.

Miller, E. M. (1997). Eugenics: Economics for the Long Run. *Research in Biopolitics* 5, 391–416.

Mintz, S. (2004). *Huck's Raft: A History of American Childhood.* Cambridge, MA and London: The Belknap Press of Harvard University Press.

Morris, J. T. (1893). Twentieth Annual Report of the Maryland School for the Colored Blind and Deaf-Mutes. Baltimore: Maryland School for the Colored Blind and Deaf-Mutes.

Pfeiffer, D. (1993). Overview of the Disability Movement: History, Legislative Record, and Political Implications. *Policy Studies Journal* 21(4), 724ff.

Quimby, N. F. (1940). *A Study of the Curriculum for Residential Schools for the Blind.* New York: American Foundation for the Blind.

Roberts, C. D., Stough, L. M., & Parrish, L. H. (2002). The Role of Genetic Counseling in the Elective Termination of Pregnancies Involving Fetuses with Disability. *Journal of Special Education* 36(1), 48ff.

Roberts, F. K. (1986). Education for the Visually Handicapped: A Social and Educational History. In G. T. Scholl, ed., *Foundations of Education of Blind and Visually Handicapped Children and Youth: Theory and Practice* (pp. 1–18). New York: American Foundation for the Blind.

Ross, I. (1951). *Journey into Light: The Story of the Education of the Blind.* New York: Appleton-Century-Crofts, Inc.

Sacks, S. Z., Tierney, D., & Wolfe, K. E. (1998). Lifestyles of Students with Visual Impairments: Preliminary Studies of Social Networks. *Exceptional Children* 64(4), 463ff.

Safford, P. L., & Safford, E. J. (1996). *A History of Childhood and Disability.* New York: Teachers College Press.

Thomas, S. B., & Russo, C. J. (1995). *Special Education Law: Issues & Implications for the 90's.* Topeka, KS: National Organization on Legal Problems of Education.

Winzer, M. A. (1997). Disability and Society before the Eighteenth Century. In L. J. Davis, ed., *The Disability Studies Reader* (pp. 75–109). New York: Routledge.

3 The Progressive Movement and the Child with Physical Disabilities

Brad Byrom

At the turn of the twentieth century, children with physical disabilities faced a wide array of hardships. Among other things, they found themselves the subjects of frightening medical experimentation and social ostracism. To reformers of the time, however, the greatest difficulties facing those whom contemporaries referred to as "cripples" were the social and cultural barriers that prevented disabled children from attending school. In an era renowned for its sense of social justice and for its emphasis upon providing education to the masses, such conditions signaled an obvious neglect. Joseph F. Sullivan, who experienced firsthand the difficulties facing cripples and later became an ardent proponent of education for disabled children, demonstrated the frustration that many felt concerning this matter. With a good deal of sincerity (and a bit of hyperbole), Sullivan described the barriers to education that he and other disabled children faced as "the most damnable neglect that the United States as a nation has ever perpetrated" (Sullivan 1914, p. 11).

While other reformers may not have felt quite as passionately about the issue as Sullivan, a large number of reform-minded Americans agreed that something needed to be done to improve the lives of disabled children. A loose coalition of socially conscious reformers—including businessmen, philanthropists, nurses, doctors, and others—pushed forth what became a nation-wide movement to aid crippled children during the first decades of the twentieth century. The movement they forged bore the hallmarks of the larger movement known as progressivism. Typically, progressive reformers exhibited a strong sense of social justice that led them to come to the aid of many marginalized groups in American society. Immigrants, children of the poor, criminals, and many others became the subjects of progressive reform efforts. And though their solutions varied greatly from one reform issue to the next, certain imperatives drove virtually all of the era's reforms, including those aimed at disabled children. Confident in the ability of experts and modern science to solve social problems, progressives took an approach characterized by a blend of pragmatism and expediency, then directed this approach at a highly complex reform agenda.

While historians differ greatly in their interpretations of this era (particularly when explaining the motivations for reform), there is general agreement on at least two important points. First of all, the reform agenda established by progressives reflected the remarkable optimism of the time—an optimism inspired largely by a faith in science and scientific experts. Secondly, progressives experienced only limited success and oftentimes failed to bring about deep and lasting social change. The combination of pragmatism and expediency brought about a remarkable volume of reform, yet much of it proved too simplistic to untangle the intricate social and political problems that progressives addressed. Perhaps nowhere in the historical record is the failed optimism of progressivism clearer than in the attempts of reformers to improve the lives of crippled children.

As with most progressive reform failures, the roots of their disappointment can be found in their inability to fully appreciate the complexity of the problem. Specifically, reformers failed to understand the nuanced meaning of disability in American society. Yet, despite the serious limitations of their reforms, reformers did manage to establish an approach to aiding crippled children that remains important to this day. This chapter attempts to explain how the progressive emphasis on science and education affected the shape of new charitable and public policies regarding crippled children and in the process helped to create a new and lasting paradigm for understanding the problem of physical disability. Exploring this topic also reveals a larger lesson regarding the matter of disability in American history. When one scrutinizes closely the efforts of reformers it soon becomes apparent that disability is not a static concept that remains the same over time. Rather, the meaning of disability—along with the reality of living with a disability—changes and is affected by the same forces that shape such concepts as gender and race. Just as the meaning of being an African American or a woman has changed across time, so too has the meaning of disability. And in no period of time did that meaning undergo more profound change than in the progressive era.

In typical progressive fashion, reformers began their crusade to aid crippled children with detailed studies of the problem. When combined with anecdotal evidence from disabled people such as Sullivan, their studies revealed that multiple layers of physical and cultural impediments formed a substantial barrier between disabled children and the public school system—a system that was evolving into the institutional forms that we recognize today (Wright 1920; Faries 1918; Hathway 1928; Hamburger &

Wright 1918). The outer, most visible layer of impediment involved physical obstacles such as cobbled streets, dirt roads, and innumerable flights of stairs. Combined with the near absence of the accessibility features that we often take for granted today (features such as elevators, ramps, and curb cuts), physical barriers served as a major obstacle to the inclusion of disabled people in American society. In combating these hindrances, personal mobility aids provided little help. Wheelchairs and braces were cumbersome and inefficient, making it difficult to navigate even in those few public spaces where physical barriers did not impede the movement of the mobility impaired.

The story of Joseph Sullivan illustrates the difficulties that faced such children. Growing up in rural Arkansas, Sullivan displayed both intellectual curiosity and stubbornness in his pursuit of knowledge. Yet, after losing the use of his legs and one arm following the onset of polio at the age of four, Sullivan encountered a series of major difficulties in his quest for knowledge. That he eventually succeeded in graduating from high school with honors is a testament to his personal tenacity. As a grammar school student, he was loaded into a wagon and pulled along bumpy dirt roads by his older brothers, then lifted upstairs to get to class. By his early teenage years, however, his brothers could no longer manage to get him to school. His increasing physical size, coupled with a long and rough commute, temporarily ended his pursuit of education. Only as a result of his own extraordinary efforts did he succeed in returning to school and completing his studies. After taking to the streets of Imboden, Arkansas, as a newspaper boy, Sullivan invested the proceeds in a cart and a team of goats that provided him with the mobility needed to obtain his diploma. Even then, he often suffered through long days spent at his desk, unable even to use the restroom. Upon graduation he hoped to attend college but could find no campuses with the accessibility necessary for him to attend (Gray 1921, pp. 11–13).

Even in those instances where a determined soul such as Sullivan did manage to run the gauntlet of physical barriers and enter the public arena, perhaps the most daunting obstacles of all remained. Disabled children faced frequent taunts and penetrating stares from their peers and adults alike that deterred all but the most thick-skinned from making frequent ventures into the public realm. As one disabled woman explained, cultural prejudices against disabled people made forays out of the home a traumatizing experience that made the heart "throb with pain" (Norris 1921). As a youth Sullivan repeatedly felt the sting of a label that, in his words, begrudged him a "normal" childhood; he felt the discomfort of stares from both adults and children, and experienced the humiliation of being denied access to public spaces. Reflecting on his childhood, Sullivan later wrote, "almost everybody you met—yes, the grownups especially—stared at you— blinked and rubbed their greedy eyes" (Sullivan 1921, p. 12).

Along with many nondisabled reform leaders, Sullivan and other outspoken members of the disabled community condemned the pity and stares that met crippled children who ventured into the public. Sullivan wrote of the pity often heaped upon these children as a force "that stifles, pains and punishes" the crippled child "to the very depth of his better self" (Sullivan 1923, p. 3). Others described pity as a moral evil that eroded the human will and robbed the individual of self-respect and pleasure (Anonymous 1919; Blake 1917; Heydon 1918). Writing in *American Magazine*, Mary Dickerson Donahey concluded from having grown up with a disability that pity was "the worst curse that the devil ever laid on mankind." Along with Sullivan and others, she believed that pity destroyed the will of the individual. By way of example, she wrote of an acquaintance whose hand was amputated, and whose family showered her with pity. Eventually, the "family pitied her into a state of perpetual sorrow, into the loss of all pleasure, and, finally, I have been told, into loss of life. She was killed by pity, and maybe it was just as well. For all her joy in living had been killed before her!" (Donahey 1918, p. 32).

The difficulty in eliminating the cultural and physical barriers facing disabled children is made clear by the fact that even the well-coordinated efforts of disability rights activists in recent decades have failed to entirely remove either physical or cultural barriers. The absence of any such rights-based movement in the early twentieth century exacerbated the problem of making meaningful change at that time.

Nevertheless, the emergence of the large-scale and broad-ranging progressive reform movement promised some hope for improvement in the lives of disabled children. Perhaps the largest reform movement in American history, progressivism was inspired by the rapid changes brought on by industrialization, immigration, and urbanization in the nineteenth century. Extending roughly from 1900 to 1920, it brought forth a remarkable energy particularly evident among the mostly middle-class reformers who led the movement. These reformers were responding to a century's worth of social and economic change that took America from its rural, agricultural origins to an increasingly modern, industrial, and urban society. American institutions and culture were simply not prepared for such changes, and a broad array of problems ensued. Thus, reformers of this period sought to adjust American society to the changing reality of the modern world. Progressives like Jane Addams and Jacob Riis are famous for having built settlement houses for immigrants, for legislating against children in the workplace, for exposing the horrors of tenement dwellings, and for dozens of other campaigns intended to create "social justice" for the less privileged.

To understand fully the impact of progressive reform on children in this era, it is helpful to first understand the social and economic motivations behind the movement. In both rural and urban areas, economic modernization brought profound change to the lives of many disabled Americans. Early in the nation's history, most farms functioned within a semi-subsistence, barter economy, where individual productivity mattered less than in a modern, capitalist society. In early America, all family members contributed to the productivity of the household to the extent that their age, gender, and physical ability allowed. Farmers operating in this system produced the variety of goods necessary for survival in a semi-subsistent economy. Employment, therefore, was not reliant upon one's productive capacity, but simply upon membership in the family. And, since the families engaged in such an economy resulted in a wide array of tasks in need of completion, it was possible to match one's particular abilities—however limited they may be—to a particular task. In such a system, the very young, the very old, and the disabled all found their niche. This is not to suggest that the adult males who stood atop this system did not discriminate based upon physical difference. Inequality and bigotry existed, even within the family unit. Still, such discrimination rarely resulted in the social ostracism of disabled individuals; such measures simply did not make sense in a semi-subsistence economy.

However, as canals, steamships, and railroads linked more and more of rural America to the emerging market economy, small family farms began to give way to large-scale farming enterprises that functioned more like factories than traditional farms. This slow process of economic change eventually resulted in the exclusion of many disabled people from the work-place. The emergence of large-scale farms or "factories in the field," as one historian described them, contributed to a rapid expansion in farm productivity and along with it a steady drop in the price of farm commodities in the second half of the nineteenth century. Falling prices and heavy competition placed enormous pressure on small farmers. While some managed to adapt to the changes in farm operations by expanding their productivity and entering the market economy, others succumbed to the harsh economic realities. Particularly in the 1870s, 1880s, and 1890s, small-scale farmers struggled and many failed. As they failed, family members were forced into competitive, wage labor positions. Not surprisingly, disabled workers found such employment difficult to find (Faragher 1988; Oliver 1990; Sellers 1991).

For the most desperate of these newly marginalized, disabled workers, urban mendicancy presented an unhappy alternative. Anglo tradition (in both England and the United States) accepted the legitimacy of disabled beggars in cities. For example, both London and New York banned begging in public for all but those licensed to beg. The presence of a physical disability was generally enough to secure such a license. Yet life in urban areas was also rapidly changing. In the smaller urban areas of the early republic, disabled people who lacked family support could be accommodated through an existing framework of charitable agencies and individual acts of assistance. As cities became larger, and as poor immigrants from foreign lands and poor migrants from rural America flooded American cities, the existing network of private charity became overwhelmed. The sheer size and anonymity of metropolitan life compounded the problem by making it easier upon the well-off individual's conscience to ignore or even condemn the disabled poor. By the 1890s, the act of begging by crip-ples—a behavior that had once been readily accepted—came to be seen by many as something of a plague and served as a constant reminder of the problems that the urban, industrial transformation of America pre-sented (Rothman 1971; Trent 1994).

To combat the many social problems that emerged during the late nine-teenth century, reformers tested a wide array of solutions, most of which were rooted in the broad fields of education and science. In fact, reformers not only came to rely upon these fields for possible answers to society's problems, but came to demonstrate a remarkable faith that with the proper application of science and the wholesale education of the masses, they could all but eliminate problems associated with the modern world. The faith in science was largely a byproduct a number of truly impressive ad-vances in fields ranging from electricity to surgery. These remarkable de-velopments helped create an unprecedented and often uncritical acceptance of scientific authority. Electric lights appeared to turn night into day. Steel-framed buildings reached into the clouds. Telephones al-lowed people to communicate over hundreds of miles. It is no wonder that progressives demonstrated so much confidence in both science and the experts who developed it (Wiebe 1967; Buenker 1973; Crunden 1982; Hays 1957).

Scientific advances also swept the medical field. From x-rays and anes-thesia, to modern hospitals and medical specialization, changes in medical practices provided physicians and surgeons with newfound respect. Mean-while the establishment of professional medical organizations, the creation and refinement of medical journals, the development of an increasingly specialized medical lexicography, and the reform of medical schools in-creased the prestige of the medical profession and allowed physicians to gain unprecedented control over matters of the mind and body. As a direct result of such changes, pediatrics, obstetrics, and many other medical spe-cialties were firmly established as legitimate and sovereign professions by the second decade of the twentieth century (Starr 1982).

Of the powers that medical practitioners assumed, one of the most im-portant was the ability to define illness. It is probably safe to say that in today's world most people understand disability to be a product of medical conditions such as blindness, paraplegia, and the like (although it is im-portant to point out that a substantial number of people today—including a good many with disabilities—would argue that disabilities are a product of cultural and social barriers rather than physical impairments). This assumption, however, has not always held sway. Prior to the progressive era, most viewed disability as a result of divine affliction. That is, they believed that God (or perhaps the Devil) created disability (Baynton 1996). The impressive advances in medical science provided one basis for challenging and eventually discrediting the divine affliction explanation for disability.

In redefining what it meant to be a cripple, medical specialists in the field of orthopedics would have the most important voice. Once a small, marginalized group viewed more with derision than respect by both the medical establishment and society at large, orthopedists began establishing their specialty as a respected medical field during the progressive era. The process would take time—more, in fact, than many comparable fields. Nevertheless, by creating their own medical journals (including the *American Journal of Orthopedic Surgery*), through surgical innovation (such as bone grafting), and by developing specialized institutions (such as orthopedic hospitals), orthopedists succeeded in gaining sway over reform efforts directed at crippled children. To be sure, their power was not absolute. Businessmen, wealthy philanthropists, women's clubs, and even a handful of disabled men played important parts in shaping reforms. Still, orthopedists steadily gained influence between 1900 and 1930, and as they did other reformers increasingly deferred to their judgment.

The growing authority of the orthopedist with regards to crippled children extended beyond issues of impaired bones and muscles to include matters of moral behavior, psychology, and even parental guidance. Orthopedist Augustus Thorndike, for instance, wrote about the effect of "misguided home influences" that created "a fixed impression in the mind" of the cripple that neither education nor work was necessary (1914). He stressed the need for reformers to remove the child from such influences whenever necessary, and to create a moral environment in their institutions that would counteract the negative influences of a pampered home life. Charles H. Jaeger, one of the most important orthopedic surgeons involved with the work performed for crippled children, argued along similar lines, and even developed a theory explaining how cripples became both dependent and immoral as a result of the pity and pampering they received at home. As he explained matters, "well-intentioned but ill-advised friends and relations" had the tendency to "coddle the patient," a behavior that led to a loss of ambition and self worth (Jaeger 1914, p. 68). The credence reformers outside of the orthopedic profession gave to orthopedists such as Jaeger and Thorndike, who ventured into such decidedly non-orthopedic matters as psychology and parenting, demonstrates the growth of orthopedic sovereignty over matters of physical disability. Numerous other orthopedists and their allies expressed similar views (Cabot 1915; Davis 1914; Willard 1928; Stein 1918). That reformers would provide power to a group of specialists who, only a few decades earlier, were labeled "saw-bones" and even quacks, demonstrates the degree to which progressives embraced the scientific expert.

In addition to the application of medical science and the expert advice of orthopedic surgeons, education played a major role in shaping reform in the first decade of the twentieth century. In fact, science and education shared important bonds. The new field of "social science" applied the techniques of the scientific method to the problems of society. Much like their counterparts in fields such as biology and chemistry, social scientists such as Lester Frank Ward and Robert Hunter (both of whom worked in the emerging field of sociology) made use of detailed, quantitative studies to gauge the cause of social problems (Hunter 1904). In particular, Ward's findings led him to insist that a lack of opportunity, educational or otherwise, provided the main impetus for poverty (Burnham 1956). Though generally accepting of the new industrial order and wage labor, progressives like Ward came to harbor a "deep outrage against the worst consequences of industrialism" (Link & McCormick 1983, p. 21).

Those who recommended education as a means to avoid the "worst consequences" concluded that the sufferings of people with disabilities were better understood as a product of social and economic circumstances than as a result of individual sloth, lower intelligence, or simply bad breeding (Ringenbach 1973). Whether reform efforts were directed at criminals, juvenile delinquents, or "cripples," progressives proceeded with the assumption that "rehabilitation could result only from policies that respected the unique personality and circumstances of each individual" (Katz 1986, p. 118). The writings of Ward, Hunter, and other progressive social thinkers like Richard T. Ely and the well-known educator John Dewey helped to convince a generation of reformers that education held a near-limitless power to surmount the difficulties of childhood (Dubofsky 1985; Degler 1991). Much as developments in medical science help to explain the important role that orthopedists played in reform efforts, the undeniable influence of social scientists on the understanding of childhood development helps explain the outpouring of support for education as a solution to the problems of the disabled child.

The impact of orthopedics and education within this reform movement is most evident in the types of institutions that reformers created. By the 1910s, virtually all institutions for crippled children included both education and orthopedics. The dozens of orthopedic hospitals that were constructed during the first two decades of the new century not only emphasized medical and surgical care, but most also provided large doses of schooling to their patients. Conversely, in most schools for crippled children orthopedic doctors made regular visits, searching for potential surgery candidates and making recommendations on topics ranging from moral behavior to the ideal desk for a student using a wheelchair.

These hybrid institutions first began to appear in the late nineteenth century along the northeastern seaboard, where urban reformers created institutions both large and small, particularly in New York, Philadelphia, and Boston. As the century drew to a close, the movement began to appear in the Midwest. The metropolitan areas of Cleveland, Detroit, Chicago, and Minneapolis, along with a number of smaller communities, became home to substantial rehabilitation efforts that produced hospitals, convalescent homes, and vocational training programs exclusively for cripples. By 1920, Oregon, Washington, and California brought regional rehabilitation centers to the West. The South proved somewhat more hesitant in adopting rehabilitation programs, but nevertheless the movement became a national one as southerners in North Carolina, Tennessee, and elsewhere created institutions modeled on their northern forerunners by the late 1910s and early 1920s.[1]

Even with the slow growth of reform efforts in the South and West, by 1912 more than 80 institutions in a dozen states provided various types of educational or medical attention to crippled children.[2] Of these, 37 were residential institutions where children remained as inmates, patients, or "pupil-patients" for an extended period of time beyond that required for medical treatment. Taken together, these institutions were capable of housing 2,474 children. Over the next decade the number of institutions and their capacity more than doubled to 76 residential institutions with a capacity of 5,729 children—a growth rate of over 300 percent. Meanwhile, the number of crippled children receiving education in special classes increased from zero in 1890 to 988 students in 51 classes by 1912. By 1924 approximately 6,225 children were educated in 162 special classes (Reeves 1914; Abt 1924).

To change the environment, reformers created specialized institutions. This may seem an obvious solution, but it is important to realize that in choosing to focus upon the creation of new institutions in order to achieve reform, progressives chose to overlook both the social barriers that proved such an obstacle to Joseph Sullivan's education, and the cultural barriers that made childhood so distressing for Mary Dickerson Donahey. The institutions progressive reformers built for crippled children were often set in rural settings, and in all cases isolated children from the mainstream of society. In fact, it could be argued that these institutions did more to create distance between disabled children and the mainstream than had existing

1. The term rehabilitation, though employed by some as early as 1910, did not come into common usage until at least the mid-1920s. My use of the term to describe events of the early twentieth century differs substantially from the definition of rehabilitation as it is commonly used today and therefore should not be confused with modern definitions.

2. States with institutions serving crippled children by 1925 included Connecticut, Illinois, Maine, Maryland, Massachusetts, Michigan, Minnesota, Nebraska, New Jersey, New York, Ohio, Pennsylvania, Rhode Island, and Washington.

circumstances. Rather than designing reforms that addressed the essential problems facing disabled children, reformers created institutions that reflected their affinity for science and the expert. They created institutions in which experts could apply their knowledge, yet in the process they further separated disabled children—literally and symbolically—from their nondisabled peers.

Though outwardly different in appearance, the various institutions that reformers created shared many traits that lent a degree of symmetry across the movement. One of the most common traits was a willingness to experiment with new therapeutic techniques. For example, most institutions adopted a popular early-twentieth-century treatment known as fresh air therapy. From tuberculosis to polio, medical experts prescribed heavy doses of fresh air for patients with virtually any physical ailment or impairment. Its benefits were considered to be such that it was administered even during cold northeastern winters. As a result, children found themselves literally out in the cold (or heat). Even in the midst of a New England winter, heavily bundled, disabled children could be found shivering on "sleeping porches" to receive the benefits of fresh air. The willingness of various institutional leaders to experiment with such fashionable therapies is simply one manifestation of the progressive commitment to expert opinion.

The willingness of doctors to experiment with new surgical procedures, and the support offered these doctors by medical laypersons within the movement provides another sign. At least one prominent orthopedist who began practicing during the era wrote of surgeons who employed "makeshift and often grotesque methods."

> In many instances, surgeons resorted to metal gadgets in their practice. In the course of my professional experience, I have come upon cases in which metal plates, screws, nails, and wires ranging from silver threads to piano strings had been used. Much of this bizarre practice in the past was due to necessity, of course, but even at the present time, metal gadgets are too often used. (Albee 1943, p. 81)

Such devices inevitably failed over time and often resulted in massive infections. Many general practitioners and surgeons scorned orthopedists, viewing their methods as "a style of quackery" (Rosenberg 1987, p. 169).

A 1914 nationwide survey of institutions for crippled children and other sources reveal that orthopedists were not the only experts who received the implicit trust of reformers and the access to institutions that went with it. In addition to the somewhat unsettling use of fresh air therapy and new surgical procedures, experts across the institutional spectrum employed a fairly uniform set of educational treatments. In addition to traditional academic lessons, institutionalized children received vocational instruction and moral training. While institutions such as orthopedic hospitals and schools for crippled children seem to have little in common, these outward differences obscured a number of common characteristics. As one might expect, orthopedic hospitals such as the Minnesota State Hospital for Indigent Crippled and Deformed Children focused upon surgical care, yet generally they also provided academic and vocational education in keeping with what one might find in a school. In fact, even the staunchest proponents of orthopedic surgery agreed that "The education of crippled children is intimately associated with their bodily care. The two cannot be separated but must be considered together" (Davis 1914, pp. 5–6). Likewise, schools such as the Dowling Memorial provided children with regular examinations by orthopedic surgeons, daily oversight by trained nurses, and programs tailored to the physical needs of the child (Sullivan 1922).

The overlapping functions that gave the various institutions a certain consistency were a product of the reformer's belief that education and orthopedics served a similar function. Put simply, education was seen as therapeutic, and orthopedic treatment was seen as instructive. The therapeutic value of education related to the common belief that physical disability was not simply a matter of the body, but also of the mind. Perhaps the clearest explanation of this connection came from orthopedists such as Thorndike, Jaeger, and others, who shared the bigoted opinion that disabled children were somehow less industrious and were inclined toward a selfish indolence (Thorndike 1914; Jaeger 1914; Cabot 1915). Those who believed that a peculiar "mental warp" existed in crippled children recommended combating it with large doses of education and moral training—what some simply referred to as the "work cure" (Harris 1919, p. 208; Albee 1943, p. 202).

The connection between hard work and medicine was not limited to reform efforts directed at crippled children. The famous journalist and social reformer Jacob Riis once described work for children of the poor by using frank medical analogies that correspond well to those applied to work for crippled children. Comparing the efforts of the Children's Aid Society to that of doctors, Riis explained that "their pill is the Industrial School, their plaster a Western farm and a living chance in exchange for the tenement and the city slum. The wonder-cures they have wrought by such simple treatment have been many" (Riis 1902, p. 187). By instilling a strong work ethic in the child, reformers like Riis believed that one of the major problems associated with both physical disability and poverty could be overcome.

Much as education was thought to have the potential to "cure" disability, surgical and therapeutic regimes were thought to have the potential to educate children. Within the ideal institution for crippled children, wrote one doctor, patients would develop an "esprit-de-corps that frowns upon the slacker and shows favor to him who pluckily surmounts the discomforts of the long treatment" (Willard 1928, p. 102). The suggestion here was that a clear benefit, not directly related to one's physical well being, came from enduring the painful procedures and long periods of recovery and therapy that orthopedic practice demanded. Self-discipline was a major goal of reform efforts. In fact, at least one leading orthopedist suggested that doctors should substitute plaster casts for removable braces, particularly when the patient seemed unlikely to follow doctors' orders regarding the wearing of painful orthotic devices (Orr 1916, p. 338).

Of the differing institutional types—special schools, asylums, hospitals, and hospital-schools—none so fully represented all that was important to the progressive as did the hospital-school. Also described as convalescent hospitals or homes, institutions like the 250-bed Massachusetts Hospital School were considered by many contemporaries to be a more vital part of the rehabilitation process than the orthopedic hospital. In fact, many viewed the orthopedic hospital as simply the jumping-off point in the rehabilitation process, while the bulk of the journey to self-support would occur in the hospital-school. Many hospital-schools established connections with hospitals, taking on children who had recently undergone surgery. Some existed solely for the purpose of providing extended rehabilitation to specific hospitals; others performed surgery on-site, while still others managed both functions.

This unique institution not only represented virtually all of the competing values of its time, but as its name reveals, the contradictions of a complex era. In hospital-schools, cutting edge medical practice was blended with the latest child development techniques emerging from the social sciences. The missions of these institutions were rarely clear, and never specific. Goals always included both medical and educational objectives, along with the ubiquitous intent of self-support.

One result of this institutional diversity was a system of shared power and authority. Orthopedists maintained the greatest single authority, but the importance given to education, the lengthy stays, and the fact that many doctors were not residents of the institutions they served no doubt undermined orthopedic authority. Resident nurses and female educators had far more contact with the children and did most of the planning of daily activities. Thus, while doctors were undoubtedly the most important symbols of authority, the daily contact with children by nurses and educators, along with the administrative responsibilities of matrons, gave non-orthopedists a more important role in shaping the day-to-day reality of hospital-school life. Philanthropists and businessmen, meanwhile, put their own stamp on the structure of hospital schools. P.A.B. Widener, who provided a multimillion-dollar endowment for the creation of the Widener School, insisted upon the creation of an institution that placed self-support above any other single objective, and played a critical role in shaping virtually every aspect of the institution, from its architectural design to the status of the patients admitted (Hodge 1908; Reeves 1914). Finally, experts in the burgeoning field of vocational rehabilitation also frequently influenced the nature of the hospital-school experience. Those behind the hospital school movement pointed to education, surgery, and therapy as a prescription for the liberation of the crippled child. A combination of these ingredients was administered in the hospital-school, where reformers hoped to provide cripples with a life free of physical suffering and economic despair, while excusing governmental and charitable agencies from the burden of care for cripples.

The result was a uniquely progressive institution in which the influence of experts from the fields of education and orthopedics drove not only reform, but a new and evolving definition of physical disability. The influence of educators and behaviorists placed a fair amount of blame for disability upon society. Misguided family and friends discouraged the ambitions of the disabled people in their company. Schools and businesses underestimated the ability of disabled people and thus felt justified in excluding them. In placing a substantial degree of blame upon society for disability, reformers seemed to be suggesting that disability was in fact a product of culture. In other words, it was not the physical impairment that caused problems for the disabled individual, but society's treatment of the individual. Such language mirrors that of the more modern "social model" of disability that is at the core of the disability rights movement.

The actions of progressive era reformers, however, belie their rhetoric. If in fact the problem of disability resided in society as a whole, then it would make sense that a solution would be found there as well. Again, it is instructive to consider recent trends in order to fully appreciate the contradiction inherent in progressive reform rhetoric. Today, those who support a social model of disability quite logically press for reforms ranging from improving physical access by adding such features as elevators, curb cuts, and the like, to changing negative cultural perceptions of disabled people.[3] Such reforms place the impetus for change upon society rather than the individual by asking or demanding that society accommodate everyone and that society change its way of thinking about people with disabilities. In the progressive era, however, few such reforms were attempted. Instead, the impetus for change was placed upon the individual. Hospitals, special schools, and the like segregated disabled children into institutions intended to change the individual both physically (through orthopedics) and mentally (particularly through moral training intended to reverse the "warped mindset" of the crippled child). In today's modern disability rights movement, the bulk of the reforms created during the progressive era are considered to be part of the emerging medical model of

3. An example of attempts to change cultural perceptions would be the rejection by many of the "poster child"—a fund-raising icon intended to elicit sympathy and donations but makes the disabled person an object of pity.

disability—a way of thinking about disability that locates the central problem of disability within the individual.

The contradiction between reform rhetoric and reform thought in the early twentieth century is largely a product of the progressives' commitment to science and the expert, and to the pragmatic simplicity of the reform agenda. While reformers recognized that at least part of the blame for disability resided within society, the complexity of solving a problem so vast as to reside in the minds of nearly all Americans was simply too great for the simple solutions that progressives preferred. Simply put, reforming several thousand cripples whom virtually everyone agreed had serious flaws seemed a lot more practical than reforming several million Americans confident that good intentions equaled equality.

REFERENCES

Abt, H. (1924). *The Care, Cure, and Education of the Crippled Child*. Elyria, OH: The International Society for Crippled Children.

Albee, F. (1943). *A Surgeon's Fight to Rebuild Men*. New York: E. P. Dutton.

Baynton, D. (1996). *Forbidden Signs: American Culture and the Campaign Against Sign Language*. Chicago: University of Chicago Press.

Blake, N. (1917). How One Man Overcame. *The Ladies' Home Journal* 34, 64.

Buenker, J. (1973). *Urban Liberalism and Progressive Reform*. New York: W. W. Norton.

Burnham, J. (1956). *Lester Frank Ward in American Thought*. Washington, DC: Public Affairs.

Cabot, R. (1915). Work for the Handicapped. *American Journal of Care for Cripples* 2, 49–51.

Crunden, R. (1982). *Ministers of Reform: The Progressives' Achievement in American Civilization, 1889–1920*. New York: Basic Books.

Davis, G. (1914). The Education of Crippled Children. *American Journal of Care for Cripples* 1, 5–11.

Degler, C. (1991). *In Search of Human Nature: The Decline and Revival of Darwinism in American Social Thought*. New York: Oxford University Press.

Donahey, M. (1918). Don't Pity Us Folks Who Have Physical Defects! *American Magazine* 86, 32.

Dubofsky, M. (1985). *Industrialism and the American Worker, 1865–1920*. Arlington Heights, IL: Harlan Davidson.

Faragher, J. (1988). *Sugar Creek: Life on the Illinois Prairie*. New Haven, CT: Yale University Press.

Faries, J. (1918). The Economic Consequences of Physical Disability: A Case Study of Civilian Cripples in New York City. *Publications of the Red Cross Institute for Crippled and Disabled Men* 1, 23–32.

Gray, A. (1921). Joe Sullivan's Body Is Weak, But Not His Will. *American Magazine* 91, 11–14, 27.

Hamburger, A., & Wright, L. (1918). *Education and Occupation of Cripples, Juvenile and Adult.* New York: Red Cross Institute for the Crippled and Disabled.

Harris, G. (1919). *The Redemption of the Disabled.* New York: D. Appleton and Company.

Hathway, M. (1928). *The Young Cripple and His Job.* Chicago: University of Chicago Press.

Hays, S. (1957). *The Response to Industrialism, 1885–1914.* Chicago: University of Chicago Press.

Heydon, H. (1918). The Supremacy of the Spirit. *Annals of the American Academy of Political and Social Science* 80, 51–57.

Hodge, J. (1908). Widener Memorial Industrial Training School for Crippled Children. *National Proceedings of the Conference of Charities and Corrections* (pp. 285–294).

Hunter, R. (1904). *Poverty.* New York: Macmillan Press.

Jaeger, C. (1914). Trade Training for Adult Cripples. *American Journal of Care for Cripples* 1, 68.

Katz, M. B. (1986). In the Shadow of the Poorhouse: A Social History of Welfare in America. New York: Basic Books.

Link, A., & McCormick, R. (1983). *Progressivism.* Arlington Heights, IL: Harlan Davidson.

Norris, H. (1921). Those Looks of Pity. *Hospital School Journal* 9, 10.

Oliver, M. (1990). *The Politics of Disablement: A Sociological Perspective.* New York: St. Martin's Press.

Orr, H. (1916). A Critique of Present Methods in the Treatment of Infantile Paralysis. *American Journal of Orthopedic Surgery* 14, 336–339.

Reeves, E. (1914). *Care and Education of Crippled Children in the United States.* New York: Russell Sage Foundation.

Riis, J. (1902). *The Children of the Poor.* New York: Charles Scribner's Sons.

Ringenbach, P. (1973). *Tramps and Reformers, 1873–1916: The Discovery of Unemployment in New York.* Westport, CT: Greenwood Press.

Rosenberg, C. (1987). *The Care of Strangers: The Rise of America's Hospital System.* Baltimore: Basic Books.

Rothman, D. (1971). *The Discovery of the Asylum: Social Order and Disorder in the New Republic.* Boston: Little, Brown.

Sellers, C. (1991). *The Market Revolution: Jacksonian America 1815–1836.* New York: Oxford University Press.

Starr, P. (1982). *The Social Transformation of American Medicine: The Rise of a Sovereign Profession and the Making of a Vast Industry.* New York: Basic Books.

Stein, G. (1918). Placement Technique in the Employment Work of the Red Cross Institute for Crippled and Disabled Men. *Publications of the Red Cross Institute for Crippled and Disabled Men* 1, 10.

Sullivan, J. (1914). *The Unheard Cry.* Nashville, TN: Smith and Lamar.

———. (1921). Big Aches in Little Hearts. *Hospital School Journal* 9, 3.

————. (1922). The Dowling Memorial School for Cripples. *Hospital School Journal* 10, 7.

————. (1923). The Cripple in the House. *Hospital School Journal* 11, 3.

Thorndike, A. (1914). Industrial Training for Crippled Children About Boston. *American Journal of Care for Cripples* 1, 19.

Trent, J. (1994). *Inventing the Feeble Mind: A History of Mental Retardation in the United States.* Berkeley: University of California Press.

What I Faced in My Life. (1919). *Ladies' Home Journal* 30, 13, 64.

Wiebe, R. (1967). *The Search for Order, 1877–1920.* New York: Hill and Wang.

Willard, D. (1928). The Mental Attitude of the Crippled Child in Relation to Orthopedic Treatment. *The Crippled Child* 5, 101–103.

Wright, H. (1920). *Survey of Cripples in New York City.* (Reprint, 1980.) New York: Arno Press.

4 A Matter of Difference: A Contextual Perspective on the History of Children with Mental Retardation in the United States

Elizabeth L. Brennan

Who, helpless, hopeless being, who
Shall strew a flower upon thy grave;
Or who from mute oblivions power
Thy disregarded name shall save?
From "Lines to the Memory of an Idiot Girl" (1844)

CHILDREN'S CHRONICLES: LOST VOICES

In *Growing up in America*, one of the five basic questions that Hiner and Hawes (1985) maintain should guide scholarship in the history of child-hood is: "What has been the subjective experience of being a child in the past?" This is a key question because "the essence of childhood is the child's special mode of experiencing life, his or her own unique way of being in the world" (p. xxi). Certainly, no one is better qualified to describe this subjective experience than children themselves, and that essential element of history includes children with significant cognitive disabilities. For much of the history considered in this chapter, however, that potential has been lost, because children with significant cognitive difference from the "norm" were not provided a documented means to express their voice (Richards & Singer 1998). In fact, being a child labeled with significant cognitive disability has led to varying degrees of invisibility (Stiker 1999) and external control, or what Safford and Safford (1996, p. 155) describe as a history of

I would like to gratefully thank James Meadours, Liz Obermayer, and Nancy Ward for their thoughtful help and direction with this chapter.

being "done to" and "done for." This is illustrated in the opening quote from "Lines to the Memory of an Idiot Girl," a poem dated September 21, 1844, which reflects a nineteenth-century view of children with cognitive disabilities as being anonymous "unfortunates." Thus, in attempting to capture the experiences of children with significant cognitive difference, one must begin with an understanding that certain limitations in voice exist.

A HISTORY OF DEFINING DIFFERENCE

Throughout the nation's history, vast shifts in attitudes toward, and definitions of, children with intellectual disabilities have colored their experiences by creating environments that have shaped these children's destinies. The history of American children who have been considered cognitively impaired, or experiencing mental retardation, reflects momentous shifts in environments over time. Mental retardation is now officially defined as beginning in childhood, "characterized by significant limitations both in intellectual functioning and in adaptive behavior as expressed in conceptual, social, and practical adaptive skills," and reflecting the "fit between the capabilities of individuals and the structure and expectations of their environment" (American Association on Mental Retardation 2002). That definition stresses that "Limitations in present functioning must be considered within the context of community environments typical of the individual's age peers and culture." Clearly, although it has only been recognized in the most recent iterations of the definition of mental retardation, the concept of *environment,* of factors extrinsic to the individual, must be a cornerstone of any analysis of the history of the experiences of children with significant cognitive disabilities.

The term *significant* is an important part of this definition as well. Based on the notion of quantifiable intelligence, "significant" refers to the degree of difference from the norm. That mental retardation is a social construct is evidenced by the changes across time with respect to who has been considered "significantly" different or disabled, as well as the labels associated with such differences, although many terms intended to denote levels of cognitive impairment, such as *moron, trainable,* etc., have mercifully been abandoned. What has remained the same, as Smith (2001) points out, is that "some disability labels carry greater stigma than other labels, and degree or level of involvement of disability is a cofactor" (p. 182). Thus, children with "significant" cognitive disabilities have been highly likely to find themselves in environments that were significantly "different" from those of their age-peers.

In view of the changes over the course of American history concerning the definition of mental retardation, it is important to identify the children about whom this chapter is written. For purposes of this chapter, mental retardation and analogous terms, such as intellectual impairment, cognitive disability, and developmental disability, refer to children whom society has historically identified as such in order to classify or to establish services. However, if viewed from the child's perspective, the meaning of the construct of mental retardation is a definition of experience. Given that over the last three centuries the experiences of and environments for children with significant cognitive disability have been products of what society views as different, those experiences and environments have changed with societal changes. Several histories (Braginsky & Braginsky 1971; D'Antonio 2004) tell the stories of children who were not necessarily intellectually disabled but who nonetheless were handed the experiences associated with that label. Understanding of such experiences thus gives us more information than a more elusive definition of cognitive disability as an intrinsic quality.

From an early age, children form a notion of what is "different" (Miller & Sammons 1999), while adults strive to define "otherness" by adopting defining labels (Brantlinger 2001; Kliewer & Fitzgerald 2001; Smith 2001; Stiker 1999). However, even given that need to define, Braginsky and Braginsky (1971) noted that "we are no closer to [defining mental retardation] than were the ancient Greeks" (p. 12). The problem, they note, has not been with too few definitions but with too many, commenting that "mental retardation is a symptom, yet to be described, that can be associated with anything and everything, permanently or temporarily" (p. 14). Almost 100 years earlier, this need for classification was addressed in Wilbur's *Classifications of Idiocy* (1877), and the need to relook at definitions is still present as we move into the twenty-first century (Biersdorff 1999; Borthwick 1994; Smith 2003).

There is a history of shifts in identification of persons with mental retardation based on changes in the construct. The "Flynn Effect," i.e., a rise in measured IQ in the general population (Kanaya, Scullin, & Ceci 2003); recognition of overrepresentation of minority students based on the achievement variable (Hosp & Reschly 2004); the 1972 redefinition of mental retardation (two standard IQ deviations rather than one, below the mean of 100) and the ensuing 80 percent "decrease" in the number of individuals with mental retardation (Winzer 1993); and debate concerning the 1992 American Association on Mental Retardation redefinition are all additional evidence of this history of shifts in, and disagreement about, how mental retardation is viewed in the United States. Emerging conceptions of different types of intelligence will further challenge current definitions, as will those who contest the notion of quantifiable intelligence defined by IQ tests (Rice 2002).

Even in the persistent absence of a clear, permanent, and universal definition of mental retardation, children have been historically grouped and labeled purportedly for research, educational, legal, and medical purposes, although some scholars argue that the groupings have often had more sinister underlying purposes (Kliewer & Fitzgerald 2001; Stiker 1999). Since the early 1900s, children with significant cognitive disabilities have been identified primarily through the use of IQ scores (Dybwad 1960; Kanaya, Scullin, & Ceci 2003), although "different" (as with disorders on the autism spectrum) may or may not be "less." Prior to adoption of mental testing, nineteenth-century classifications drew distinctions between degrees of intellect using the terms "moron," "imbecile," and "idiot." The 1880 Jasper County, Illinois, census schedules drew a distinction between the definitions of "idiot" (beginning in infancy) and "stupidity which results from idiocy, and that which is due to the loss or deterioration of mental power in consequence of insanity." The census records describe that condition as not "true idiocy, but dementia or imbecility." The record goes on to state that enumeration for census purposes should be of "true idiots" only and that "special pains should be taken to indicate all idiots from birth." Wilbur's 1880 definition also emphasized age of onset to include "such an early period of life as to precede the customary development of childish intelligence."

In addition to being influenced by defining systems of identification, environments for children with cognitive disabilities have been framed for much of the nation's history by the infantilization and perpetualized dependency pervasive for children so labeled. Although the notion of "mental age," a term still widely used today, was introduced in a 1908 revision of the Stanford-Binet scale, the notion had been implied in 1854 in Whittier's *Peculiar Institutions in Massachusetts.* This report on the condition of "cases of idiocy" in the commonwealth noted that some were "helpless as children at seven years of age," some "seemed as helpless as children at two years of age," and others "in the condition of mere infants." Accordingly, the notion of mental age, even defined informally for children with mental retardation, has had impact on their contexts until the very recent recognition of the importance of "age appropriate" environments and activities. Previously, older children and youths with cognitive disabilities often found themselves provided early childhood games, books, and music with the notion that these were a better match to their "mental age" (e.g., Gifford-Smith & Brownell 2003; Taylor & Searl 2001).

As Noll and Trent note in *Mental Retardation in America* (2004), others have provided detailed histories that chronicle the history of services for children. While providing a history of children's services is important, the perspective of the child, including children with significant cognitive disabilities who did not receive services, needs to be examined. Those contexts and environments and the children's experiences in them hold evidence that lead us to the child's perspective. In addition, although histories of their own childhood offered by adults are viewed through the "reconstructive lens of maturity" (Safford & Safford 1996, p. viii), those reflections are valuable in recreating this history. Those personal histories along with a narrative description of environments from a more child-centered perspective over this span of time and place may give us a reference point in attempting to grasp a greater sense of the subjective experiences of children.

ENVIRONMENTS AND COMMON GROUND

The history of childhood in the United States from the colonial period forward includes the individual perspectives and stories of children who are distinct in background and experience. The history of children during the eighteenth and nineteenth centuries is framed by the global influence of immigrants as well as American and Hispanic natives and children born to slavery (Wortham 2002). The twentieth century brought more entrenched waves of influence, creating greater distinctions based on regional, educational, and socioeconomic differences. As we embark on the twenty-first century, "a confluence of changes—social, economic, technological—has led many authors and child-development experts to warn that the very concept of childhood is in danger" (Jacobson 1999, p. 32). The extent to which a child in the twenty-first century is exposed to those stressors will create huge distinctions in childhood experiences (Elkind 1999, 2001). While certain common experiences have existed for many children in the past, they were often depicted in books, photos, stories, and family communications. In recent years, popular culture (as reflected in language, dress, games, and pastimes) has become more commonly shared through television and other media. While such experiences have changed over time, they form a context or "common ground" of what is "childhood" for many American children.

Environments and experiences in them also provide common ground for children whom society has labeled variously as cognitively, intellectually, or developmentally disabled. History often shows that it is not their divergent disabilities that have most often pulled children so labeled together but the common experiences of children who have been treated differently or who have been segregated (Smith 2001; Snow 2004). Although environmental childhood images for children with significant cognitive disabilities have changed over time, at any given place or time in American history the images of these children generally differ from those of children who are considered "normal." Longmore and Umansky (2001) point out that "experiences of cultural devaluation and socially imposed restriction, of personal and collective struggles for self-definition and self-determination . . . recur across the various disability groups and throughout their particular histories" (p. 4). The difference historically, then, between the typical experiences of childhood and those of children with significant cognitive disabilities can be measured by the degree of loss of some commonalities and the creation of new ones.

For children with mental retardation, historical contextual differences have been experienced in both concrete and abstract ways. Concrete differences can be more easily identified and described. For example, children with significant cognitive disability in the late twentieth and early twenty-first century might still not share common space in school with other children who are not disabled. But even with some degree of inclusion in school and community activities, children with significant cognitive impairment often experience a more abstract isolation. Friendships and play based on true membership or sense of belonging in school and community are often altered for these children (Williams & Downing 1998). As research and theory widely recognize, environments, and children's experiences in them, are critical determining factors in the nature and progress of development. It is therefore important to learn about how environmental images and experiences for children with cognitive disabilities have impacted their lives and have framed their history over time (Rice 2002).

CHRONOLOGY OF ENVIRONMENTAL SHIFTS

Colonial Period to the Mid-nineteenth Century

In the hindsight process of constructing a sense of what it was like to be a child with significant cognitive disability in America in times past, one can see that absence of voice or visibility lends some clues as to the environments in which such children found themselves. Shifts in environment and locus of control reflect movement that has occurred from periods of protection and community in colonial times through the early nineteenth century; confinement marked by invisibility, hopelessness, and absence of rights from the mid-1800s through the first half of the twentieth century; acceptance, greater visibility, and inclusion marked by participation, membership, and advocacy beginning in the 1960s; and today, movement forward in visibility, voice, self-determination, and self-advocacy. However, boundaries of these phases are not distinct and progress has often been followed by retrenchment. What is pertinent to this discussion is the effect such shifts are likely to have had for children.

Beginning in late-seventeenth-century Massachusetts, the laws of colonial New England began to establish protective provisions for people labeled as "idiots" based on the English conception of idiocy as the basis for a focus on protection from harm, in turn derived from Elizabethan "Poor Laws"(Wickham 2001). Later in colonial America, children with cognitive disabilities "blended into the community" and "for all practical purposes, were not mentally retarded" because at that time the demands for reading, writing, and technical skills were lower (Taylor & Searl 2001, p. 18). Some children were kept quietly in their homes. Elizabeth Jefferson, the sister of

Thomas Jefferson who was described by Jefferson himself as an "idiot girl," lived with her family (Wickham 2001). In 1774, a series of earthquakes rocked Virginia, and amid the confusion at Monticello Mountain, Elizabeth wandered away from the mansion. Her body was found a few days later (Provence 2003). For children with mental retardation during this span of time, strong communities defined their environments and provided them with a certain measure of protection from the "outside."

Census headings in the late 1800s highlighted the identification of "idiots" (e.g., 1880 Jasper County Census; United States 1870 Federal Census), including notations of "cause of idiocy" and "size of head," culminating a trend that been gathering momentum for several decades. However, not until the first moves toward segregation of the "feebleminded" in the mid-1800s was a wave of intense identification efforts sparked. Developing processes of identification led to new notions of what to do with people identified as idiots or mentally "deficient." While initial efforts were motivated by altruistic concern for the welfare of the children themselves, what was to follow were years of various forms of confinement and containment, with the associated absence of rights.

The Era of the Asylum

It is often recognized that a shift of focus in the United States to institutionalization began with the asylum established in 1848 by Samuel Gridley Howe, director of the Perkins Institution for the Blind in Watertown, Massachusetts (Ferguson, 1994). However, Howe's vision, based on principles of family and community, in no way resembled the system of institutions that emerged, causing Howe himself to declare that "we should build up public institutions only in the last resort" (quoted in Richards 1909, p. 516). More disturbing "solutions"—those almost too painful to contemplate—would within decades frame environments and experiences for children with significant cognitive difference, creating a transition from "benevolence" of the mid-1800s to an ominous plan of segregation and sterilization (Goodheart 2004). The move toward segregation in the 1800s led to a shift in environments that reflected a "solution" to the societal concern that feeble-minded children were a burden or a problem, a shift that continued to influence environments for children with mental retardation for more than a century.

This custodial perspective that distinctly characterized American institutions was already growing when in 1876 the Association of Medical Officers of American Institutions for Idiots and Feeble-minded Persons was formed to determine a comprehensive plan managing the problem of mental retardation. The influence of this plan, which relied on institutions to provide training to children with cognitive disabilities and to release them with the skills necessary to live in their communities, continues to be felt, even into the twenty-first century (Goode 1998). But the reality was markedly different from the plan due to the fact that, with the rapid growth of institutions across the country in the mid-to-late nineteenth century, the institutional choice was the primary option available to parents. Secondly, the conviction was increasingly growing that earlier hopes for the enterprise, especially inspired by the work of Eduoard Seguin, recently arrived from France, had been ill-founded; institutionalization was more and more expected to be a lifelong experience. While often children with mental retardation were exploited as free laborers on the institution grounds (Goode 1998), leaders of institutions pointed out that other, less fortunate children experienced abusive conditions as workers in factories (Rokker 1894). A few private schools and a "tradition of teachers of special children who boarded a small number of them in their homes" were options available only to wealthy families (Goode 1998, p. 6).

While institutions were seen as a way to alleviate the "burden" of feeblemindedness, this increasingly meant the burden on society rather than on the individuals themselves. Begun as "training schools," they in time became primarily custodial in nature. Barr (1899) described the situation this way: "The idiot or unimprovable class and the idio-imbecile, the direction of whose feeble powers so far as to aid in the care of himself or his weaker brother can hardly be dignified by the term training, we will not discuss here, although they are unfortunately found in large proportion in the custodial departments of all training schools in this country."

While the late 1800s also brought greater conversation surrounding "training" and "education" in asylums for the "feeble-minded" (Boen n.d.), only about half of American children at that time were receiving an education at all (Safford & Safford 1996). Education for children with mental retardation grew along separate, non-parallel lines, and from 1879, when the first class for "backward" children began in Cleveland, Ohio, through 1900 when compulsory education mandates began to affect all children, most "day classes" for children with mental retardation were stated to have "failed" for a myriad of reasons (Winzer 1993, p. 321). However, within the first decade of the twentieth century, an *ungraded class* approach for students who "didn't fit," pioneered in New York by Elizabeth Farrell (1908–1909) and influenced by a day class model pioneered in Germany, was being replicated in other large urban school districts. The leadership in the field, however, represented in the Medical Officers (i.e., institution superintendents) organization, considered this enterprise, at best, a holding operation until the children enrolled were "sent to the institutions for safety" (Johnstone 1908, p. 115).

Children Forever

One reason for the lack of attention to education for children considered mentally retarded in the latter nineteenth and early twentieth centuries is that these children were often infantilized and seen as children forever. This perception is underscored in the story of "Blind Tom" (Schmidt n.d.), which illustrates both the complexities and environmental implications of this perspective. Thomas Greene Bethune ("Blind Tom") was born in 1849 as the son of slaves and was the first African American to perform at the White House (Kirk 1995). Thomas was born blind, described as an "idiot" by his teacher, and described in historical accounts as mentally retarded (Kirk 1995). In fact, because of his blindness and perceived lack of intelligence, he was considered to be of no worth—literally included at no cost when his mother was sold into slavery.

However, endowed with the Bethune family's musical talent, Thomas began at a young age to play back what he heard from memory and, by the age of six, was composing his own works. The potential for income did not escape his owner and soon Tom was given over to a concert promoter. At age nine, "Blind Tom" began to travel the country and to be exhibited at four shows a day. Mark Twain also helped to make Blind Tom famous by providing firsthand accounts of his performances (Schmidt, n.d.). Thomas's childhood history is one of control and abuse at the hands of opportunists. When he died at the age of 59, the *New York Times* obituary headline read: "Old Negro with Strange Mastery of Music Ends His Days in Hoboken—A Child All His Life." The "normal" progression and development of independence and self-determination as one moves from childhood to adulthood was altered for Tom. A child in the eyes of others, a slave not only by virtue of the difference in his color but also by his cognitive difference, he was never allowed to become a free, autonomous, independent individual.

For other children without the celebrity of Blind Tom, the rise of institutions in the mid-1800s created new environments where children with significant cognitive disabilities lived and learned. Their worlds were the institution. Everything they did was framed by the walls that surrounded them and the people within them. Yet other children were sent to "poor farms," as was one young girl named "Molly Unknown." Molly was a resident of the Decatur County (Iowa) "Farm" in 1883 (Hoffman n.d.). She was found abandoned and believed to be feeble-minded; she was sent to join other children, mostly poor, at the farm, where she lived into adulthood until her death. Still others lived in frightening isolation. Jaroslav Huptuk was a sixteen-year-old "feeble-minded dwarf" when the 1894 inspection of an Illinois factory found him finishing knife blades on an emery wheel (Rokker 1894).

However, many stories indicate that families were instrumental in setting living environments for children with cognitive disabilities. Richards and Singer (1998) point out the importance of family, stating that even in the face of institutionalization, "the family remained first, and for many the main, context in which disability was defined and experienced" (p. 444). The stories they tell of children in early-nineteenth-century America show positive family supports and education. However, this was by no means the case for all. A report on conditions for children with cognitive disabilities in the Commonwealth of Massachusetts in 1848, chronicled by J. G. Whittier (1854), found that those children were in the most deplorable state when in private homes. The author describes "idiotic" children found "with their heads covered over with cold poultices of oak bark" which the parents thought would help them remember their lessons. Thereafter, professionals increased their efforts to persuade families whose children evidenced cognitive delays to place them in institutions as early as possible so they could be properly cared for. But within decades, as White and Wolfensberger (1969) expressed it, the focus shifted from "sheltering the deviant from society" to "protection of society from the deviant."

"Negative" Eugenics: Segregation, Sterilization, and Exploitation

Because the worth of children with mental retardation was so diminished at this point in time, it was a small but dark step to the notion that these children were good candidates for research subjects. Turn-of-the-twentieth-century medical experimentation included children who were "idiots" without thought of informed consent. Medical interventions took additional ominous turns as the eugenics movement swept the nation in the early 1900s. By the 1930s, sterilizations were routinely performed on individuals "diagnosed" as mentally retarded and often on their family members as well in an effort to cleanse the gene pool (University of Virginia Health Sciences Library). Estimates through the mid-twentieth century place the number of people who were sterilized in the tens of thousands (Franklin 1980). Even children, some as young as ten years old, were sterilized (Railey & Begos 2002). In 1926, Carrie Buck, then a seventeen-year-old girl, was the center of a legal contest regarding involuntary sterilization of the "feeble-minded." She and her sister Doris were sterilized under the program as the Supreme Court upheld the right in the formal opinion in the case of *Buck v. Bell* delivered in 1927 (University of Virginia Health Sciences Library). Later research would establish that Carrie had been falsely "diagnosed."

Earlier perspectives persisted well into the twentieth century as evidenced when Dr. F. J. Russell, superintendent of a school for feebleminded children, referred to "feeblemindedness" as a "blight on mankind" (1917). He went on to note that "low grades" did not constitute a serious problem but that "morons" ("high-grade feebleminded" individuals) constituted a greater problem because "nearly every effort . . . [to] reclaim" them as normal persons had been fruitless. Russell believed that to give feebleminded children training and then return them to society was a "moral as well as an economic mistake." This was echoed at about that same time in Lucas County, Ohio, where the Trustees of the Lucas County Children's Home were hesitant to accept children who were "feeble-minded," sending them instead to other institutions including the Home for Feeble-minded in Columbus, Ohio (The History of Lucas County Children Services). Ironically, while the label of feeblemindedness was used as a screen to keep many children out of orphan asylums, the label also kept many children from being adopted. Henry Goddard, the Director of the Training School for Backward and Feeble-Minded Children in Vineland, New Jersey, worked actively against the adoption of "feeble-minded" children and for their permanent segregation in institutions (University of Oregon n.d.).

With swelling enrollments in institutions and the Depression and World War II decreasing available staff, the 1930s and 1940s brought age restrictions on children who could be admitted to institutions. While until 1945 children under the age of five were not allowed under law to be placed in institutions, "by 1943, 32% of beds in institutions were filled with children aged five to ten years" (Goode 1998, p. 11). Beyond the common horrors of institutionalization, the need for subjects for dysentery research during World War II led to the use of orphans and children who were mentally retarded (Rothman 1991).

Return to the Charity Model and Prelude to Deinstitutionalization

As the middle of the twentieth century approached, ideologies about children with disabilities built from a hierarchical agenda of benevolence, which then gave way to a rise in sympathy toward children with significant cognitive difference. Eventually, the "Poster Child" (Block 1998) notion of support and aid emerged and was manifested in new environments for children with significant cognitive difference characterized by the charity model. These environments were perhaps not so frightening but were still quite different from those experienced by other children. However, while a wave of sympathy altered environments for some children, photo depictions through the mid-twentieth century continued to show images of children with significant cognitive disabilities in institutions and segregated programs—often under dire conditions that reflected cruelty, neglect, and abuse (Blatt & Kaplan 1966). While clearly not all children with mental retardation over this span of history were treated in such ways, it is clear that many children were maltreated, even if their treatment was not viewed as such at the time.

Carol Buck's story is different as told from her famous mother's perspective in Pearl Buck's *The Child Who Never Grew* (1992). Carol was born in 1920, around the same time as Rosemary Kennedy, the sister of John F. Kennedy (O'Brien 2004). Both prominent families dealt with the public disclosure of the childhood of these women in a climate of shame. The attention garnered by their public stories led to improved conditions in some institutions. However, by 1945, institutions were 20–30 percent overcrowded, with as many as 200 children sleeping on mattresses on the floor (Goode 1998).

Mid-twentieth-century perspectives moved to some levels of acceptance and visibility for children with mental retardation, but that sympathy was most often coupled with attitudes of negative expectation and motivation to control. Numerous instances—some gruesome—of control measures continued. In some areas of the country, involuntary sterilizations contin- ued into the mid-1970s (Castles 2002; Reinhold 1980). In 1968, fourteen- year-old Elaine Riddick Jessie, who lived with her grandmother, was sterilized at a hospital in North Carolina (Railey & Begos 2002). Jesse was described as feebleminded although she scored above 70 on an IQ test (70 and below was the standard for sterilization), and her environmental con- ditions were never taken into consideration.

Since the inception of institutionalization, the institutional environment has been the chief framework for defining and experiencing disability for many children with cognitive disabilities—and others so labeled. It is im- portant to note that not all children who experienced institutional envi- ronments after being labeled "feebleminded" were indeed cognitively impaired, as with the experiences of some boys in the Fernald School in Connecticut; but many became so in the course of a lifetime in an insti- tution (D'Antonio 2004). However, with the label came the experiences.

Institutional contexts for children's experiencing of significant cognitive disability were most often bleak at best, if not abysmal. In 1946, Gordon Zahn described the Rosewood Training School in Maryland as a "dead-end street," failing even to provide "adequate care and reasonable pleasant sur- roundings." His descriptions of children being herded into "playrooms" included that the "smell, sight and sounds" would cause nausea. Growing awareness of such conditions in these facilities and in those for persons with mental illness gave rise in the 1970s to a nationwide "deinstitutional- ization" movement, coupled with the growing influence of a concept intro- duced in the Scandinavian countries termed "normalization," which explicitly focuses on *environments* experienced by persons, including chil- dren, with mental retardation. This concept, which its authors translated into specific implications for day-to-day living, was defined as "making avail- able to the mentally retarded patterns and conditions of everyday life which are as close as possible to the norms and patterns of the mainstream of society" (Nirje 1976, p. 52).

Advocacy Brings about New Environments

Families at this point in history, beginning in the years following World War II and continuing through the period of the civil rights movement, began to play an extraordinarily critical role in framing experiences and environments for children with labels of mental retardation. A self-advocate who was born in 1966 describes a wonderful childhood with a "loving and inclusive family." Still, she described her discovery of labels and their impact on her life this way: "There was one time I came off of the bus and I heard from kids that I was 'MR' (you know the word) well, anyway I always heard that I had a learning disability, so I went home and asked mom, and she was somewhat embarrassed/ashamed. That was the first I knew I was MR" (personal e-mail communication, July 29, 2004).

While many children with mental retardation had experienced a type of "de facto" (Richards 2004, p. 67) inclusion prior to the mid-nineteenth century, the institutional movement spun "specialized" education out on a separate trajectory, distinct from the common school. These environmental differences are deeply entrenched. Howe's work in the mid-1800s toward the "training" of children who were mentally retarded to become productive citizens anticipated developments that would take over a century to materialize, and the crossing of a chasm of custodial care. In 1975, the Education for All Handicapped Children Act was passed, founded on critical court decisions. It guaranteed all children with disabilities, irrespective of severity, a free appropriate public education in the least restrictive environment, based on an individual education program. Subsequently renamed the Individuals with Disabilities Education Act (IDEA), this legislation has radically changed the environments experienced by children with significant cognitive disabilities, who had previously been excluded from schools and schooling as a matter of public policy (United States Office of Special Education Programs 2000).

For most children with significant cognitive disabilities in the United States from the mid-1800s to the mid-1970s, school was a separate experience, quite distinct from that of their age-peers (Winzer 1993). The 1917 report from Dr. F. J. Russell highlighted the "mistake" of trying to train children who were cognitively disabled and return them to society. However, a short sixteen years later, in Cuyahoga County, Ohio, the parent advocacy movement was born when the families of five children identified as mentally retarded, protesting their exclusion from schools, fought for equal environments for their children (Morse 2000). Family advocacy, critically important in bringing about legislative change, would drastically reform school environments for children with cognitive disabilities over the next half century and onward. However, data at the end of the twentieth century indicated that the more significant the disability, the less chance that a child shared common educational experiences with children in the regular education classroom (United States Department of Education 2002).

From the first notion of institutional "special education" to key legislation in the mid-1970s, education for children with mental retardation, if provided at all, had been a segregated enterprise, premised on a "deficit model" of people with disabilities (Lipsky & Gartner 1997, p. 51). The Individuals with Disabilities Education Act of 1997 moved its precursor leg-islation forward and set an increasing mandate for change under the concept of least restrictive environments, although it did not change the definition of such environments. Although this legislation focused closer attention on educational environments for these children, change has been slow, and while school continued to reflect a separate image for many children with cognitive disabilities, those children were also a separate image in the experience of children who were "nondisabled" or "typical." Since it was assumed that most children who were nondisabled had mini-mal or no experience interacting with children with disabilities, puppets were used to set the stage for the new wave of "mainstreaming." Accord-ingly, attempts have been made to "prepare" the environment to be ac-cepting, a notable example of which was Kids on the Block, Inc., created in 1977 in direct response to U.S. Public Law 94-142.

With the movement toward normalization, mainstreaming, and inclu-sion, strides have been made in the United States to create common learning environments and experiences for children. However, from an environmental perspective, during the 1999–2000 academic year, children in the United States labeled with mental retardation age six through twenty-one represented almost one-quarter of all the children with disabilities who were served in separate public educational facilities. Another 26.9 percent, although enrolled in public schools, were served outside of the regular classroom for over 60 percent of their school day. Additionally, 16.8 per-cent of children educated in separate facilities were classified as children with multiple disabilities, most of whom have significant cognitive disabil-ities (United States Department of Education 2002).

Even when children with cognitive disabilities shared common schools with other children, other barriers existed that altered the environment. Often children with cognitive differences were educated in separate class-rooms and maintained different schedules. Viewing these contexts over time from a child's perspective, the most important consideration would arguably be a sense of membership and belonging. The inclusive education movement has a focus that goes beyond common physical environments and addresses issues of "normalcy" in terms of peer interactions and com-mon meaningful activities (Williams & Downing 1998), including access to literacy opportunities and challenge (Kliewer & Biklen 2001).

Because physical environments have often been different for children with cognitive disabilities across time, and because other barriers exist due to the perception of "difference," a focus on facilitating friendships has grown with the movement toward membership and inclusion (Salend 1999). Even in inclusive environments, young children with disabilities en-gage in less frequent social interaction with children who are typically de-veloping (Odom 2000). Lacking good historical records from earlier times, we can infer that the road to friendship was usually a difficult one for children with mental retardation. That inference is confirmed through oral histories of adults. One self-advocate recounts his struggle to make friends in the 1970s. He describes being teased: "I think my first self advocacy I did was have mean person call me retard and handicap. I remember ride the bus back home he was still tease me. I tell him I am not retard [sic] or handicap went the bus stop the next stop I walk home I think it was go 3 miles for me to walk it." (personal e-mail communication, July 29, 2004). Recognition of the importance of natural environments and interactions for children have framed services for young children with cognitive disabilities in the United States since 1970 (Bricker 2000). Those Early Intervention services provided in homes and community environments immediately impact the lives and friendships of those children.

While contexts have been a critical aspect determining friendships for children with mental retardation in the United States, friendships have been a critical aspect in those contexts. Despite the importance of friendships to the subjective experience of all children, we know the least about this aspect of the history of children with cognitive disabilities. For children, friendships and membership represent an all-important step in social-emotional development and self-image. "What happens in children's peer groups and friendship relations affects development and functioning in probably every other aspect of children's lives, including the family, the school, and the community" (Gifford-Smith & Brownell 2003, p. 235).

SELF-DETERMINATION AND MOVEMENT FORWARD

As Noll and Trent state in *Mental Retardation in America* (2004), "A word is a label when it has a history" (p. 1). The history of the use of "words" becoming "labels" for children with mental retardation is long. From the historical intellectual gradation terms of "idiot" (lowest), "imbecile" and "moron" (highest), to the term "feebleminded," to distinctions between "trainable" and "educable," to present-day failures to use person-first language (Snow 2004), labels have set the stage for children's experiences. Families continue to play a critical role in advocating for natural environments and supports for their children. However, to the present, examples of recommendation for institutionalizing children with mental retardation continue to be found (Brennan & Safford 2001). By 2001, 8.6 percent of individuals living in intermediate care facilities for the mentally retarded and developmentally disabled were under the age of seventeen. While over half of those children lived in smaller institutions of fewer than six children (an institution is defined as four or more beds), in 1998 more than 25 percent of those children lived in facilities that had more than sixteen children in long-term residence (American Health Care Association).

"Normalcy" connotes different environments to different families. New environmental options for children with cognitive disabilities may frame the future as, with a current focus on home schooling in the United States, the numbers of children with disabilities in the United States who are being home-educated continues to rise (Pavlides 2004). In 1999, over 8 percent of the parents of children who were home-schooled chose that option because of the child's disability or special needs (Bielick & Chandler 2001). While "home-schooling" as a contemporary trend carries certain implications, family responsibility for teaching children with mental retardation has roots over the past centuries. Prior to the initiation of special education day classes in the first decade of the twentieth century, and then the legislation now known as the Individuals with Disabilities Act, mothers who chose to have their children live at home were also handed the responsibility for "training" them—and without much direction and support (Brockley 2004). An adult self-advocate who was born in 1966 and labeled mentally retarded remembers being taught by his mother: "During summer months my mom teach me how write and teach me basic words and other school things. My mom was not teacher. She did it because she care about me hold alot of me" (personal e-mail communication, July 29, 2004). The complexities in the structure of charter schools present new challenges and options for families of children with cognitive disabilities. In the 2000–2001 academic year, 12 percent of students in charter schools were identified as having needs for special education support services, close to the 13 percent of students receiving special education supports nationally in the public schools (Hendrie 2004).

The "What do you want to be when you grow up?" question is not one that would have been asked of many children with cognitive disabilities for much of the history under discussion. The possibilities for these children as they moved into their adult years were so limited as to render the question meaningless. Currently, many of those children who were not asked that self-determining question are answering it themselves by leading purposeful lives that include marriage, community, and work. To document the movement and achievements of children with significant cognitive difference, we look to the present-day voice of young adults with cognitive disabilities as they share recollections of their childhood.

Many of those adults are now active self-advocates and members of advocacy organizations such as TASH—formerly known as The Association for Persons with Severe Handicaps—and People First self-advocacy organizations for people with developmental disabilities. TASH is an international organization "of people with disabilities, their family members, other advocates, and professionals fighting for a society in which inclusion of all people in all aspects of society is the norm" (TASH 2005). Many persons with significant disabilities who are self-advocates maintain vital positions on the organization's board of directors in addition to their other positions of advocacy, leadership, and training. As a self-advocate who was born in 1950 expressed, "To learn how to advocate for myself took five years. There was no one to teach me" (personal communication, August 5, 2004). This recollection reflects the struggle for many children with cognitive disabilities to reach toward increasing levels of self-determination and choice over their environments. There is ample empirical evidence that "individuals with significant disabilities can learn to self-regulate and self-manage their own behavior, become less dependent on others, and express preferences and use those preferences to make choices" (Wehmeyer 1998, p. 15). Considerations of the ability of children with mental retardation to self-determine should increasingly be reflected in schools (Palmer, Wehmeyer, Gipson, & Agran 2004), communities, and homes, so that the question of what one wants to be when one grows up is directed to all children in meaningful ways.

As we see movement through history toward a greater common ground in environments for all children, the future holds promise that while children will naturally have varied experiences based on differing environments, those varied experiences will not be due to disability or labels of disability. The importance of oral histories in capturing the experiences of individuals with mental retardation has been increasingly recognized (Dillon & Hoburn 2003; Kliewer & Biklen 2001) and should include the voices of children with cognitive disabilities. Moving into the twenty-first century, personal stories from children with mental retardation will then create a more accurate first-person historic record of that subjective experience.

REFERENCES

American Association on Mental Retardation. (2002). *Definition of Mental Retardation.* Retrieved December 21, 2004, from http://www.aamr.org/Policies/faq_mental_retardation.shtml.

American Health Care Association. (n.d.). *A Guide to Residential Services for Persons with Mental Retardation or Developmental Disabilities (MR/DD).* Retrieved December 20, 2004, from http://ahcaweb.org/brief/mrdd_guide.pdf.

Barr, M. W. (1899). The How, the Why, and the Wherefore of the Training of Feeble-minded Children. *Journal of Psycho-Asthenics.* Retrieved December 7, 2003, from Disability History Museum, http://www.disabilitymuseum.org/lib/docs/1392card.htm.

Bielick, S., & Chandler, K. (2001). *Homeschooling in the United States: 1999.* National Household Education Surveys Program. National Center for Education Statistics. United States Department of Education, Office of Educational Research and Improvement.

Biersdorff, K. K. (1999). Duelling Definitions: Developmental Disabilities, Mental Retardation and Their Measurement [Electronic version]. *Rehabilitation Review* 10(7). Retrieved August 28, 2004, from http://www.vrri.org/rhbindx.htm.

Blatt, B., & Kaplan, F. (1966). *Christmas in Purgatory.* Boston: Allyn and Bacon.

Block, L. (1998). (Producer). Inventing the Poster Child [Radio broadcast] in

Beyond Affliction: The Disability History Project. http://www.npr.org/pro grams/disability/ba_shows.dir/index_sh.html.

Boen, J. L. (n.d.). From Asylum to Developmental Center. *Fort Wayne News-Sentinel Projects: Fort Wayne State Developmental Center.* Retrieved August 4, 2004, from http://jordan.fortwayne.com/ns/projects/devcenter/devcenter1.php.

Borthwick, C. (1994). Mental Retardation, Dementia, and the Age of Majority [Electronic version]. *Disability & Society* 9(4). Retrieved August 4, 2004, from http://home.vicnet.au/~borth/MAJORITY.HTM.

Braginsky, D. D., & Braginsky, B. M. (1971). *Hansels and Gretels: Studies of Children in Institutions for the Mentally Retarded.* New York: Holt, Rinehart & Winston.

Brantlinger, E. (2001). Poverty, Class, and Disability: A Historical, Social, and Political Perspective. *Focus on Exceptional Children* 33(7), 1–19.

Brennan, E. L., & Safford, P. L. (2001). The Meaning of Disability for Grandparents of Young Children with Special Needs. In L. Rogers & B. Swadener, eds., *Semiotics and Dis/ability: Interrogating Categories of Difference.* Albany: State University of New York Press.

Bricker, D. (2000). Inclusion: How the Scene Has Changed. *Topics in Early Childhood Special Education* 20(1), 14–19.

Brockley, J. (2004). Rearing the Child Who Never Grew: Ideologies of Parenting and Intellectual Disability in American History. In S. Noll & J. W. Trent, eds., *Mental Retardation in America* (pp. 130–164). New York: New York University Press.

Buck, P. S. (1992). *The Child Who Never Grew.* Bethesda, MD: Woodbine House.

Castles, K. (2002). Quiet Eugenics: Sterilization in North Carolina's Institutions for the Mentally Retarded, 1945–1965. *Journal of Southern History* 68(4), 849–879.

D'Antonio, M. (2004). *The State Boys Rebellion.* New York: Simon & Schuster.

Dillon, M., & Holburn, S. (2003). Preserving Oral Histories: Example of the Institutional Experience. *Mental Retardation* 41(2), 130–132.

Dybwad, G. (1960). *Are We Retarding the Retarded?* Presentation at the Tenth Anniversary Convention of the National Association for Retarded Children, Minneapolis, MN. Retrieved August 11, 2004, from http://www.disability museum.org/lib/docs/1722.htm. Disability History Museum, http://www. disabilitymuseum.org.

1880 Jasper County, IL Federal Census Schedules of Handicapped, Dependent & Delinquent Inhabitants of Illinois in *Illinois Trails: History and Genealogy of Jasper County, Illinois.* Retrieved September 10, 2003, from http://www. iltrails.org/Jasper/1880schedule.html.

Elkind, D. (1999). The Social Determination of Childhood and Adolescence. *Education Week* 18(24), 48–50.

———. (2001). *The Hurried Child.* Cambridge: Perseus Publishing.

Farrell, E. K. (1908–1909). Special Classes in the New York City Schools. *Journal of Psycho-Asthenics* 13, 91–96.

Ferguson, P. M. (1994). *Abandoned to Their Fate.* Philadelphia: University Press.

Franklin, B. A. (1980). Teen-ager's Sterilization an Issue Decades Later. *New York Times*, March 7, p. A16.

Gifford-Smith, M. E., & Brownell, C. A. (2003). Childhood Peer Relationship: Social Acceptance, Friendships, and Peer Networks. *Journal of School Psychology* 41, 235–284.

Goode, D. (1998). *And Now Let's Build a Better World: The Story of the Association for the Help of Retarded Children, New York City 1948–1998.* Retrieved August 23, 2004, from http://www.ahrcnyc.org/index.htm.

Goodheart, L. B. (2004). Rethinking Mental Retardation: Education and Eugenics in Connecticut, 1818–1917. *Journal of the History of Medicine and Allied Sciences* 59(1), 90–111.

Hendrie, C. (2004). Charters: An Uneasy Fit. *Education Week* 23(17).

Hiner, N. R., & Hawes, J. M. (1985). *Growing up in America: Children in Historical Perspective.* Chicago: University of Illinois Press.

The History of Lucas County Children Services. (n.d.). Retrieved August 19, 2004, from http://www.co.lucas.oh.us/LCCS/history.asp.

Hoffman, H. V. (n.d.). Copied from *History of Decatur County Iowa 1839–1970*, 105–108. Retrieved August 12, 2004, from http://www.rootsweb.com/~iadecatu/CountyFarm.html.

Hosp, J. L., & Reschly, D. J. (2004). Disproportionate Representation of Minority Students in Special Education: Academic, Demographic, and Economic Predictors. *Exceptional Children* 70(2), 185–199.

Individuals with Disabilities Education Act Amendments and Regulations of 1997. (n.d.). Retrieved January 10, 2005, from http://www.cec.sped.org/law_res/doc/law/index.php.

Jacobson, L. (1999). Changing Versions of Childhood. *Education Week* 18(24), 32–34.

Johnstone, E. R. (1908). The Functions of the Special Class. *National Education Association Journal of Proceedings* (pp. 114–118). Washington, DC: National Educational Association.

Kanaya, T., Scullin, M. H., & Ceci, S. J. (2003). The Flynn Effect and U.S. Policies: The Impact of Rising I.Q. Scores on American Society via Mental Retardation Diagnosis. *American Psychologist* 58(10), 778–790.

Kirk, E. K. (1995). Black Performers at the White House: A Picture History. *American Visions* 10(1), 22–24.

Kliewer, C., & Biklen, D. (2001). "School's Not Really a Place for Reading": A Research Synthesis of the Literate Lives of Students with Severe Disabilities. *JASH* 26(1), 1–12.

Kliewer, C., & Fitzgerald, L. M. (2001). Disability, Schooling, and the Artifacts of Colonialism. *Teachers College Record* 103(3), 450–470.

Lines to the Memory of an Idiot Girl. (1844). *Littell's Living Age*, September 21. Retrieved December 7, 2003, from Disability History Museum, http://www.disabilitymuseum.org.

Lipsky, D. K., & Gartner, A. (1997). *Inclusion and School Reform.* Baltimore: Paul H. Brookes Publishing Co.

Longmore, P. K., & Umansky, L. (2001). Disability History: From the Margins to the Mainstream. In P. K. Longmore & L. Umansky, eds., *The New Disability history: American Perspectives* (pp. 1–29). New York: New York University Press.

Miller, N. B. & Sammons, C. C. (1999). *Everybody's Different: Understanding and Changing Our Reactions to Disabilities.* Baltimore: Paul H. Brookes Publishing Co.

Morse, T. E. (2000). Ten Events That Shaped Special Education's Century of Dramatic Change. *International Journal of Educational Reform* 9(1), 32–38.

Nirje, B. (1976). The Normalization Principle. In R. B. Kirgel & A. Schearer, eds., *Changing Patterns in Residential Services for the Mentally Retarded* (rev. ed., pp. 51–58). Washington, DC: President's Committee on Mental Retardation.

Noll, S., & Trent, J. W. (2004). *Mental Retardation in America: A Historical Reader.* New York: New York University Press.

O'Brien, G. (2004). Rosemary Kennedy: The Importance of a Historical Footnote. *Journal of Family History* 29(3), 225–236.

Odom, S. L. (2000). Preschool Inclusion: What We Know and Where We Go from Here. *Topics in Early Childhood Special Education* 20(1), 20–27.

Palmer, S. B., Wehmeyer, M. L., Gipson, K., & Agran, M. (2004). Promoting Access to the General Curriculum by Teaching Self-determination Skills. *Exceptional Children* 70(4), 427–439.

Pavlides, M. (2004). Homeschooling Children with Disabilities: Balancing Freedom and Responsibility. *The Review of Disability Studies* 2(1).

Provence, L. (2003). Charlottesville Rocks: 4.5 Strikes Us. *The Hook*, December 18. Retrieved December 11, 2004, from http://readthehook.com/stories/2003/12/10/newsCharlottesvilleRocks45.html.

Railey, J., & Begos, K. (2002). Still Hiding. *Against Their Will: A Special Report from the Winston-Salem Journal.* Retrieved November 14, 2004, from http://againsttheirwill.journalnow.com.

Reinhold, R. (1980). Virginia Hospital's Chief Traces 50 Years of Sterilizing the "Retarded." *New York Times*, February 23, p. 6.

Rice, S. (2002). The Social Construction of "Disabilities": The Role of Law. *Educational Studies (American Educational Studies Association)* 33(2), 169–80.

Richards, L. E. (1909). *Letters and Journals of Samuel Gridley Howe, the Servant of Humanity* (vol. 2). Boston: Dana Estes & Co.

Richards, P. L. (2004). Beside Her Sat Her Idiot Child: Families and Developmental Disability in Mid-nineteenth-century America. In S. Noll & J. W. Trent, eds., *Mental Retardation in America: A Historical Reader* (pp. 65–87). New York: New York University Press.

Richards, P. L., & Singer, G.H.S. (1998). "To Draw Out the Effort of His Mind": Education of a Child with Mental Retardation in the Early-nineteenth-century America. *The Journal of Special Education* 31, 443–466.

Rokker, H. W. (1894). "Filthy Shops," and "Injurious Employments." First Annual Report of the Factory Inspectors of Illinois (pp. 10–13). Retrieved August 4, 2004, from http://womhist.binghamton.edu/factory/doc16.htm.

Rothman, D. J. (1991). *Strangers at the Bedside: A History of How Law and Bioethics Transformed Medical Decision Making.* New York: Basic Books.

Russell, F. J. (1917). The Deficient Child. *Proceedings of the Second Annual Vermont Conference of Charities and Correction,* 31–33. Retrieved August 12, 2004, from http://cit.uvm.edu:6336/dynaweb/eugenics/orfrvcs012417.

Safford, P. L., & Safford, E. J. (1996). *A History of Childhood & Disability.* New York: Teachers College Press.

Salend, S. J. (1999). Facilitating Friendships among Diverse Students. *Intervention in School and Clinic* 35(1), 9–15.

Schmidt, B. (n.d.). Archangels Unaware: *The Story of Thomas Bethune Also Known as Thomas Wiggins Also Known as "Blind Tom" (1849–1908).* Retrieved July 14, 2004, from http://twainquotes.com/archangels.html.

Smith, A. (2001). A Faceless Bureaucrat Ponders Special Education, Disability, and White Privilege. *JASH* 26(3), 180–188.

Smith, J. D. (2003). Abandoning the Myth of Mental Retardation. *Education and Training in Developmental Disabilities* 38(4), 358–361.

Snow, K. (2004). *People First Language.* Retrieved August 26, 2004, from http://www.disabilityisnatural.com/peoplefirstlanguage.htm.

Stiker, H. (1999). (Trans. Sayers, W.). *A History of Disability.* Ann Arbor: University of Michigan Press.

TASH website. (2005). Retrieved January 10, 2005, from www.tash.org.

Taylor, S. J., & Searl, S. J. (2001). Disability in America: A History of Policies and Trends. In E. D. Martin, ed., *Significant Disability: Issues Affecting People with Significant Disabilities from a Historical, Policy, Leadership, and Systems Perspective.* Springfield, IL: Charles C. Thomas.

United States Department of Education. (2002). Twenty-Fourth Annual Report to Congress on the Implementation of the Individuals with Disabilities Education Act. Retrieved January 7, 2005, from http://www.ed.gov/about/reports/annual/osep/2002/toc-execsum.pdf.

United States Federal Census. (June 1, 1870). Retrieved August 4, 2004, from http://familyresearchlibrary.com/uscensus/abt_census.htm.

United States Office of Special Education Programs. (2000). *History: Twenty-five Years of Progress in Educating Children with Disabilities Through IDEA.* Retrieved January 10, 2005, from http://www.ed.gov/policy/speced/leg/idea/history.pdf.

University of Oregon. (n.d.). Feeble-minded Children. In *Adoption History Project.* Retrieved July 14, 2004, from http://darkwing.uoregon.edu/~adoption/topics/feeblemindedchildren.htm.

University of Virginia Health Sciences Library Web Document. *Eugenics.* Retrieved January 5, 2005, from http://www.healthsystem.virginia.edu/internet/library/historical/eugenics/3-buckvbell.cfm.

Wehmeyer, M. L. (1998). Self-determination and Individuals with Significant Disabilities: Examining Meaning and Their Interpretations. *The Journal of the Association for Persons with Severe Handicaps* 23(1), 5–16.

White, W. D. & Wolfensberger, W. (1969). The evolution of dehumanization in our institutions. *Mental Retardation* 7, 5–9.

Whittier, J. G. (1854). Peculiar Institutions in Massachusetts. *Literary Recreations and Miscellanies.* Boston: Tickner and Fields. Retrieved August 11, 2004, from Disability History Museum, http://www.disabilitymuseum.org/lib/docs/1530. htm.

Wickham, P. (2001). Idiocy and Law in Colonial New England. *Mental Retardation* 39(2), 104–113.

Wilbur, H. B. (1877). The Classifications of Idiocy. *Proceedings of the Association of Medical Officers of American Institutions for Idiotic and Feeble-minded Persons.* Philadelphia: J. B. Lippincott. Retrieved December 7, 2003, from Disability History Museum, http://www.disabilitymuseum.org.

———. (1880). Instinct Not Predominant in Idiocy. *Proceedings of the Association of Medical Officers of American Institutions for Idiotic and Feeble-minded Persons.* Philadelphia: J. B. Lippincott Company. Retrieved December 7, 2003, from Disability History Museum, http://www.disabilitymuseum.org.

Williams, L. J., & Downing, J. E. (1998). Membership and Belonging in Inclusive Classrooms: What Do Middle School Students Have To Say? *The Journal of the Association for Persons with Severe Handicaps* 23(2), 98–110.

Winzer, M. A. (1993). *The History of Special Education: From Isolation to Integration.* Washington, DC: Gallaudet University Press.

Wortham, S. C. (2002). *Childhood, 1892–2002.* (2nd ed.). Wheaton, MD: Association for Childhood Education International.

Zahn, G. C. (1946). Abandon Hope. *The Catholic Worker,* October. Retrieved December 7, 2003, from Disability History Museum, http://www.disability museum.org.

5 Children Being Different, Difficult, or Disturbed in America

Philip L. Safford and Elizabeth J. Safford

Nicholas Hobbs (1982) famously characterized the range of differences considered in this chapter with the phrase "troubled and troubling child." This duality of concern is apparent throughout history, manifest in efforts both to understand and care for children in pain or in conflict and to protect society from troublesome youth. As long as there have been schools, there have been students who challenged teachers' authority, created disruption in the classroom, could not seem to learn or perform as expected, or just did not fit. And surely there have always been parents who were concerned about a moody, withdrawn, "high-strung," oppositional, impulse-driven, or "quirky" child or teen.

UNDERSTANDING OF CHILD DEVIANCE

While childhood "insanity" was occasionally reported in the nineteenth century, and wayward, unsupervised children and youth were becoming an increasing concern, especially in the cities, the concept *emotionally disturbed child* was a twentieth-century invention (Despert 1965). The more than 300 disorders recognized by the American Psychiatric Association include many conduct, regulatory, and mood disorders, even psychotic conditions, specific to childhood. Although American children have presumably experienced such "conditions" since colonial times, their manifestations were attributed to willfulness and inclination to disobedience, if not demonic possession.

The authors wish to thank Nancy J. Kortemeyer, public relations director for Beech Brook (formerly the Cleveland Protestant Orphan Asylum) for her assistance.

With accounts of girls convulsing and unintelligible speech, the witch-craft accusations in 1692 in Salem, Massachusetts, are often associated with mental illness. That it was most often adolescent girls who claimed to have been bewitched poses the question of whether girls were more susceptible than boys to disturbance. Were the girls' "admissions" evidence of insanity, youthful impressionability, or malicious lying? Elizabeth Reis (1997) attrib-utes the witchcraft accusation phenomena to prevalent views of gender: females' "weaker nature" made them more vulnerable to Satan, while the Puritan doctrine of females' "inherent vileness" made young girls more likely to be persuaded of their guilt. Steven Mintz (2004) suggests that making these accusations was a way of experiencing power, otherwise im-possible for girls in that setting (p. 23).

Whether through inheritance or nurture, parents have always been blamed for children's deviance, and mothers have been especially prone to link the child's destiny to their own misdeeds. Hawthorne (1850/1983) describes Hester Prynne's fear that her daughter, Pearl, must have familial taint, signified by the scarlet letter A she has been condemned to wear: "Day after day she looked fearfully into the child's expanding nature; ever dreading to detect some dark and wild peculiarity, that should correspond with the guiltiness to which she owed her being" (p. 194).

The eighteenth century saw major reforms in the treatment of mentally ill persons, long chained, abused, and displayed for public amusement. While the individual most identified with "removing the chains" was Phi-lippe Pinel, in Paris, Vincenzo Chiarugi had instituted similar reforms in Florence, Italy, two decades earlier (Barton 1987). A contemporary whose *moral treatment* approach had the most direct impact on practices in Amer-ica was William Tuke, an English Quaker. Appalled by the inhumane treat-ment in London's infamous Bethlehem Hospital (known as "Bedl'm"), Tuke pioneered a radically different approach, using kindness and calm structure in the Retreat he established at York. Philadelphia's Friends Asy-lum (1813), founded by American Quakers, drew heavily on the Retreat model. Over the next several decades, as the superintendent of the Lunatic Asylum at Utica, New York, Dr. Amariah Brigham (1845) explained in "Schools in Lunatic Asylums," moral therapy was considered an educational intervention to teach patients acceptable attitudes and behaviors.

The first American mental asylum was established in 1773 in Williams-burg, Virginia, although the Pennsylvania Hospital Benjamin Franklin co-founded in 1751 had a section for "lunatics." Neither could be described as employing moral treatment until Benjamin Rush (1745–1813), the new nation's preeminent physician and signer of the Declaration of Independ-ence, took a leadership post at the Pennsylvania facility in 1787. Although Rush described childhood insanity as rare, he did acknowledge its exis-tence, especially having had the personal experience of a son and a brother who had been hospitalized for mental problems (Hawke 1971). But other than attributing memory impairment in children to "idiotism," his descriptions are of adults.

Rush (1812) differentiated "partial insanity" (e.g., hypochondriasis and melancholia) and "general intellectual derangement" from *dementia* or *fatuity* (i.e., "idiotism"). But he thought mental health a matter of character—a belief that undergirded moral treatment's blend of benevolence with authoritarianism (Foucault 1965). In a lecture to Franklin's American Philosophical Society, Rush (1786) distinguished a "weakened" moral faculty (*micronomia*) from its total absence (*anomia*) (p. 16), noting that this faculty can be affected by climate, diet, alcohol, excessive sleep, or heredity. Critical in strengthening the moral faculty in the young are "steady labor," cleanliness in food preparation and personal hygiene, and "solitude" to permit calm, silent reflection and freedom from excessive excitement—all elements of moral treatment.

Although Jean Etienne Esquirol (1838) had both described childhood psychosis and differentiated mental illness from mental subnormality, they long continued to be conflated, while persons with mental retardation were long burdened with attributions of dangerous, even criminal tendencies. After his 1909 visit to Clark University, Freud's theories of intrapsychic conflict, informed by work with adult neurotic patients, presented a new understanding of the inner lives of children that profoundly changed the way childhood mental illness was understood. Before Freud, alienists "blamed the victim." Kaufman (1993) reports a laundry list of firmly held nineteenth-century notions linking mental illness to licentious thoughts, masturbation, excessive excitement, religious fervor, sedentary habits, reading "vile books," or excessive studiousness. Parents were enjoined to correct such behaviors in the interest of the child and of society. To prevent "masturbatory insanity," parents were cautioned about fondling or hugging children, and to be concerned about a child who has a "downcast look" or chooses to be alone. The only cure, parents were instructed, was total abstinence.

Many thought that the increasing educational attainment of girls, given their female anatomical and emotional vulnerability, placed them at risk for such disturbances as hysteria and melancholia. In 1881, George Beard introduced the term *neuresthenia*, or nervous exhaustion, to address what were considered specifically "female complaints" of young women of well-educated middle- or upper-class families. However, sensitive young men were also susceptible to such complaints, the remedy for which was "a strident dose of 'the strenuous life' " (Noll 2004, p. 598). Neuresthenic symptoms in girls and young women were sometimes reflected in eating disorders. While *anorexia nervosa* was identified in the 1870s, a predecessor called "chlorosis" was seen in anemic middle-class adolescent girls who deprived themselves of nourishment—an extreme means of living up to societal expectations in the era of corsets (Brumberg 1982).

Such concerns were class-specific. Deviance from accepted norms on the part of working-class youth, Irish, and by the 1880s immigrants from southern and eastern Europe, was ascribed to genetic inferiority associated with "foreignness." Neither they nor African American nor Native American youth were represented within the practice of physicians addressing mental problems in the young. Reports by alienists working in institutions tended to bear out prevailing sentiments that immigrant pauper stock, like that of Blacks and Indians, was constitutionally inferior.

DISCIPLINE AND CONTROL

The concept of *control* is central to any understanding of the disturbed or disturbing child, although beliefs have differed widely concerning how best to help the child develop *inner* control. The colonists, reflecting European practices, approached child rearing and discipline very differently from the Native Americans, who, socializing the young with the values of pride, courage, and independence, generally did not employ harsh punishment or restraint or forced weaning or toilet training with infants. As Mintz (2004, p. 10) noted, "A Puritan childhood is as alien to twenty-first century Americans as an Indian childhood was to seventeenth-century New Englanders," who believed even newborns potential sinners whose willful nature must be suppressed.

During the Great Awakening of the 1730s and 1740s, sermons and religious tracts attacked youthful anger and disobedience, which had earlier been a capitol offense, as highly undesirable traits that needed to be corrected. Insubordinate children needed to be "broken," for their own good as well as that of society. A premium was placed on responsibility, the converse of which was waywardness, and on self-control, rather than expressing anger or, for girls, offenses with sexual implications, such as disobeying or lying to parents to keep company with boys. This repressive approach was not universal throughout the colonies, however; Quaker childrearing stressed guidance and encouraged children's sense of worth and independence (Mintz 2004).

In the nineteenth century this expectation of filial responsibility was fostered by education, as well as peer influence through young men's organizations (Wallach 1997). Boys were socialized to live up to their fathers' expectations and demonstrate "manly virtues" of self-control and a strong sense of familial responsibility. However, this no longer implied countering the child's innate vileness, but rather appealing to his better nature. Pamphlets and articles on child rearing, increasingly addressed to mothers, advised using appeals to guilt, rather than punishment, to keep their sons and daughters on the right path. As Freud's writings would later suggest, this was a double-edged sword.

Relatedly, by the 1840s opposition was growing to the use of corporal punishment as a corrective for miscreants. Reformers who opposed beatings in schools, notably Horace Mann, or cruel treatment of mentally ill persons, notably Dorothea Dix, followed a tradition begun by Benjamin Rush (Glenn 1984). If parents do employ corporal punishment, Rush (1792/1972) had advised that it be "moderate" rather than "violent" (p. 22), and that cruel or public punishments are counterproductive, for they tend to harden the offender's "sensibility . . . the avenue to the moral faculty" (p. 32). Rather than attempting to beat the devil out of them, parents and teachers should bring out the good within them. This seemed a role for which women were uniquely suited.

Although best known as leader of the Common School movement, Horace Mann (1796–1859) also had an important role in establishing the first state mental institution, as well as one of the first "oral" programs for deaf students in the United States. His second wife Mary Peabody worked with her sister Elizabeth Peabody to establish America's first English-speaking Froebellian kindergarten in Boston in 1860, seeing in "child-gardening" the full expression of women's role (Weber 1969).

Educational reformers thought the natural attributes of womanhood well suited to teaching. Henry Barnard (1840) extolled women's "gentleness," "forbearance," "refined manners," and "purer morals" as positive influences. Mann's (1853) championing of the shift to a predominantly female teaching profession reflected his distaste for punitive disciplinary practices such as he had experienced as a boy. He believed that women's more "mild and gentle" qualities would be an effective counterforce to the rampant use of physical punishment by male teachers. But women didn't necessarily conform to this expectation; correspondence of women teachers in New England between 1830 and 1850 recounted resorting to "pinching," "cuffing," and whipping for disruptive behavior, insubordination, rebelliousness, truancy, and poor work (Preston 1993).

THE "GOOD BAD BOY"

The malefactors were generally boys, whose misdeeds Mann clearly did not view—disturbing as they were to their teachers—as evidence of innate depravity or pathology. While Mann's belief that woman's touch held the key to their redemption oversimplified the matter, many adults were inclined to view youthful misbehavior more tolerantly. This trend was apparent in post–Civil War literature, as Alison Lurie (2004) noted in an essay linking the story of Pinocchio to Tom Sawyer, titled "The Good Bad Boy."

In colonial New England, misconduct reflected two dangerous youthful inclinations. Excessive pride caused disobedience, expressed in "contempt for authority, rebellion against family government, boasting, Sabbath-breaking, and blasphemy, while sensuality encouraged company keeping, reveling, drinking, masturbation, and fornication" (Chamberlain 2002,

p. 184). However, a greater tolerance for boys' misdeeds was apparent in an early 18th century episode of "boys" (actually young men in their twenties) accused of lascivious speech in the presence of young women after surreptitiously reading medical manuals depicting female anatomy. Despite Cotton Mather's call for public condemnations, the outcome revealed a cultural change from a single, church-monitored standard to a double standard, treating such male misbehavior as a private matter to be handled within the family (Chamberlain 2002).

As a source of moral instruction, children's literature "exhorted, intimidated, cajoled, or threatened . . . the tragic consequences of misbehavior" (Baskin & Harris 1977, p. 39), illustrating the rewards for the child who chooses the path of virtue. Children were enjoined to obey their parents, be industrious, be considerate of others, and guard against impure thoughts. Stories portrayed models who learned from their minor mistakes with the help of wise and forgiving elders. Mark Twain (1875) satirized this ideal in his "Story of a Bad Little Boy" and "Story of a Good Little Boy," parodies of Horatio Alger's books for boys, the first of which, *Ragged Dick*, appeared in 1867. The former is an unregenerate young miscreant named Jim (not "James"), the latter the too-good-to-be-true Jacob. The irony is that Jacob's is a tale of no good deed going unpunished, while Jim—unlike Sunday School portrayals of evildoers—gets away with every misdeed. "This Jim," Twain recounts in mock amazement, "bore a charmed life" (p. 58).

In contrast to these satirically drawn archetypes are "real boys" in whom right and wrong are less distinguishable. In a moment of remorse for the "wrong" he has done in aiding Jim's escape, Huckleberry Finn writes a letter telling Jim's owner where she can find her runaway slave—then tears it up, thinking this represents persistence in his evil ways: "All right, then, I'll go to hell . . . and take up wickedness again, which was in my line, being brung up to it. . . . And for a starter, I would . . . steal Jim out of slavery again; and if I could think up anything worse, I would do that, too; because as long as I was in, and in for good, I might as well go the whole hog." (Twain 1884/1995, pp. 330–331).

Although considered a bad influence, Huck represented a more empathic understanding of misbehavior and underlying virtue in young (male) Americans reflected in a long-popular literary genre that "depicts a child's world that is antagonistic to the world of adults," (Crowley 1985, p. 385). The original "boy-book," *The Story of a Bad Boy*, by Thomas Bailey Aldrich (1895), recounts young Tom's escapades while staying with his grandparents in a New Hampshire port town in the 1840s. In portraying Tom as "not such a very bad, but a pretty bad boy," the author distinguished his young self from the idealized model portrayed in Sunday School. His pranks were usually harmless, and when one goes bad he is remorseful. His grandfather's response to Tom's black eye from fighting is "you rascal! Just like me when I was young" (p. 258).

Boys will be boys. While girls are self-sacrificing, dutiful "little women," boys, in the words of Henry Cabot Lodge, are "natural savages" (Crowley 1985), epitomized by the most famous youth in American literature: "Huckleberry was cordially hated and dreaded by all the mothers of the town because he was idle, and lawless, and vulgar, and bad—and because all their children admired him so and delighted in his forbidden society.... [E]verything that goes to make life precious, that boy had. So thought every harassed, hampered, respectable boy in St. Petersburg" (Twain 1876/1971, pp. 61–62).

Nor is Tom Sawyer a model of deportment. In fact his lying, truancy, running away, and choice of companions suggest he is "seriously delinquent," although he is "basically good at heart" (Lurie 2004, p. 15). In another setting—the city—or at a somewhat later time, Tom, or certainly Huck—orphan and "half-orphan" respectively, with inclinations for misconduct like the Horatio Alger protagonists—might well have found themselves "served" within the emerging network of social agencies.

AN "INSTITUTIONAL WEB" TO CONTAIN DEVIANCE

In their efforts to manage deviance and preserve social order, nineteenth-century reformers on both sides of the Atlantic created what Foucault (1977) termed an "institutional web" of reformatories, asylums, training schools, and orphanages. With compulsory school attendance laws, the web later extended into the common schools in the form of "special" schools or classes. Each of these has had a role in the history of services for troubled and troubling children.

Asylums and Conflation of Disturbance and Retardation

Foucault (1965, p. 36) considered confinement the stage after embarkation in managing the deviant, the "madhouse" succeeding the "ship of fools"; once asylums were established in the colonies debtors, felons, and poor Irish youth sent as indentured servants became the preponderance of inmates. He ascribed the continuing inhumane conditions in mental asylums, even in the moral treatment era, to the association of madness with animality, noting that even Pinel and Tuke were impressed with the apparent ability of "lunatics," confined naked in cells, to endure cold temperatures and pain (p. 75). Moreover, moral treatment, while a great advance over the persecution of earlier times, involved treating mentally ill adults like children (Grob 1973).

While nearly all inmates in the numerous asylums established in the United States by the mid-nineteenth century were adults (Grob 1973), there were some children. Among the 164 patients treated at the Lunatic Asylum at Worcester, Massachusetts, in 1833 were two boys, ages fourteen and sixteen, and two nineteen-year-old females (Worcester Lunatic Asylum 1833). Kaufman (1993, p. 73) cites a superintendent's report that in 1841, nine of 122 patients in Western Lunatic Asylum (in Virginia) were younger than twenty, with two under fifteen. Mary Mann (1877, p. 120) provided this account of how childhood mental disorders were understood: "A distinguished and most successful superintendent of an insane hospital once assured me, that in the majority of cases, self-control was all that was needed as a remedy for insanity. I asked him if he had ever known of insane children? He said he had known many; and that it usually appeared in the form of *unmanageableness*."

Many children who could not be managed at home found willing reception in asylums for the feebleminded. S. G. Howe (1852) described children in his experimental school whose aberrant behavior falsely suggested feeblemindedness with the term "simulative idiocy," a precursor to notions of "moral idiocy" and "juvenile affective insanity," terms coined by Dr. Isaac Kerlin, superintendent of the Elwyn Training School at Media, Pennsylvania. Kerlin (1885, pp. 254–258) warned, "there is free in the community a great host of crime-doers who are not so much criminals as mental and moral imbeciles." Like the "Juke" family, they reflected the "taint" causing "their crime, pauperism, and bestiality . . . living stocks of half-witted bastards, criminals, and paupers, who will continue to roll up the bill of expense for petty crime and misdemeanors and the untold expense of ruined character. . . . How many of your incorrigible boys, lodged in the houses of refuge to be half educated in letters and wholly unreached in morals, are sent out into the community the moral idiots they were at the beginning, only more powerfully armed for mischief?"

Walter Fernald (1909, pp. 859–862), superintendent of the Massachusetts School for the Feeble-Minded, described adolescent inmates illustrating "the imbecile with criminal instincts." Despite "degenerative stigmata," all can carry out work responsibilities under supervision, and even have modest academic skills, but their commonalities involve sexual acting out, noncompliance with authority, aggressive behavior toward peers, habitual lying, and profane and obscene language. A girl is "cunning . . . selfish and grasping . . . deceitful, unreliable." A boy is "contemptuous . . . egotistical [and a] cruel practical joker"; another is "never in sympathy with the officers . . . in charge [and] always sly and cunning in his mischief-making." A third "lies persistently, purposely, and maliciously [and is] a great thief . . . impatient of control."

Rather than illustrating a propensity of young "imbeciles" to engage in antisocial behavior, the descriptions imply the likelihood of undesirable behavior earning the perpetrator the label of "imbecile." Similarly, students referred for placement in public school special classes for "mental defectives" as these were established in the twentieth century tended to be those who were troublesome or difficult to manage (Sarason & Doris 1969). Concerns persist even today that children of poor or minority status, thus "culturally different" from the institutional norm, are disproportionately represented in special education classes.

Reform or Transport: Child-saving for the "Deserving Poor"

In accordance with English Poor Laws, parishes or "unions" comprising several parishes in the colonies were authorized to impose taxes to establish poorhouses and provide nominal sums of "poor relief" for some families of young children (Thurston 1930). Indenturing, or "binding out" provided for older children to be "farmed out," their work monitored by designated overseers of the poor. What of young children without families? Howard Zinn (1995, p. 49) quotes a 1737 description of "the poor street urchin of New York as 'an Object in Human Shape, half starv'd with Cold, with Cloathes out at the Elbows, Knees through the Breeches, Hair standing on end. . . . From the age about four to Fourteen they spend their Days in the Streets . . . then they are put out as Apprentices, perhaps four, five, or six years.' " Within the next century, these urban waifs, reduced to begging, thieving, and prostitution, would be perceived as a social menace.

For boys, delinquency was mainly defined as involving property offenses, while for girls it usually involved status offenses (runaways, sexual acting out). Of particular concern were youth considered "wayward" or who "lacked parental guidance" (Richardson 1989, p. 11), characteristics explicitly associated with the poor. Hence, both delinquency and dependency were identified with "pauperism," and in 1824, the Society for the Prevention of Pauperism became "the Society for the Prevention of Delinquency," its aim to establish Houses of Refuge. John Griscom, a Quaker, founded the first such reformatory in New York in 1825, followed by others in Boston, Philadelphia, New Orleans, Rochester, Baltimore, and Cincinnati. However, the ideal of a compassionate environment for poor children who had been led astray to become virtuous through productive work was soon thwarted; environments were prison-like, punishments severe, and the children generally exploited as cheap labor (Hawes 1971).

To address these concerns, reformers looked to an alternative model: a colony established in 1839 in a rural setting at Mettray, France, by Judge Frederic Auguste Demetz. While discipline was strict and labor arduous, the Mettray model's intent was to maintain a healthful, humane, and democratic environment. The beneficial influence of productive work was assumed in American facilities established as extensions of the common school. The Lyman School for Boys, established at Westboro, Massachusetts, in 1847, was followed in 1849 by the State Industrial School at Rochester, New York, and in 1856 by a school in Lancaster, Ohio. The first girls' "family style" reform facility, the State Industrial School for Girls, opened at Lancaster, Massachusetts, in 1856 (Brenzel 1980).

The dual motives of "child-saving" and protecting society continued to be reflected in the institutional web, illustrated by the founding in 1875 of the New York Society for the Prevention of Cruelty to Children and the concurrent spread of reformatories. Both motives can be seen in the founding of the Children's Aid Society by Charles Loring Brace, suggested by Brace's (1872, pp. 16–17) warning that, "This dangerous class . . . when these boys and girls are mature . . . will poison society." His concept involved "placing-out" vagrant children roaming the city with midwestern farm families. Approximately 20,000 children were gathered from New York's streets between 1854 and 1874, processed by professional social workers, and placed on trains to their rural destinations, where the older ones were expected to provide a source of labor in exchange for the benefits of home, family, and country life. By 1929, when the society extended its focus to community child mental health services, this prototypical foster care system had placed out more than 100,000 children (CAS website).

During the last half of the nineteenth century, more and more American children of newly emerging "middle class" families were experiencing a safer and more nurturing domestic life. However, as Mintz (2004, p. 134) summarized, "at no point in American history was childhood as diverse" with African American children subjected to unimaginable psychological as well as physical cruelty that did not end with emancipation, and many immigrant children still essentially sold into servitude and subjected, whether in factory or domestic service, to severe, often abusive discipline.

There has surely been nothing in American history more damaging to children's psychological well-being, over generations, than slavery of African Americans (Berlin, 2002). The post–Civil War years also brought conditions conducive to childhood disturbance in white as well as black children, from post-traumatic stress disorder likely among extremely young combatants to children left fatherless or homeless. In ensuing decades, homeless children joining in "bread riots" to avoid starvation included orphans and runaways often escaping abusive home situations (Mintz 2004). While social Darwinists called for reformatories to protect society, as "the Century of the Child" dawned, a leader (Butler 1901, p. 210) called reform schools "prominent factors in the work of child-saving . . . the lower dam which catches those not stopped by other effects higher up the stream. . . . Their charges are but children, neglected, untrained, wayward boys and girls. They need discipline, education, training, and correct adjustment to the proper conditions of life."

By 1925 there were more than 150 reform schools in the United States, housing nearly 24,000 children. In addition to their rural settings, cottage living arrangements, and intent to reform through strict discipline and productive labor, these "schools" had in common two characteristics: the lack of a meaningful educational program, although school truancy was often a factor leading to placement, and a clientele virtually entirely drawn from the poorest families, or those who had no families at all (Caddey 1963).

Orphan Asylums: Forerunners of Residential Treatment

The first orphanage in the colonies was founded at the Ursuline Convent in New Orleans in 1727. George Whitefield, a Methodist itinerant preacher, founded another in 1738 in Savannah, Georgia. By 1800, there were private orphanages in New York, Philadelphia, Baltimore, and Boston, a public orphanage in Charleston, South Carolina, and in 1822 Quakers opened the first "colored" orphan asylum in Philadelphia. By 1851, there were seventy-seven private orphan asylums, as well as public asylums established to remove children from almshouses where they had been intermixed with adults (Butler 1901). The number grew rapidly as Civil War deaths added to parents lost as a result of epidemics and work-related accidents. A century later, as maintenance of children with families, their own if possible, was favored over institutional care, many redefined their role to that of providing *residential treatment* for children with emotional problems.

A prototypical example of this shift is seen in the history of the Cleveland (Ohio) Protestant Orphan Asylum. The asylum, later renamed Beech Brook, began in 1852 consequent to a charitable project by a women's group, the Martha Washington and Dorcas Society, based at what is now known as the Old Stone Church, a Cleveland historic landmark. While their original intent was to collect and distribute food and clothing for poor children, the women soon decided instead to devote their efforts to founding an asylum for the "purpose of sheltering orphaned and destitute children" in the wake of a cholera epidemic (Cleveland Protestant Orphan Asylum 1879).

The "little frame house" sheltering the first eleven children was outgrown by 1855, so the "family" of twenty-five children was moved to another donated location. Responding to the "increasing call for shelter for orphans," Leonard Case donated land to construct a new building, and the agency officially became the Cleveland Protestant Orphan Asylum (CPOA) in 1876. A gift of a "country" site in 1916 enabled the asylum to develop a farm, as did many such agencies, for the dual purpose of feeding the children and availing the older ones the wholesome benefits of work. A more homelike atmosphere was created by replacing dormitories with Tudor cottages and matrons with house parents.

Although the agency's name and location changed, its mission continued to be "to gather up the homeless and destitute children of the city, feed them clothe them, send them to school, and in every way possible fit them to go out into permanent homes, where they will have the advantages of a Christian education, and where they will be treated and respected as one of the family" (CPOA 1879, p. 16). The goal was that every child be either "returned" or "placed out," since "the ultimate aim of all asylum work should be to establish the child in family relations as soon as possible" (p. 12). The annual report for 1878 showed that of the 209 children served, 70 had been adopted and 91 returned to "friends" (usually the child's parents or other relatives). One, due to behavior problems, had been sent to the Industrial Home for Girls. Two had died.

In the early years, despite the neglect and mistreatment they may have experienced previously, the children were not seen as difficult to manage: "As a general thing we found them in good health, happy and contented; their physical wants abundantly supplied, and their mental and moral training carefully looked after" (1879, p. 11). Superintendent A. H. Strunk insisted that no one should think them inferior to any children because they "come from hunger, from cold, from nakedness, from neglect and abuse. Their poverty is not of their own misdeeds" (p. 13). Nor were all children in need of "asylum" without families. In an all-too-typical case, "the old, old story of drunkenness and abuse was the cause of [Lulu's] coming to the Asylum. [She] . . . scarcely heard anything from the lips of her parents but profanity and obscenity" (p. 14).

But it was becoming increasingly apparent that children who came from homes of parental addiction, mental illness, abuse, and neglect needed help to "unravel the mental snarls" (a phrase mentioned repeatedly in the agency's annual reports) so that their prospects for successful adoptive or foster placement could be enhanced. While parental deaths in Cleveland as throughout the nation in the 1918 flu epidemic had a major effect on enrollment in the 1920s, increasing numbers of children who were referred were neither "full" nor "half" orphans, but children who were "disturbed or disturbing."

By the 1920s, child profiles quite different from the descriptions of earlier residents as contented and docile are implied by log entries such as: "lazy physically and morally," "sly and will not properly do the simplest task," "habitually disobedient, a liar and a most persistent troublemaker," "sly and disobedient," "has managed to keep in hot water during most of his stay here," "difficult to control—has to be supervised every minute," "will flout authority and sweetly smile while he is doing it," "inclined to be sneaky," "stubborn and willful," "[sexually] precocious and a habitual liar," "a crybaby and destructive," "steals other boys' things," "babyish," "a liar and a shirker," "a biter." Two young brothers who "have tempers" must be restrained by their older brother.

Rather than being noncompliant or "sly," some children manifest anxiety, such as "an uncontrollable masturbator," two brothers who both had "an uncontrollable terror of physicians," and a boy whose anxieties were expressed in the form of "queer animal noises while sleeping." A girl "will go into a tantrum and shriek and yell should anything displease her." Another "screams and cries upon the least provocation." A boy "needs a continuous show of affection to keep him going straight." Two sisters were bed wetters.

Placements were not always successful. In some cases, the child's rejection seems cruelly arbitrary; a girl "did not quite appeal to the people who had her"; another seemed "not quite normal." A foster family decided they "wanted an older girl." One boy was returned "for observation, but we could find nothing wrong with the lad." In some instances the concern was sexual acting out. A girl was "returned because she was intimate with a chance acquaintance"; another for having "sex experiences"; another had "tampered with a younger boy in the family." A boy "was not obedient and caused his foster parents much expense and concern"; another's "foster parents thought he was subject to fits [and were advised] . . . there is a possibility that he will be epileptic sometime in the future." One had again run away from his own family's home, while three brothers returned from unsuccessful placement with their own family are described as "the roughest we have had in some time. Troublemakers all."

This change in the clientele served by Beech Brook and other orphanages heralded a change in function from providing temporary placement for poor children to "the provision of individual attention to badly behaved, difficult, or troubled children" (Morton 2000, p. 443). Having sought psychiatric consultation for several years, in 1932 Beech Brook, as it was now called, hired its first psychiatrist. In 1958 it officially stopped accepting orphans and became a full-time Residential Treatment Center.

Another that followed this course was the Methodist Children's Home (now Berea Children's Home and Family Services), whose campus and nearby farm were also located in the Cleveland area. That agency's shift was prompted by an analysis by the Child Welfare League of America (1960, pp. 7–8), which noted, "There are only 1/16 as many orphans in the United States as there were as late as 1920 even though the child population is much larger. . . . Only a small percentage of mothers die in child-birth today as contrasted with 1920 or even 1935. Industrial and farm accidents have been greatly reduced and epidemics and plagues have been eliminated." The need for care of orphans, the report continued, had been replaced by a need for professional treatment for "troubled children, problem children, emotionally disturbed children, children who need to have their capacity to love and be loved restored" (p. 8).

Many orphanages joined the few agencies that had been established as treatment facilities, such as the Sonia Shankman Orthogenic School, established in 1913 at the University of Chicago's Rush Medical Center and made famous by Bruno Bettelheim, principal and then director from 1944 until his death; the Child Guidance Home in Cincinnati, Ohio (1920); and the Menninger Foundation's Southard School (1926) in Topeka, Kansas, which also served "feeble-minded" children. By the 1970s, there were 340 residential treatment centers in the United States, in addition to twenty-six public and private psychiatric hospitals exclusively serving children under sixteen (Witkin 1974). The fact that most instituted an on-site school program was due to two concerns: many of the children could not tolerate "regular" school, and schools often could not tolerate many of the children. Soon "educational therapy" came to be considered a key component of the therapeutic milieu, and the teacher an ancillary member of the ortho-psychiatric team.

MENTAL HYGIENE, CHILD STUDY, AND CHILD GUIDANCE

While interest in children's mental and emotional development, virtually a new phenomenon in the nineteeth century, had grown, the first professional to apply the tools of social science to these issues was G. Stanley Hall, first president both of the American Psychological Association and of Clark University. Beginning in the 1880s, Hall pioneered the use of questionnaires to elicit the "content of children's minds," later enlisting teachers he trained in observation and interview techniques—beginning what was soon called the Child Study Movement. While Hall's concepts and methodology contributed greatly to their understanding of childhood and adolescence, they provided little guidance for helping children who experienced problems.

The Psychoeducational Clinic and the Mental Hygiene Movement

Psychological *services* for children began in 1896 with Lightner Witmer's clinic at the University of Pennsylvania, whose first client was a fourteen-year-old boy with a spelling problem that might today be considered a *specific learning disability* (although it turned out that glasses helped considerably). In the course of work with the boy and other clients referred to him for learning or behavioral difficulties, Witmer (1909) developed a diagnostic teaching, or "orthogenic" approach, pioneering the basic methodology subsequently employed with children with specific learning disabilities. While Witmer applied his methods successfully with children reported to have serious learning problems—including some the institution for feebleminded children at Media, Pennsylvania, considered "uneducable"—he believed the approach applicable with all children. In fact, the journal he founded for sharing case studies, *Psychological Clinic*, was subsequently subtitled *A Journal of Orthogenics for the Normal Development of Every Child* (French 1990, p. 4).

Witmer's model inspired clinics in institutions, universities, and—beginning with Chicago's Department of Scientific Pedagogy and Child Study, established in 1899—the larger school districts. By the 1930s school-based clinics and the newly designated *school psychologists* and other professionals who staffed the clinics had major roles in determining students' eligibility for special education, need for personal counseling, and even fitness for schooling. A study of school-based clinics by J.E.W. Wallin (1914), published as *The Mental Health of the School Child*, urged greater attention to children's psychological problems. A growing number of child mental health specialists like D. A. Thom (1927) and Arnold Gesell (1930), the first self-identified school psychologist, amplified this concern, as research results (Wickman 1928) revealed that teachers were simply not attuned to their students' emotional needs.

These developments occurred across a backdrop of increased attention to mental illness, for which Clifford Beers merits much credit. In 1908, Beers had published *A Mind that Found Itself*, an account of his experiences following commitment to a mental hospital for a nervous breakdown. In 1909—the year of Freud and Jung's historic American visit—Beers, Adolph Meyer, and William James, America's preeminent psychologist, cofounded the National Committee for Mental Hygiene. Though a neurologist, Meyer opposed the then dominant organic view of mental illness, with its associated "typologies" and pessimistic prognoses. Maintaining that psychopathology could be explained on the basis of "learned habit patterns," he believed that Freud's insights had implications for healthy child rearing and pedagogy (Hale 1971, p. 18).

Nonetheless, problems with delinquency continued. Authorities had long expressed concerns about the effects of urbanization on children, unless well supervised by parents and kept in school rather than turned loose on the streets. L. Emmett Holt (1897) warned against the susceptibility of the young to the excessive stimulation and excitement of urban environments. Jane Addams (1909) of Chicago's Hull House warned that, without parks and playgrounds to provide recreational outlets, the innate curiosity of youth exposed them to vice. By 1918, the approximately 400 settlement houses in American cities were working to counter the stresses of poverty through a variety of health, educational, and recreational services (Mintz 2004).

In his address at the Twenty-eighth National Conference of Charities in 1901, social reformer Jacob Riis said, "I have found that a boy's club is vastly more effective in dealing with slum problems than a policeman's club" (p. 18). Riis recalled how society "used to put the little lads in jail for nothing else in the world than not going to schools that were like dungeons." (p. 19). Responding to the increasingly influential "doctrine of despair" of the eugenics movement, he enjoined his fellow reformers to counter fatalistic hereditarian arguments that the poor, the malefactors, and those with disabilities or mental illness are doomed by their "germ-plasm."

Jane Addams and her colleague Julia Lathrop (charter member of the National Committee for Mental Hygiene, and in 1912 appointed to head the new U.S. Children's Bureau) were key influences in bringing about what came to be termed child guidance. The mental health professionals working in this area were especially concerned with the prevention of serious mental health problems through education, counsel to parents, and outpatient treatment. Although it crossed socioeconomic class lines, by the 1920s child guidance had increasing response from middle-class parents concerned about childhood or adolescent rebelliousness or other misbehavior (Horn 1984; 1989).

While also employing short-term "psychopathic hospital" stays, child guidance's main venue was the clinic, illustrated by the shift made by the Children's Aid Society to community mental health services. At the peak of American "negative eugenics," William Healy opposed ascribing delinquency to genetic predisposition; neither did he associate it with mental retardation. Maintaining that delinquents should not be considered qualitatively different from other youth, Healy (1915) endorsed psychological rather than punitive approaches. In 1909, through Addams's efforts, he founded the Juvenile Psychopathic Institute in Chicago in conjunction with the juvenile court, which had been established ten years earlier (Schowalter 2003). In 1912, a Children's Clinic opened in Boston Psychopathic Hospital, and the next year the new Henry Phipps Psychiatric Clinic in Baltimore opened a department for children. In 1917 Boston's Judge Baker Guidance Center was established, which Healy directed until his retirement in 1947 (Jones 1999).

Another of Healy's important contributions was cofounding with Dr. Karl Menninger and others the American Orthopsychiatric Association (AOA) in 1924. This new professional organization reflected a key innovation of child guidance professionals: the orthopsychiatric team. In this model, a psychiatric social worker "worked" with parents, while the child was seen by a clinical psychologist (the specialization Witmer had pioneered) and psychiatrist, in order to develop a comprehensive understanding of the child's needs.

From "Pathogenic Parent" to Parent Advocacy

While the orthopsychiatric team approach exonerated families in one sense, implicitly countering the eugenic association of disturbance and delinquency with "familial taint" (Jones 1999), it tended to implicate the family, in the words of a leader in the field, in having "failed in its socialization task" (Devereaux 1956, p. 52). Ascribing children's social-emotional problems to faulty parenting, especially mothering, professionals such as Bettelheim considered the child's "therapeutic removal" from the home essential, at least in the short term. Thus, despite the community-based innovations of child guidance, as late as the 1960s, the "treatment of choice" for many emotionally troubled children and adolescents suggested a return to the era of the asylum—and of parental iatrogenic guilt.

> On a Monday in 1961, Cliff was carried, kicking and screaming, into the treatment center. His wailing continued through the afternoon and into the night, until at last he slept. The history revealed a bright boy who, despite poor school attendance, performed well on achievement measures, but now refusing to go to school, he was admitted with a diagnosis of "school phobia." It soon emerged that Cliff had become convinced that if he should leave his mother, a chronic invalid, she would die. After daily struggles, his father had called for help.

Sometimes, although the interpretation of the dynamics of the problem seemed warranted, the corrective measures—separating child and parents—often, as in Cliff's case, avoided the problem rather than addressing it. In *Girl, Interrupted*, author Susanna Kaysen (1993), who entered historic McLean Hospital in Massachusetts when she was seventeen, reflects on the context of hospitalization for mental illness experienced by her fellow patients: "Our families. The prevailing wisdom was that they were the reason we were in there, yet they were utterly absent from our hospital lives. . . . Lunatics are similar to designated hitters. Often an entire family is crazy, but since an entire family can't go into the hospital, one person is designated as crazy and goes inside" (p. 95).

Several factors have combined to bring about greater partnership with parents. Advances in understanding of childhood disorders such as childhood schizophrenia and autism (e.g., Rimland 1964), due in no small measure to advocacy, initially by parents and today self-advocacy through the Disability Rights Movement, increasingly pointed to biogenic causation, rather than bad parenting. Rather than reverting to the pessimism of psychiatry's organic era, however, these advances have accompanied advances in intervention, especially *early* intervention, beginning in the first years of life.

Relatedly, *ecological* interpretations of childhood disturbance (Hobbs 1982) emphasized the transactional nature of parent-child relationships and the fact that children's behavior—at home, at school, and in the community—never occurs in a vacuum, but in an ecological context. This understanding contributed to more frequent use of day treatment alternatives, encouragement of parent involvement in residential as well as day programs, family diagnosis and family therapy, and, for young children, the concept of *family-focused* services reflected in Part C of the Individuals with Disabilities Education Act. A growing movement today, informed by new awareness of the impact on very young children, even infants, of domestic violence, physical and sexual abuse, and other environmental stresses, is the interdisciplinary field of *infant mental health*. Like other areas of early intervention, this specialized area recognizes the critical importance of the first years of life in influencing the subsequent course of development, as well as the indivisible nature of the child-caregiver relationship.

"Laggards in Our Schools" and the Emergence of Special Classes

Over the course of the nineteenth century, as in the case of mental retardation, there was a shift from a focus on understanding and "saving" children and youth who presented disturbing behavior to containment and segregation in the interest of protecting society (Macmillan 1960). With enactment of compulsory school attendance laws, troublesome youngsters represented a source of disruption that could less readily be addressed by simply expelling them. Consequently, classes for "unruly" boys, in New Haven, Connecticut, in 1871 and in New York City in 1874 were the first special classes to be established for exceptional students in American public schools. These and similar groupings established in other large cities tended to lump together "incorrigibles" with others who, for a variety of reasons including immigrant children's difficulties with English, "didn't fit" (Kaufman 1993).

These formed the basis for what became known as "ungraded classes," the first of which, in New York City, was assigned to nineteen-year-old Elizabeth Farrell (1870–1932), who coined the term. The class of eight-to-sixteen-year-old boys, as Farrell (1908–1909) recalled, "grew out of conditions in a neighborhood which furnished many serious problems in truancy and discipline. [It] . . . was made up of the odds and ends of a large school. . . . They were the children who could not get along in school. . . .so-called naughty children . . . [who] had to be convinced that . . . school was a privilege not a punishment" (pp. 91–92).

By the 1911–1912 school year, there were 131 "ungraded" classes in 95 New York schools under Farrell's direction, enrolling about 2,500 pupils (Goddard 1912). Although they were designated for students with mental retardation, with the advent of school-based clinics, psychiatric problems rather than low IQ were often identified as primary concerns, and some class groupings were created accordingly. It was not until 1946, however, that New York organized special programs specifically geared to the needs of emotionally disturbed students through what were identified as "600 schools." These included residential as well as day school settings, beginning with the program Dr. Lauretta Bender, a pioneer in identifying and treating childhood schizophrenia, had inaugurated in 1935 on a new children's ward at Bellevue Psychiatric Hospital. Teachers in that setting, and subsequently in many of the 600 schools, were guided in incorporating therapeutic principles in instruction in basic skills, as well as therapeutic uses of the arts (Berkowitz & Rothman 1960).

While Farrell and Wallin (1914) viewed special classes as important in meeting children's diverse needs, they both saw these as but one facet of comprehensive services, coordinated by the psychoeducational clinic. In addition to children whose physical or psychological needs interfered with learning or school adjustment, the pupil diversity resulting from compulsory school attendance, in combination with massive immigration, had revealed many others who had great difficulty learning. In a report tellingly titled *Laggards in Our Schools*, Ayres (1909) claimed more than a third of American elementary pupils were academically deficient and, when held back in grade, constituted an economic burden as well as a social one. Eventually, according to Christine Sleeter (1990, p. 33), American educators created, or *constructed*, five "categories" to explain school failure, "called slow learners, mentally retarded, emotionally disturbed, culturally deprived, and learning disabled"; the last group "created to explain the failure of children from advantaged social groups, and to do so in such a way that it suggested their eventual ability to attain relatively higher status occupations than other low achievers."

With increased use of IQ testing for sorting purposes, for children who didn't fit, segregated special classes seemed the answer. For those who "didn't fit" the special classes—children with low IQ, epilepsy, or excessive acting out—the predominant strategy by the 1930s involved explicit policies of exclusion. Even after federal law (P.L. 94-142) mandated free, appropriate public education in the least restrictive environment and "zero exclusion" in 1975, emotional disturbance is more likely than other disabilities to be associated with such "restrictive" settings as residential centers and segregated day schools (Kaufman 1993).

As with physical disabilities, some children with serious emotional disturbance have experienced a highly medicalized, nonnormative period in hospital settings during their childhood or adolescence. As Susanna Kaysen (1993, p. 84) recalls, "[The doctors] had a special language: *regression, acting out, hostility, withdrawal, indulging in behavior.* This last phrase could be attached to any activity and make it sound suspicious: indulging in eating behavior, talking behavior, writing behavior. In the outside world people ate and talked and wrote, but nothing we did was simple."

Further reflecting on her own and her fellow patients' illness, treatment, and "interrupted" youth, she concludes, "We were probably better than we used to be, before we went into the hospital. . . . Many of us had spent our hospital years yelling and causing trouble and were ready to move on to something else. All of us had learned by default to treasure freedom and would do anything we could to get it and keep it" (p. 124).

As with mental retardation and adult mental illness, the *deinstitutionalization* movement favored a more *normalized*, community-based service model for children experiencing emotional and behavioral problems, which meant an increased role for public school programs. By the 1960s, a national study by Morse, Cutler, and Fink (1964) identified more than 300 special classes for children with emotional problems, based in community schools as well as in residential treatment settings. As states developed standards for eligibility, program requirements, and teacher qualifications in the 1970s, and colleges and universities developed teacher preparation programs, the number of such classes grew rapidly, as did the number of students identified as "*seriously emotionally disturbed* (SED)."

A persisting problem, however, has been that of definition. Since many, if not most, children at some time manifest the behavioral characteristics identified in "official" definitions, the SED label is based on severity, chronicity, and context of the behavior, a matter of clinical judgment (Kaufman 1993). For special education purposes, only one psychiatric diagnosis—schizophrenia—automatically signals eligibility, while "social maladjustment" does *not*, unless the social maladjustment is *caused by* serious emotional disturbance—another "judgment call." (Since 1990, the IDEA legislation and regulations have distinguished *autism* from other categories.)

In addition to definitional issues, the study by Morse, Cutter, & Fink (1964) highlighted the diverse "approaches" used in working with disturbed children, each reflecting its own understanding of the origin and nature of the problem, and each with certain implications for intervention. Consequently, in the 1970s considerable study was invested in the differentiation of psychodynamic, behavioral, biomedical, sociological, and ecological "conceptual models" (Rhodes & Tracy 1972).

These developments paralleled the emergence of the disability classification, largely due to parent advocacy, that is by far the largest; *specific learning disabilities* accounts for more than half the students receiving special education services in American schools. The other "new" category introduced in the 1990 legislation along with autism was not new at all. Accounts in antiquity, and even archaeological finds from prehistory, reveal that there have always been humans who experienced *traumatic brain injury* (TBI). What these three highly diverse "groups," as well as another recognized by the Americans with Disabilities Act as a disability—*attention deficit hyperactivity disorder* (ADHD)—have in common is their presumed (established, in the case of TBI) underlying, biological basis.

CONCLUSION

It is now generally understood that children's differential traits, predispositions, and styles reflect the interaction of a host of genetic factors—many of them as yet poorly understood—with a multitude of environmental factors, some of which, such as lead, clearly have dire biological effects. The great many American children who have experienced physical, sexual, and/or psychological abuse, instability, or exposure to violence are at great risk for "derailment," if not irreparable damage, in the course of development (Zigler, Finn-Stevenson, & Hall 2002). In addition, advocacy and empirical research in the areas of learning disability, autism, TBI, and ADHD continue to increase public understanding of, and appreciation of, the variety of human differences.

Yet, in the era of inclusive schools that are learning to celebrate diversity, including diversity associated with disability, students with all of these labels suggesting "difference, difficulty, or disturbance" continue to be major concerns to educators, policy makers, and certainly parents. Despite a century of progress in understanding children's emotional needs, and in learning to recognize when a child's "acting out" is a way of reaching out, many children and adolescents continue to be overlooked, misunderstood, blamed, and often punished for what, as Beech Brook's first superintendent insisted, was no fault of their own. Child mental health services are underfunded and often unfocused while prisons proliferate, and educational policy intended to do precisely the opposite leaves many children behind, including the "troubled and troubling child."

REFERENCES

Addams, J. (1909). *The Spirit of Youth and the City Streets*. New York: Macmillan.

Aldrich, T. B. (1895/1990). *The Story of a Bad Boy*. Boston: Houghton Mifflin; Hanover and London: University Press of New England.

Ayres, L. P. (1909). *Laggards in Our Schools: A Study of Retardation and Its Elimination in City School Systems*. New York: Charities Publications Committee.

Barnard, H. (1840). Second Annual Report of the Board of Commissioners of Common Schools in Connecticut. Hartford, CT.

Barton, W. E. (1987). *The History and Influence of the American Psychiatric Association*. Washington, DC: American Psychiatric Association.

Baskin, B., & Harris, K. H. (1977). *Notes from a Different Drummer*. New York: R. R. Bowker.

Beers, C. W. (1908). *A Mind That Found Itself: An Autobiography*. New York: Longmans, Green.

Berkowitz, P. H., & Rothman, E. P. (1960). *The Disturbed Child: Recognition and Psychoeducational Therapy in the Classroom*. New York: New York University Press.

Berlin, Ira. (2002). *Generations of Captivity: A History of African-American Slaves*. Cambridge, MA: Belknap Press of Harvard University Press.

Brace, C. L. (1872). *The Dangerous Classes of New York and Twenty Years' Work Among Them*. New York: Wynkoop and Hollenbeck.

Brenzel, B. (1980). Domestication as Reform: A Study of the Socialization of Wayward Girls, 1856–1905. *Harvard Educational Review* 50(2), 196–213.

Brigham, A. (1845). Schools in Lunatic Asylums. *American Journal of Insanity*, 1, 326–340

Brumberg, Joan J. (1982). "Chlorotic Girls, 1870–1910: An Historical Perspective on Female Adolescence." *Child Development* 53, 1468–1474.

Butler, A. (1901). Saving the Children. Report of Committee on Destitute and Neglected Children. In *Proceedings*, 1901 Conference on Charities and Corrections (pp. 205–213).

Caddey, J. W. (1963). The Church-Related Residential Treatment Center for Emotionally Disturbed Children. Unpublished thesis, Oberlin Graduate School of Theology, Oberlin, OH.

Chamberlain, A. (2002). Bad Books and Bad Boys: The Transformation of Gender in Eighteenth-Century Northampton, Massachusetts. *The New England Quarterly* 75(2), 179–203.

Child Welfare League of America, Inc. (1960). *Report of Survey of the Methodist Children's Home, Berea, OH.* New York: Child Welfare League of America.

Children's Aid Society (CAS). http://www.childrensaidsociety.org/about/history.

Cleveland Protestant Orphan Asylum. (1879). *Annual Report: 1878.* Cleveland, OH: Cleveland Protestant Orphan Asylum.

Crowley, J. M. (1985). Little Women and the Boy-Book. *The New England Quarterly* 58(3), 384–399.

Despert, J. L. (1965). *The Emotionally Disturbed Child: Then and Now.* New York: Brunner.

Devereaux, G. (1956). *Therapeutic Education: Its Theoretical Bases and Practice.* New York: Harper & Brothers.

Esquirol, J. E. (1838). *Des Maladies Mentales: Considerees sous Hygieniques, et Medico-legau, 1772–1840.* Paris: Bailliere. Trans. E. K. Hunt. *A Treatise on Insanity.* Philadelphia, PA: Lee & Blanchard, 1845.

Farrell, E. K. (1908–1909). Special Classes in the New York City Schools. *Journal of Psycho-Asthenics* 13, 91–96.

Fernald, W. E. (1909). The Imbecile with Criminal Instincts. *American Journal of Insanity* 65, 734–743. In R. H. Bremner, ed., 1971, *Children and Youth in America: A Documentary History.* Volume II: 1866–1932, Parts Seven and Eight (pp. 859–862). Cambridge, MA: Harvard University Press.

Foucault, M. (1965). *Madness and Civilization.* New York: Random House.

———. (1977). *Discipline and Punish.* New York: Pantheon.

French, J. L. (1990). History of School Psychology. In T. B. Gutkin & C. R. Reynolds, eds., *The Handbook of School Psychology* (2nd ed., pp. 3–20). New York: John Wiley & Sons.

Gesell, A. (1930). A Decade of Progress in the Mental Hygiene of the Preschool Child. *Annals of the American Academy of Political and Social Sciences* 151, 143–148.

Glenn, M. C. (1984). *Campaigns Against Corporal Punishment: Prisoners, Sailors, Women, and Children in Antebellum America.* Albany: State University of New York Press.

Goddard, H. H. (1912). Report on Educational Aspects of the Public School System of the City of New York to the Committee on School Inquiry of the Board of Estimate and Appointment: Ungraded Classes. New York: Board of Education of the City of New York.

Grob, G. N. (1973). *Mental Institutions in America: Social Policy to 1875.* New York: The Free Press.

Hale, N. G. (1971). *Freud and the Americans: The Beginnings of Psychoanalysis in the United States, 1876–1917.* New York: Oxford University Press.

Hawes, J. J. (1971). The Treatment of Delinquent Children. In T. R. Frazier, ed., *The Underside of American History: Other Readings.* Vol. 1: To 1877. New York: Harcourt Brace Jovanovich.

Hawke, D. (1971). *Benjamin Rush.* New York: Bobbs-Merrill.

Hawthorne, N. (1850/1983). *The Scarlet Letter.* New York: Literary Classics of the United States, Inc.

Healy, W. (1915). *The Individual Delinquent: A Text-Book of Diagnosis and Prognosis for All Concerned in Understanding Offenders.* Boston: Little, Brown.

Hobbs, N. (1982). *The Troubled and Troubling Child.* San Francisco: Jossey-Bass.

Holt, L. E. (1897). *The Diseases of Infancy and Childhood.* New York: D. Appleton.

Horn, M. (1984). The Moral Message of Child Guidance, 1925–1945. *Journal of Social History* 18, 25–36.

———. (1989). *"Before It's Too Late": The Child Guidance Movement in the United States, 1922–1945.* Philadelphia: Temple University Press.

Howe, S. G. (1852). Third and Final Report of the Experimental School for Teaching and Training Idiotic Children; Also, the First Report of the Trustees of the Massachusetts School for Idiotic and Feebleminded Youth. *American Journal of Insanity* 9, 20–36.

Jones, K. W. (1999). *Taming the Troublesome Child: American Families, Child Guidance, and the Limits of Psychiatric Authority.* Cambridge, MA: Harvard University Press.

Kaufman, J. (1993). *Characteristics of Emotional and Behavioral Disorders of Children and Youth* (5th ed.). New York: Merrill/Macmillan.

Kaysen, S. (1993). *Girl, Interrupted.* New York: Vintage Books.

Kerlin, I. N. (1885). Provision for Idiotic and Feeble-minded Children. In I. C. Barrows, ed., *Proceedings of the National Conference of Charities and Corrections at the Eleventh Annual Session* (pp. 246–263). Boston: Georgett Ellis.

Lurie, A. (2004). The Good Bad Boy. *New York Times Book Review,* June 24, 2004.

Macmillan, M. B. (1960). Extra-scientific Influences in the History of Childhood Psychopathology. *American Journal of Psychiatry* 116, 1091–1096.

Mann, H. (1853). A Few Thoughts on the Powers and Duties of Women: Two Lectures. Syracuse: Hall, Mills, and Company.

Mann, M.T.P. (1877). *Moral Culture of Infancy* (rev. ed.). New York: E. Steiger. Accessed in Making of America, http://www.hti.umich.edu/cgi/t/text/text-idx?c=moa;idno=ABJ6024 (11/9/04).

Mintz, S. (2004). *Huck's Raft: A History of American Childhood.* Cambridge, MA: The Belknap Press of Harvard University.

Morse, W. C., Cutler, R. L., & Fink, A. H. (1964). *Public School Classes for the Emotionally Handicapped: A Research Analysis.* Washington, DC: Council for Exceptional Children.

Morton, M. J. (2000). Surviving the Great Depression: Orphanages and Orphans in Cleveland. *Journal of Urban History* 26(4), 438–455.

Noll, S. (2004). Mental Illness. In Paula S. Fass, Editor-in-Chief, *Encyclopedia of*

Children and Childhood in History and Society (pp. 597–99). New York: Macmillan Reference USA.

Preston, J. A. (1993). Domestic Ideology. School Reformers, and Female Teachers: Schoolteaching Becomes Women's Work in Nineteenth-Century New England. *The New England Quarterly* 66(4), 531–551.

Reis, Elizabeth. (1997). *Damned Women: Sinners and Witches in Puritan New England.* Ithaca: Cornell University Press.

Rhodes, W. C., & Tracy, M. L. (1972). A Study of Child Variance. Volume 1: Conceptual Models (Research/Technical Report, Conceptual Project in Emotional Disturbance). Ann Arbor: Institute for the Study of Mental Retardation, University of Michigan. (ERIC No. ED135120.)

Richardson, Theresa R. (1989). *The Century of the Child: The Mental Hygiene Movement and Social Policy in the United States and Canada.* Albany: State University of New York Press.

Riis, J. A. (1901). A Blast of Cheer. *Proceedings*, Twenty-eighth National Conference of Charities (pp. 18–24).

Rimland, B. (1964). *Infantile Autism.* New York: Appleton-Century-Crofts.

Rush, B. (1786). An Enquiry Into the Influence of Physical Causes Upon the Moral Faculty: An Oration Delivered Before the American Philosophical Society. Philadelphia: Charles Cist. Reprinted in Rush, B. (1972). *Two Essays on the Mind.* New York; Brunner/Mazel, Inc.

———. (1812/1962). *Medical Inquiries and Observations Upon the Diseases of the Mind.* New York: Haafner. (Facsimile, New York: Harper, 1962).

Sarason, S. B., & Doris, J. (1969). *Psychological Problems in Mental Deficiency* (4th ed.). New York: Harper & Row.

Schowalter, J. W. (2003). A History of Child and Adolescent Psychiatry in the United States. *Psychiatric Times* 20(9). http://www.psychiatrictimes.com/p030943.html.

Sleeter, C. E. (1990). Learning Disabilities: The Social Construction of a Special Education Category. In S. Sigmon, ed., *Critical Voices on Special Education: Problems and Progress Concerning the Mildly Handicapped* (pp. 21–35). Albany: State University of New York Press.

Thom, Douglas A. (1927). *Everyday Problems of the Everyday Child.* New York and London: D. Appleton.

Thurston, H. (1930). *The Dependent Child.* New York: Columbia University Press.

Twain, M. (1875/1906). *Sketches: New and Old (The Writings of Mark Twain, Vol. XIX, Hillcrest Edition).* New York and London: Harper & Brothers.

———. (1876/1971). *The Adventures of Tom Sawyer.* New York: Western Publishing Co.

———. (1884/1995). *The Adventures of Huckleberry Finn.* Hertfordshire, UK: Wordsworth Editions Ltd.

Wallach, Glenn. (1997). *Obedient Sons: The Discourse of Youth and Generations in American Culture.* Amherst: University of Massachusetts Press.

Wallin, J.E.W. (1914). *The Mental Health of the School Child: The Psychoeducational Clinic in Relation to Child Welfare.* New Haven: Yale University Press.

Weber, L. (1969). *The Kindergarten: Its Encounter with Educational Thought.* New York: Teachers College Press.

Wickman, E. (1928). *Children's Behavior and Teachers' Attitudes.* New York: Commonwealth Fund.

Wishy, B. W. (1968). *The Child and the Republic: The Dawn of Modern American Child Nurture.* Philadelphia: University of Pennsylvania Press.

Witkin, M. J. (1974). *Residential Treatment Centers for Emotionally Disturbed Children 1973–74.* (Mental Health Statistical Note No. 130.) Washington, DC: U.S. Department of Health, Education, and Welfare.

Witmer, L. (1909). The Study and Treatment of Retardation: A Field of Applied Psychology. *Psychological Bulletin* 6(4), 121–126.

Worchester Lunatic Asylum. (1833). First Report of the Superintendent of the Lunatic Asylum at Worcester. Worcester, MA.

Zigler, E. F., Finn-Stevenson, M., & Hall, N. W. (2002). *The First Three Years and Beyond: Brain Development and Social Policy.* New Haven: Yale University Press.

Zinn, H. (1995). *A People's History of the United States, 1492–Present* (rev. ed.). New York: HarperPerennial.

II Resource Documents

The documents included in this section were compiled by the several contributing authors and coeditors. Those selected are intended to represent the variety of resources for inquiry in this area.

Deafness and Childhood

1. *Report of the Committee of the Connecticut Asylum for the Education and Instruction of Deaf and Dumb Persons* **(June 1, 1817)**

The following excerpt is from the first annual report of what was later called the American School for the Deaf.

It will be very gratifying to the patrons and friends of this institution to learn, that through the blessing of a kind providence, its doors are now opened, notwithstanding the numerous obstacles and disappointments which have been encountered from the commencement of our labours. A numerous and interesting family of the unfortunate are already assembled, and we behold those minds which were like a waste hedged about with thorns, now yielding to the cultivation of science, and daily affording promise of abundant intellectual improvement. Are any still skeptical on the subject of promoting the happiness of the deaf and dumb by education? Let them visit the Asylum, and behold the social circle in the evening hour, delighted in exhibiting those first rudiments of learning which they have already acquired. . . . It cannot be expected that any very interesting details respecting the pupils, should at this time be communicated: but it may be of use to record, in a very brief manner, the origin and progress of that institution, which takes the lead in this western world, in the instruction of those who have hitherto remained neglected and forgotten.

Source: Hartford, CT: American School for the Deaf, Hudson and Co. Printers, http://disabilitymuseum.org/lib/docs/1734card.htm, paragraph 8, Disability History Museum, http://www.disabilitymuseum.org (January 5, 2004).

2. "Alice Cogswell to Emily Phillips, May 30, 1821"

Alice Cogswell, the first pupil admitted to the Connecticut Asylum, wrote to a family friend when she was sixteen.

My dear Mrs. Phillips,

I felt great gladness to receive your sweet letter last April and to hear that you was restored to health. Before you wrote me, I felt anxious to receive letters from you for many days. You say that you and that your good girl Susan are in probability to come here to see me in July or August. This fills my mind with sweet hopes to see them.

I expect riding from Philadelphia to here will improve your health and spirits. I am so ashamed as not to answer your letter immediately. I will tell you the reason. I hope you will excuse me for the delay. In the beginning of my vacation I accidentally pricked a needle in the end of my right finger of which I did not care. But one day as I held the needle by the finger it hurt my nerves, so I could not sew. My mother told me I had to use something. Then the nerves of my arms felt very feeble and cold. I rested my arm on the handkerchief across my neck during almost all the vacation. I once put the blister on the finger which felt very hot. However, I must amuse myself at reading books and sometimes riding with my Father. I was surprised to hear that you had formerly had a dangerous lameness of your arm by the needle.

You cannot imagine how I was glad at the arrival of Mr. Clerc. Every Hartford body is extremely happy to see him. He is fleshy, happy, and healthy. He has made a great deal of travels in the part of Europe. When you come here you will undoubtedly feel glad to see him again. I suppose you have not heard of this, that the new Asylum is completely finished, and the deaf and dumb persons live already there now. I used to go to school nowadays, sometimes in a chaise when it rains. But I dine with the D. and D. [deaf and dumb] every noon. It is a most delightful and cool place and has as fine a prospect as I ever saw or felt. When you are in this town I will show you the apartments of the new Asylum. In the highest story it is a very large garret called the hall and has four arched windows. You will be delighted to view the prospect.

The new Asylum has been dedicated about a few weeks ago. A great number of people assembled to hear Mr. Gallaudet's sermon, and a dedicatory hymn written by Mrs. Sigourney was sung. I will tell you about circumstances of this when I see you for it is too long an account.

Tell Susan that I am very glad to know that she can understand French. Mr. Clerc will be happy to have her talk with him by finger for French words.

I must finish this for it is late. Give much love to Susan. I shall be very glad to meet her and you in July or August.

Goodnight,
Believe me, your sincere friend, Alice

Source: In *Father and Daughter: A Collection of Cogswell Family Letters and Diaries (1772–1830).* Hartford, CT: American School for the Deaf, http://www.disability museum.org/lib/docs/698card.htm, Disability History Museum, http://www. disabilitymuseum.org (January 5, 2004).

3. "About My Travels"

The Directors of the American School for the Deaf regularly included samples of students' written work in the annual reports prepared for the trustees. This example, by "C.W.C.," a sixteen-year-old girl, "born deaf, under instruction four and a half years," was one of several student essays in the 1863 Annual Report. While the essays were included to illustrate students' educational progress, this one provides some insight concerning peoples' response to a child who was deaf, as well as her emotional responses.

A long while ago when I was a little girl, my father and I went to the city of Boston and visited at Mr. Kasson's and staid for one day and left there for Manchester, New Hampshire. We rode in the cars for Manchester and arrived at the depot in the night. Then my father asked a driver to let us ride in the coach to our friend's house across the bridge. He and I jumped out of the coach and the driver returned to the depot again. We walked on the way to M. B's house and staid all night. In the morning early Miss E. invited us to see some cross dogs in a cage, and then a man invited my father and I to ride in the wagon to the depot, and the man went away. By and by the cars came to the depot, so my father and I rode in the cars and arrived at Wells River, Vt. We went home. Afterwards my father, mother, and I rode in a large wagon to Mr. McLure's and staid for a short time and found that his daughter Sophronia was a deaf and dumb girl, that sat on a chair near the window. I was much afraid of them. Then my parents and I went home. Afterwards my father and I went to Boston again. We rode in the cars; my father walked about in the cars, and I was alone. A stranger lady looked at me for a long while and gave five or ten cents to me. I was very glad but some ashamed because of the lady. By and by a man gave one or two dollars to me. I thanked him. I will remember this. Father and I went to the depot and went to Mr. Kasson's and knocked at the door in the dark. But Mr. Kasson did not open the door, but we found a man who told my father that Mr. Kasson and his family were gone. So my father and I went to the hotel and staid all night. In the morning we went to Mr. Kasson's and knocked at the door and found Miss Lavinia who opened the door and invited us to enter her house, and we staid for some days. My father and I went to Manchester, N.H. again, and staid all night. In the early morning we rode in the drive's coach and hurried to the depot. By and by the cars came, so my father and I rode in the cars to the depot of Wells River, Vermont, all safe. We then went home.

Source: 1863 Annual Report, http://clerccenter.gallaudet.edu/.

4. "Asylum at Hartford"

Lydia Sigourney, who had tutored Alice Cogswell when she was very young, was a well-known author and poet when she wrote a description of the "Asylum at Hartford" in 1845, from which the following is excerpted.

The female pupils out of school hours, are occupied in various feminine employments, under the charge of the matron. Gathered into this same fold, and cheered by her kind patronage, sits the deaf, dumb, and blind girl, often busy with her needle, for whose guidance her exceedingly acute sense of feeling suffices, and in whose dextrous use seems the chief solace of her lot of silence, and of rayless light.

There are at present in this Institution one hundred and sixty-four pupils, and since its commencement, in 1817, between seven and eight hundred have shared the benefits of its shelter and instruction. Abundant proof has been rendered by them, that, when quickened by the impulse of education, their misfortune does not exclude them from participating in the active pursuits and satisfactions of life. By recurring to their history, after their separation from the Asylum, we find among them, farmers and mechanics, artists and seamen, tellers of deaf mutes in various institutions, and what might at first seem incompatible with their situation, a merchant's clerk, the editor of a newspaper, a postmaster, and county-recorder in one of our far Western States, and a clerk in the Treasury Department at Washington.

More than one hundred of the pupils from this Asylum have entered into the matrimonial relation; and some, within the range of our own intimacy, might be adduced as bright examples of both conjugal and parental duty.

One of the most interesting members, who entered at its first organization, and remained during the full course of seven years, was a daughter of the late Dr. Mason F. Cogswell, who was early called to follow her lamented father to the tomb.

Source: Sigourney, L. H. (1845). "Asylum at Hartford," from *Scenes in My Native Land.* New York: James Munroe & Co., http://www.disabilitymuseum.org/lib/docs/822card.htm, paragraphs 6–9, Disability History Museum, http://www.disabilitymuseum.org (January 5, 2004).

5. "Looking Back"

The two accounts included in this "Looking Back" article from the January–February 1997 issue of World Around You *describe what it was like to be a d/D student in an "oral" school in the 1950s.*

RULERS, CORNER, MATH, KNIFE USED IN FIGHT AGAINST SIGN LANGUAGE

Oral programs—where deaf students learn through speech and lipreading—have changed a lot over the years. In the 1950s, oralists believed that use of sign language would hurt deaf children. Punishments were severe in those days, too.

Dennis Berrigan

Dennis Berrigan is American Sign Language Training and Evaluation Coordinator, in Laurent Clerc National Deaf Education Center, at Gallaudet University, Washington, D.C.

"We Knew We Were Strong . . ."

Buffalo, New York

We sat three in a row—a girl, a boy, and myself in between. We were in first grade. Our teacher was a nun and she was very strict. We were all scared of her.

All day, we wore headphones and practiced speech. The teacher did not allow any signing at all. Sign language was completely forbidden in class. We were supposed to learn through speech and lipreading.

We still signed to each other, of course, and when the teacher caught us, she would smack us on the arms. Sometimes she would hit us with a wooden rod and sometimes she would hit us with a ruler.

Once when she caught me, I knew what was expected, so I offered her my arm to hit. She slapped so hard, she broke her ruler. Another time, she hit a boy next to me until red welts rose up on his skin. I remember when he showed his arm to us.

We didn't like getting hit, but when I broke a ruler and when my friend showed me his welts, we grinned secretly at each other. We knew we were strong. . . . We even felt a little proud.

Chris Hunter

Chris Hunter is Director of the Division on Deafness, in Lansing, Michigan.

"Warning . . . We Would Lose Our Hands"
Los Angeles, California

I was young, 10 or 11, and in the fourth or fifth grade in an oral day school program. The school had a strict policy against the use of sign language. We were not allowed to gesture, sign, or fingerspell at all.

Still, many of my friends and I used made up signs to communicate in secret places. When we were caught, we were punished. Punishment took various forms. Sometimes our hands were slapped with a ruler. Sometimes we were made to sit in a corner. Sometimes we did multiplication and division drills repeatedly. One day in class, I was playing with a rubber ball, winding it around my fingers, wrist, and hand. Jokingly, I looked over and signed something to the student next to me. I laughed and the teacher turned and looked.

She stopped, called for the class to follow her, and walked out of the classroom. We were all puzzled. I could see she was upset. We arrived in the school kitchen where the teacher spoke with one of the chefs. We students crowded around a butcher block, where meat was chopped up. The teacher called for me to come forward. The chef grabbed my hand, put it on the block, and lifted the butcher knife. He raised it high above my hand and lowered it quickly. He stopped with the knife a few inches from my wrist. Then he let my hand go. I was shaky and I cried. The students gathered around me shocked. The teacher came forward and warned us that we would lose our hands if we continued to use sign language.

In 5th grade, my parents pulled me out of the school and placed me in California School for the Deaf in Riverside. Then I could use sign language. I was free.

Source: World Around You: A Magazine for Deaf Teens, published by the Laurent Clerc National Deaf Education Center at Gallaudet University, http://clerccenter. gallaudet.edu/.

6. Interview with "JJ"

As part of their research for this section and for chapter 2, the authors conducted interviews with living d/D persons, asking them to recall their experiences, especially their schooling. "JJ" (his sign name) had recently, in his senior year, been named Homecoming King at the Ohio School for the Deaf, in Columbus, when this interview was conducted. The following excerpts express his reflections about experiences in two very different school settings: a residential school specifically for d/D students, and a "mainstream" (i.e., inclusion) program in a highly regarded suburban school district that enrolls deaf students residing throughout the region. The interview, which with JJ's permission was videotaped, was translated from American Sign Language (ASL) to English in order to prepare a transcript. JJ also gave the authors permission to use his full name: John Curtis Bechold, Jr.

JJ: I am one of 4 in my family. My mother is an interpreter who works for the Deaf. I am a student now at the Ohio School for the Deaf (OSD). I first started in mainstreamed school, until 7th grade. I am also interested in playing sports. . . .

Int: Do you have deaf or hearing people in your family?

JJ: All of my family is hearing except two of my cousins who are deaf. Really, they're not related, but step-cousins. My relatives aren't fluent in ASL but they can communicate a little bit in sign language. They know some signs and fingerspelling. In my immediate family, my mother, my father, my brother and a few friends are experts and fluent in ASL. But most of my hearing friends use fingerspelling.

Int: What about yourself?

JJ: I use ASL as my primary communication. I am fluent in this language.

(When asked, JJ smiles and acknowledges that his ASL skills are better than those of his parents.)

Int: . . . are you hearing, the same as your parents, or are you deaf—big D Deaf or little d deaf?

JJ: No. I am Deaf. I use the big D. . . . The big D means that I am totally Deaf and am proud of myself being labeled as Deaf. . . .

I: Who taught you to be proud, to be Deaf?

JJ: My friends, my parents, books, and research that explained about the Deaf community. It inspired my a lot. I like the big D.

(After talking about his participation in Deaf activities, JJ reflects on his experiences in two very different school settings, the state residential school for d/Deaf students he had attended since 7th grade and a public elementary school he had previously attended, located within thirty miles of his home school district, one of two regional units in the area students classified as Hearing Impaired attend.)

JJ: Their program is Total Communication. I was mainstreamed since kindergarten . . . in classes with all hearing people. I was the only deaf person, and I had an interpreter with me. The teacher and I would use the interpreter. The interpreter relayed all information and conversations.

Int: . . . Did you like it? How did it work?

JJ: I liked it in kindergarten, but as I grew older and approached 7th grade I began to feel left out. . . . I started to notice that hearing students were in groups and I wasn't. If I tried to join their groups, problems would appear. There would be problems with communication, problems with sharing information. . . . It was just too much trouble. So I transferred to OSD.

Int: . . . Tell me more about socializing; tell me about the teachers.

JJ: In the mainstreamed class, hearing people tended to pick on me, to bully me, to give me a hard time. Or they ignored me and didn't care about me. They tended to put me down and pressure me. They also left me out of things. I was really sick of it. . . . I would blow up and lose my temper, and sometimes I would fight.

Int: You behaved badly?

JJ: Yes. I would blow up and lose my temper. . . .

(JJ is asked to describe his school day, beginning with arrival on the bus with two or three other children well before school began. The early arrivals would compare homework as they waited for the other students to arrive. Asked whether he had a favorite teacher, JJ responds "No." He explains:

JJ: I didn't really enjoy it there. . . . The communication would break down so easily. There was no communication. I couldn't learn anything. I couldn't try anything. . . . Without communication it was worthless.
      [*Despite the communication problems at school that made learning difficult*] "mostly I just read the books on my own and learned on my own."

JJ credits the fact that he "learned a lot" to his parents' support and help at home. He is asked about the teachers.)

JJ: They weren't lousy, but they didn't know anything about me or about the Deaf. We would work in the same room together, but they really didn't know or understand what Deaf kids needed or what we could do. . . .

JJ: The problems became more serious. I was fighting more, and not getting along with others. There was more physical fighting and I had had enough. I was fed up and decided to transfer to OSD when I was in the 4th grade, but, for me, they felt it would be too easy and they said I should stay in the hearing school.

(JJ talks about his experiences since coming to OSD, including seeing the Harlem Globetrotters play, traveling on a school trip to Italy, and being elected Student Body President. Attending OSD, he says, "has really changed my life a lot." But it has meant living away from his family—and family, he says, is "my number one priority." So he is asked how he felt on his first day at OSD, away from home.)

JJ: When I first arrived there, I interacted with others right away. I got along with everyone and I was introduced to Deaf people and names. I did not feel left out. I did not feel that I was just sitting there, quiet. When I first arrived I met people, and chatted and was active. That's how it felt to me—wow!

Int: Tell me about the education at OSD and at ——— (his former school)—compare them. Were they the same?

JJ: If we are talking about education, exposure, level of academics, then ——— wins. But if you are talking about vocations and other things, then OSD. OSD offers a lot of benefits and information. I can get direct advice from my advisor, counseling without an interpreter. It would be more difficult to do that at ———, and there would be more misunderstandings and wrong information. OSD could give me personal advice. . . .

Int: So you've told me that socialization was a problem at ———?

JJ: Well, I knew the same three kids since we were little. We were together, nothing much changed. At OSD I played sports such as basketball, wrestling, and soccer against other Deaf schools. Their schools then had more Deaf students and I had more opportunities to socialize. At ——— there wasn't any opportunity to socialize. . . .

Int: Do you feel that the residential school has prepared you for real life? Are you ready for real life?

JJ: So-so. . . . From my own personal opinion, and from what I see of other deaf students, so-so. At the residential school, they have strict discipline but, since I've grown up, I've learned a lot, so I know what to expect in the real world. . . .

(JJ tells about jobs he has held as a student at OSD, noting that he earns money and has a savings account. Asked what he plans to do when he graduates, he says he is in the process of applying to Gallaudet University, which he has visited.)

JJ: I may become a teacher, or an actor, or a technician.

Int: . . . Suppose you become a teacher and you could change deaf education. How would you change it? What would you save? What would you drop?

JJ: That's a good question. I don't know.

Int: (smiles) Maybe next year, when you're at Gally, you'll think of something. Let me know. What classes have you had at OSD?

JJ: English, algebra, gym, health, science, chemistry, physics. For advanced students. . . . We have vocational classes too—art, computer, business office education, technical, year book. I worked with video editing, newspaper—we used old printing machines. Home economics, sewing, cooking, wood shop. Government, American history, world geography. Recently I took an on-line class. I thought I would try and I knew I would be fine. . . . We have ASL I, II, and Drama. [*He also describes study of Deaf history.*]

(After JJ acknowledges that he had learned ASL from his mother before attending OSD, Mrs. Bechold signs some comments she wishes to add.)

Mrs. B: Before, when he was at ———, JJ was frustrated. The principal called me often saying he was a troublemaker. We decided to go to OSD. There was an interview and we sat around with people from OSD and they said that JJ should be fine in a mainstreamed program. I said no, it was very frustrating. They said that OSD didn't fit his needs, that ———'s education was fine. But it wasn't education. It was that the OSD experience is different from the mainstream program. We told them that OSD must take JJ, that if he could transfer, then maybe he would have less problems with his behavior. We were willing to take the risk to see if he would improve. Finally, we convinced them.

7. Recommendation Letter

The following recommendation letter from A. C. Manning to Dr. E. M. Gallaudet on behalf of a promising African American student reveals much about racial attitudes early in the twentieth century.

Waleska, Ga

Aug. 24, 1908

My dear Dr. Gallaudet,

I want to speak to you in behalf of Mr. Hume Battiste, one of our recent graduates of the Mt. Airy School. Last spring he took the College examinations and was admitted into your Introductory Class. But he is considered a Negro and there's the rub.

The report is being circulated that the College boys intend to make it so disagreeable for him in case he enters college that he can't stay. He appeals to me for advice and I know of no better course than to lay the case before you.

You know I am a Southern man with all the sentiments so frequently called "race prejudice," but I want to assure you that this young man is one of the most interesting boys I ever taught and so far is he above the average you naturally never think of his racial misfortunes. During the past year I taught him and found him to be an excellent character, possessing rare qualities—nor is he at all offensive in appearance or manner.

His ambition is to become a pharmacist and I also desire to have you advise him on this point. Not being acquainted with a deaf pharmacist, I hardly knew whether or not to encourage him in this hope. His mother does not want him to attend College unless there is a possibility of his becoming a pharmacist, as he already has a good trade at which he can make a living.

I hope the young man may receive favorable consideration, for I believe he will prove himself worthy.

Hoping that the summer's vacation has done you much good, I remain

Yours respectfully,
A. C. Manning

Source: Gallaudet College Archives, Gallaudet University, 800 Florida Ave. NE, Washington, DC 20002-3695.

Visual Disability and Childhood

1. Laura Bridgman's Journal

Laura Dewey Bridgman (1829–1899), who was blind, deaf, and without the senses of smell and taste, lived at Perkins from 1837 until her death. During most of those years she kept a journal, from which the following is excerpted.

October 4th, 1847

I omitted taking my shower bath when I was aroused from my slumber because our room appeared to me extremely cold. I recited my lesson from Arithmetic until our meal. We had our meal much later than usual. At quarter past [Laura inserts a cylindrical figure] my best teacher began to read to me from the Dictionary about the [?]. At 9 she read to me from Mrs. Lass's book about her good neighbors. At quarter past 10 she dismissed me for 3 quarters of an hour for a recess. Wight taught me 9 more lessons from the [?]. I was very successful.

2. A Letter from Laura Bridgman

Laura was fairly well along in her schooling when she wrote the following letter to her parents.

My dear, my mother,—I want to see you very much. I send much love to you. I send ten kisses to my sister Mary. My one pair of stockings are done. Can Mary walk with her feet? Do stockings fit her? I want you to write a letter to me sometime. Miss Swift teaches me. I want you to come to South Boston with my sister, to stay few days, and see me exercising the callisthenics. Oliver [Caswell, 1829–1899, deaf and blind from scarlet fever at age three] can talk with his fingers very faster about words. I will write a letter to you again. Miss J. [Julia Ward Howe and Dr. [S. G. Howe] send love to you. Miss Davis is married, Mrs. Davis. She has gone to live with her husband in Dudley. Is Mary well? Is my aunt well? I send love to her. I will write letter to you soon sometime. Why did you not write letter to me? I go to meeting every Sunday. I am gentle in church with Miss Rogers. I am happy there. Good bye

Laura Bridgman

Source: Quoted in Howe's *An Account of Laura Bridgman of Boston, Massachusetts, A Blind, Deaf, and Dumb Girl with Brief Notices of Three Other Blind Mutes, Pupils in the Same Institution.* London: John Wright and Co.

3. Laura Bridgman's Journal Excerpts

These excerpts from Laura's journal, with an "Introductory Note by Prof. G. Stanley Hall," is contained in the archives of the Perkins Institute in Watertown, Massachusetts. Sanford inserted and interspersed interpretative commentary in passages quoted from Laura's written recollections of her early life, before entering Perkins, and since. Here, Laura describes her first meeting with the famed educator, Dr. Samuel Gridley Howe (to whom Laura will bring much greater fame) who arranges for her admission to Perkins, where, with occasional visits home, she will spend the rest of her life.

I could not talk a single word . . . with my own fingers. I only knew how to make them comprehend some of my wishes. I offered my tiny hand unto my dear Mother, entreating her that she might know of my want for some thing to eat or drink. I stroked on my hand for some butter spread on a piece of bread. I could not assure her whatever I should like for a drink or nourishment, because I was incapable of making the deaf alphabet. I was generally satisfied with any kind of food or liquids that they procured for me. . . .

I did not know what was my region, nor any object of the world. I did know that my Parents had a farm upon which we lived. . . .

When I attained the 8th year living with my dear Mother, A gentleman went to see me at my home. I would not venture to go to her spare parlour with her; for I was so very shy and timid. she introduced me to the noblest visitor, but I shrunk myself as hastily as I had strength. He took my tiny hand and greet[ed] me most cordially. he seemed to be [such] a very unusually tall man to me, that it made me feel much repelled, because I never saw so tall a man before in my life. It was Dr. S. G. Howe whom I could not know or like. It was perfectly kind in him to leave the first Insti. and go so far to beseech [seek] me at Hanover which was so much more expensive for him to travel than of late. . . . (p. 18).

I felt much grieved and tormented to leave my native town so suddenly. My parents conducted me to the Insti. in pearl street when I was not exactly [quite] 8 years old, in Oct. I took a long ride in a chaise with them. I do not know whether we traveled in a stage or the cars, nor how long it took us on our journey from my blessed home toward the 1st Insti. I dreaded leaving home so much that it made me shed an abundance of tears from my eyes many long days. the time elapsed so very heavily and painfully that I did not know what to do with myself. I kept clinging on my dear parents, so as to not let them escape from me, but did not succeed in detaining them. I was removed from them; they attempted to avoid me as quickly as possible. At the very moment that I lost them I burst in[to] bitterest tears. . . . (pp. 18–19).

The Dr. devised a way of having some words printed on bits of paper, which he glued on a mug and spoon, knife, fork, etc., for me to begin to feel on a single word by my finger. I could not know how to spell one letter with my own fingers for some time. Dr. H. was my first instructor. Miss Drew was my first instruct[r]ess in her ladyship. I loved them so dearly for a great many excellent reasons. . . . Dr. and Miss Drew set me a most excellent example. I felt so very glad to receive education from them. I enjoyed my new lesson much more than I can say. I never felt weary of studying, as it was very difficult for me to understand such simple and short words. . . . Dr. made some signs that brought me up to understanding naturally. he boxed [patted] my head meaning 'right'; he knocked at my elbow for 'wrong.' He checked at me by his finger for 'shame' or 'folly' and when he was displeased in seeing anything which I had done wrong. He stroked my hand when he perceived how dirty or shabby I looked; he patted my cheeks expressing me his love and affection (p. 19).

Source: Quoted in *The Writings of Laura Bridgman,* by E. C. Sanford. San Francisco, CA: Overland Monthly Publishing Company, 1887.

4. Valedictory Address

Twenty-year-old Annie Sullivan, soon to become Helen Keller's famed and beloved "Teacher," had been named valedictorian of her class of eight Perkins graduates in 1887. The following is most of her valedictory address.

Today we are standing face to face with the great problem of life.

We have spent years in the endeavor to acquire the moral and intellectual discipline, by which we are enabled to distinguish truth from falsehood, receive higher and broader views of duty, and apply general principles to the diversified details of life. And now we are going out into the busy world, to take our share in life's burdens, and do our little to make that world better, wiser, and happier.

We shall be most likely to succeed in this, if we obey the great law of our being. God has placed us here to grow, to expand, to progress. To a certain extent our growth is unconscious. We receive impressions and arrive at conclusions without any effort on our part; but we also have the power of controlling the course of our lives. We can educate ourselves; we can, by thought and perseverance, develop all the powers and capacities entrusted to us, and build for ourselves true and noble characters. Because we can, we must. It is a duty we owe to ourselves, to our country, and to God.

All the wondrous physical, intellectual and moral endowments, with which man is blessed, will, by inevitable law, become useless, unless he uses and improves them. The muscles must be used, or they become unserviceable. The memory, understanding and judgment must be used, or they become feeble and inactive. If a love for truth and beauty and goodness is not cultivated, the mind loses the strength which comes from truth, the refinement which comes from beauty, and the happiness which comes from goodness.

Self-culture is a benefit, not only to the individual, but also to mankind. Every man who improves himself is adding to the progress of society, and every one who stands still, holds it back. The advancement of society always has its commencement in the individual soul. It is by battling with the circumstances, temptations and failures of the world, that the individual reaches his highest possibilities.

The search for knowledge, begun in school, must be continued through life in order to give symmetrical self-culture.

For the abundant opportunities which have been afforded to us for broad self-improvement we are deeply grateful.

Source: Quoted by Joseph P. Lash in *Helen and Teacher*. New York: Addison Wesley/ Perseus Publishing, 1980, pp. 36–37.

5. *The Achievements and Abilities of the Blind*

A number of persons with visual disability who achieved success or even fame in life, most notably Helen Keller, wrote autobiographies or memoirs describing their childhood experiences. The following excerpt is from chapter 1 of a book titled The Achievements and Abilities of the Blind, *the author of which, born in 1835, is identified as "Prof. James W. Welch, A Graduate of the Ohio Institution for the Blind." The author recalls how, following graduation, he supported himself by giving "entertainments," complementing his musical performances with demonstrations of his literacy and computational skills.*

In early childhood I contracted a cold which settled in my eyes. At the age of 4 years I lost one eye. I retained the sight of my right eye until about the age of 10, when other complications set in, causing opacity of the cornea. I could see to discern colors until 13 years of age, then I had the measles, which almost entirely deprived me of sight. I entered the School for the Blind at Columbus, Ohio, October 6th, 1846. Here my life began anew. Hope sprang up and the light of knowledge, with its genial rays, spread joy and happiness along my future pathway. My schooldays were spent very much in the same manner as most boys spend their schooldays, viz., in study and mischief.

My studies were Reading, Writing, Arithmetic, Algebra, Geometry, Trigonometry, Natural and Mental Philosophy, Chemistry, Astronomy, Geography, physical and descriptive; English Grammar, Physiology, Botany, and Latin Language. I also took a thorough course in music. I succeeded well in all my studies.

Music was most difficult for me to conquer, but by everlasting perseverance and many a lick from my old preceptor (Mr. Machold) I finally mastered that branch. . . .

We were taught trades in the work department at school, making brushes, baskets, and brooms. The girls were taught all kinds of needle and bead work.

We were allowed to take manufactured articles home with us to sell during vacations. By this means I clothed myself from the time I was 15 years old. When I graduated, I prepared myself for business by purchasing a melodeon, a horse, and a buggy.

Having an ambition to do for myself, I began life in earnest. I bought the melodeon of Mr. Penniman [superintendent of the school] for sixty-five dollars, payable in 90 days. My horse cost $100, my buggy $75, payable in one year. I succeeded in paying for the whole outfit; this I did by giving concerts. The two concerts which I gave in 1850 consisted of a few songs, accompanied by the violin and exhibiting the manner of reading, writing, and cyphering. I now added to my program a variety of songs, patriotic, amusing, and sentimental, also violin solos, still retaining the reading, writing, and cyphering.

My entertainments pleased the people and that pleased me.

Source: Columbus, OH: Fred. J. Heer, Publishers, 1905, pp. 9–11.

6. *Ten Years of Preacher-Life*

William Henry Milburn provided another account of blindness incurred in childhood in Ten Years of Preacher-Life: Chapters from an Autobiography.

I was playing with a boy about my own age, when raising his arm, to throw a piece of glass or oystershell, and not seeing me behind him, the missile entered my left eye, as he drew his hand back, and laid upon the ball just below the pupil. The sharp agony of pain and the sight of dropping blood alarmed me, and I sped like a frightened deer to find my mother. Then followed days and weeks of silence and darkness, wherein a child lay with bandaged eyes upon his little couch, in a chamber without light, and which all entered with stealthy steps and muffled tones. At last there came a morning, when I was led into a room where the bright sunshine lay upon the carpet; and though dimmer than it used to be, never had I been so glad to behold it. But my gladness was suddenly checked when I found several strange gentlemen seated there, among whom was our family physician, a tall, stern, cold man, of whom I had always been afraid. What they were going to do I could not tell; but a shudder of horror ran through me when, seated on my father's knee, my head resting on his shoulder, the doctor opened the wounded eye and he and the other surgeons examined it. They said that the cut had healed, and that all now needed to restore the sight entirely was the removal of the scar with caustic. How fearful was the fiery torture that entered the eye and burnt there for days, I need not attempt to describe! Then came once more the darkened chamber and long imprisonment; until I was led a second time into the light room, and the presence of the same men, who seemed to be my enemies, coming only to torment me. I shrunk from them, and cried aloud to my father to save me. The doctor caught me between his knees, threw my head upon his shoulder, thrust the caustic violently through the eye, and the light went out of it forever!

Matters were now worse than ever. Not only was a live coal placed in the socket of one eye, but it was feared that inflammation would destroy the other. Furiously did the inflammation rage in spite of all that skill and kindness could do. My third imprisonment lasted two years. Living in a little chamber where brooded the blackness of darkness—undergoing bleeding, leeching, cupping, besides swallowing drugs enough to dose a hospital, until the round childish form shrunk to a skeleton, and the craving of appetite was but tantalized with boiled rice, and mush without mild as an alternative—was not this a sad way for a child to spend his life, between the ages of five and seven?

Source: New York: Derby & Jackson, 1859, pp. 14–16.

7. "Blindness and the Blind"

The work of Howe and others contributed to a new public awareness of blind persons, not simply as "unfortunates" but as persons of worth and accomplishment. Curiosity and interest was not limited to readers of educational or medical publications. The following excerpt is from "Blindness and the Blind," one of eight "original prose articles" included with several poems in the June 1842 issue of Southern Literary Messenger. *Authorship is attributed to the Virginia Institute for the Blind at Staunton, Virginia. A purpose of the article was to dispel "false notions as to the blind," and this passage underscores Howe's advice to parents of young children who were blind.*

It would be a great mistake . . . to believe that the touch of all blind persons is very delicate. Individuals differ materially in that respect, owing probably to the different manner in which they have been brought up. While some persons, following the true indication of nature, allow their children to feel every object within their reach, and even assist them in the investigation of their tangible properties; other parents again, not only remove carefully out of the reach of their children any object which careless handling might injure, but even prohibit their unfortunate offspring from touching the most innocent and indestructible plaything. The result of these opposite modes of treatment is evident. While the first will astonish their beholder by the freedom and ease of their movements, by their accurate knowledge of the tangible properties of objects, and by the delicacy of their touch; the latter totter more than they walk, know not the most common objects apart, and have a touch as obtuse as that of seeing persons.

Source: Southern Literary Messenger 8(6), pp. 418–419, published in Richmond, Virginia, and edited by T. W. White.

8. "The Deaf, Dumb, and Blind Girl"

Nineteenth-century children's literature was intended to inculcate good qualities of character, such as kindness toward others, pity for the less fortunate, and gratitude for their own good fortune. This article, written by Lyman Cobb, is taken from Cobb's Juvenile Reader *(Kickok and Shugert, publisher, 1834). This short piece suggests there was at least one child at the American School for the Deaf who was also blind.*

Should any of you, my young friends, visit at any future time, the asylum at Hartford, and be induced to inquire for the deaf, dumb and blind girl, you would probably find her seated with her knitting, or needlework, in a dress, neat, and in its plainness comfortable to the humility of her circumstances.

Many strangers have waited for a long time to see her thread her needle, which is quite a mysterious process, and never accomplished without the aid of the tongue.

It will be difficult for you, my dear children, to gain a correct idea of a person perfectly blind, deaf and dumb, even after repeatedly beholding her.

Cover your eyes for a short time, and you shut out this world of beauty. Close your ears, and you exclude this world of sounds.

Refrain from speaking, and you cease to hold communion with the world of intelligence. Yet, were it in your power to continue thus for hours, even for days, you still have within your minds a treasury of knowledge to which she can never resort.

You can not picture to yourselves, the utter desolation of one, whose limited acquirements are made at the expense of such toil, and with the hazard of such continual errour [sic].

Never, therefore, forget to be grateful for the talents which you are endowed. For every new idea which you add to the mental storehouse, praise Him, who gives you with unveiled senses, to taste the luxury of knowledge. When the smile of your parents and companions makes your heart glad, or when you look at the bright flowers and fair skies of summer, think with compassion of her, who must never see the face of her fellow creatures, nor the beauty of the earth and sky.

When you hear the melody of musick [sic], of the kind voice of your teachers; strive to value and improve your privileges; and while you pour for all the emotions of your souls in the varieties of language, forget not a prayer of pity for her who dwells in perpetual silence; a prayer of gratitude to Him who has caused you to differ from her.

Source: Accessible at http://www.disabilitymuseum.org/lib/docs/792.htm, paragraphs 22–30, Disability History Museum, http://www.disabilitymuseum.org (January 20, 2005).

Other Physical Disability and Childhood

1. Edward Benton's Will

The fate of children with physical impairments was long dependent entirely on their families' circumstances, as family histories often reveal. The will of an early Connecticut settler named Edward Benton, written in 1675–1676, provides for the permanent care of one of his children.

As the Holy Providence of God has left the burden of a crippled child upon my hand to be cared and provided for, who may live and be burdensome after my decease, Zacheus Benton by name, and that affliction is an interruption to the more equal distributions of my small estate amongst all my children, I do therefore give only a sum of 5 shillings apiece unto my five children [not including Zacheus or Andrew, who was named Executor] and to my son Zacheus I give a colt, which he shall choose. Item 1 [not named, but presumably real estate] I give unto my son Andrew Benton, upon condition that he shall duly attend and provide for his brother Zacheus Benton, during the term of his natural life with all the necessaries of food and rayment, washing and lodging, suitable for him.

Source: Legacy Report: Ancestors of Frances Ann Lunan, http://www.planet shoop.com/shoop/Fran.htm.

2. First Annual Report of the Factory Inspectors of Illinois

With increasing industrialization and with inadequate policies regulating child labor, many children incurred serious injuries on the job resulting in permanent phys-

ical impairment. Children with disabilities were often particularly exploited, while unhygienic conditions, especially in the food production industries, contributed to the spread of infectious disease. Florence Kelley of Chicago's Hull House expressed concern over these issues with vivid descriptions of actual children in this report.

Filthy Shops

The medical examinations made in this office preliminary to granting health certificates reveal an incredible degree of filth of clothing and person. The children taken from the candy factories were especially shocking in this respect, and demonstrated anew, the urgent need of bathing facilities both in the workingman's home, where bath-tubs seem to be unknown, and in numerous and accessible swimming baths, where a plunge can follow the day's work.

Boys are found handling candy with open sores upon their hands, and girls wrapping and packing it whose arms were covered with an eruption which is a direct consequence of filth. Boys from knee-pants shops have presented themselves so covered with vermin as to render a close examination almost impossible.

Injurious Employments

The reckless employment of children in injurious occupations also is shown in the record of these medical examinations. A glaring example of this is Jaroslav Huptuk, a feeble-minded dwarf, whose affidavit shows him to be nearly sixteen years of age. This child weighs and measures almost exactly the same as a normal boy aged eight years and three months. Jaroslav Huptuk cannot read nor write in any language, not speak a consecutive sentence. Besides being dwarfed, he is so deformed as to be a monstrosity. Yet, with all these disqualifications for any kind of work, he has been employed for several years at an emery wheel, in a cutlery works, finishing knife-blades and bone handles, until, in addition to his other misfortunes, he is now suffering from tuberculosis. Dr. Holmes, having examined this boy, pronounced him unfit for work of any kind. His mother appealed from this to a medical college, where, however, the examining physician not only refused the lad a medical certificate, but exhibited him to the students as a monstrosity worthy of careful observation. He was finally taken in charge by an orthoaedist, and after careful treatment will be placed in a school for the feeble-minded. The kind of grinding at which this boy was employed has been prohibited in England for minors since 1883, by reason of the prevalence of "grinders' pthisis" among those who begin this work young.

Another occupation conspicuously injurious to children is the running of button-hole machines by foot-power. As a typical case: Joseph Poderovsky, aged fourteen years, was found by a deputy inspector running a heavy button-holer at 204 West Taylor street, in the shop of Michael Freeman. The child was required to report for medical examination, and pronounced by the examining physician rachitic and afflicted with a double lateral curvature of the spine. He was ordered discharged, and prohibited from working in any tailor shop. A few days later he was found at work at the same machine. A warrant was sworn out for the arrest of the employer, under Section Four of the law, but before it could be served the man left the State. This boy has a father in comfortable circumstances, and two adult able-bodied brothers.

Bennie Kelman, Russian Jew, four years in Chicago, fifteen years and four months old, father a glazier, found running a heavy sewing machine in a knee-pants shop. A health certificate was required, and the examination revealed a severe rupture. Careful questioning of the boy and his mother elicited the fact that he had been put to work in a boiler factory, two years before, when just thirteen years old, and had injured himself by lifting heavy masses of iron. Nothing had been done for the case, no one in the family spoke any English, or knew how help could be obtained. The sight test showed that he did not know his letters in English, though he claimed that he can read Jewish jargon. He was sent to the College of Physicians and Surgeons for treatment, and forbidden work until cured.

When the law went into operation, every tin-can and stamping works in Illinois was employing minors under sixteen years of age, at machines known to be liable to destroy the fingers, hands, and even the whole arm of the operator. The requirement of a medical certificate for all minors so employed has materially reduced their number, but the law should be so amended as to give the inspector power to prohibit the employment of minors at this and all kindred occupations. Until such power is conferred, the mutilation of children will continue to be a matter of daily occurrence.

The working of the law, even in its present inadequate form, is exemplified in its application to the tin-can industry by Norton's tin-can factory at Maywood. Here a very large number of boys are employed, a score having been found under fourteen years of age. In one part of the factory twenty to thirty boys work upon a shelf suspended between the first and second floors of the building. These unfortunate lads crouch, lie on their sides, sit on their feet, kneel, in short, assume every possible attitude except the normal, straight, sitting or standing posture of healthful employment. Their work consists in receiving pieces of tin sent to them by boys on the second floor, sorting them and poking them into slits in the shelf, whence the pieces of tin are conveyed to the machines on the ground floor for which they are destined. The atmosphere of the room at the height of the shelf is such that the inspector could endure it but a few minutes at a time. The noise of the machinery was so overpowering that it was impossible to make the boys hear questions until after two or three repetitions. The pieces of tin being sharp, the lad's fingers were bound up in cloths to prevent cutting, but in many cases these cloths were found to be saturated with blood. Altogether, the situation of these tin can boys was among the most deplorable discovered. Four inspections were made, and literal compliance with the wording of the law in all respects required. When the season ended, it was with the assurance upon the part of the Norton Bros. that they will open next year with no minors employed on their Maywood premises under sixteen years of age.

Source: Springfield, IL: H. W. Rokker, 1894, pp. 10–13. http://www.binghamton. edu/womhist/factory/doc16htm.

3. The Normal Child and Primary Education

Arnold Gesell and J.E.W. Wallin were two influential advocates for school medical screening and greater efforts to prevent health-related impairments in American children. In the following passage quoted from the introduction of an early textbook coauthored with his wife, Gesell notes progress since the turn of the century, crediting the Child Study Movement pioneered by his mentor, G. Stanley Hall, and seeming to presage the school-based psychoeducational clinics introduced in the 1920s and 1930s. His use of the term hygiene *refers to prevention of both physical and mental illness.*

Some day, probably, laboratories of child study and educational hygiene will be regular features of every large public-school system in America. . . . The new biological temper, which is the product of modern science, exalts hygiene and makes health the central solicitude in all the work of education.

Eleven years ago the school superintendents of America met in Chicago. Diligent search through the printed report of the meeting discloses no single mention of child health, no word about child hygiene, no address devoted to the conservation or development of the physical vigor of youth. At that time eight cities in America had systems of medical inspection in the public schools. Today the number of such systems if over four hundred. Historically *Child Hygiene*, yesterday only a phrase but already becoming a program for action, is a phase or an outgrowth of the scientific study of the child.

Source: See Gesell, A. & Gesell, B. (1912). *The Normal Child and Primary Education.* Boston: Ginn and Co., pp. 26–27.

4. National Society for Crippled Children

Franklin D. Roosevelt had not yet undertaken his campaign for the United States Presidency when in 1927 he addressed the annual convention of the newly formed organization the National Society for Crippled Children. His response to the rhetorical question "Why Bother with the Crippled Child?" reveals the conviction and advocacy that came with Roosevelt's personal identification with this particular cause. It also reveals his keen awareness of practical issues and the need to do more than appeal to sympathy in gaining public support.

Mr. Toastmaster, . . . [this] is just going to be a heart-to-heart talk . . . .

We workers have still got the task, in this nation, of selling our wares. We have still got the task of talking to the business men and women of the nation, to the taxpayers of the nation, proving our point as to why all this is worth while.

Sometimes we have to be business like. Sometimes we have to talk in terms of dollars and cents. It is a hard thing to do in a subject like this, and yet I find in talking to people throughout this country about the problem of the crippled child, and, I might add, of the crippled adult, too, they often do not see anything but the appeal to the heart. They get that. It is fine that they do, and it is right that we should emphasize that as well, but, back of it all, we have got to live in this day and generation, this time of practicality, and put things down in figures.

When you come down to that, there are many in our midst who want to know why; what good is it to spend all this time, and all these taxes, and all these gifts to bring back cripples. We have had figures presented at this gathering—an estimate of 400,000 crippled children in North America. I take it that that is a fairly accurate guess. If there are that many crippled children, how many more crippled adults are there who are getting around a little, many of them still hidden, many of them still to be found. . . .

Yes, we are young. As I said over the radio, we have only just begun our work. We still have to solve the problems of how and when and where. After we have done the principal part of restoring these people, we want to know how we can then go about making them into useful citizens. That is being solved as the days go by. We are finding new uses for people without arms, for people who can't walk with ease. The interesting thing to me about it is, and I think you will bear me out when I assert to the public of this country, that the mind, the mental capacity of the average cripple is not below the average. It isn't even just the average; I believe it is above the average. . . .

Education of the public, the dear, good, old, long-suffering public, which if you keep on driving at, and telling facts to, will come around to your point of view every time, if you tell the truth, and, heaven only knows, we have the truth.

Source: Accessed at http://www.disabilitymuseum.org/lib/docs/883.htm, paragraphs 1, 3–5, 10, and 22, Disability History Museum, http://www.disability museum.org (January 20, 2005) or through the Franklin D. Roosevelt Library.

5. "The Crippled Child's Bill of Rights"

I—Every child has the right to be well born; that is to say, the right to a sound body, complete in its member physically whole. In the securing of this right we pledge ourselves to use our influence that proper pre-natal, intra-natal and post-natal care be provided to the end that congenital deformity, insofar as it is humanly and scientifically possible, be prevented.

II—Every child has the right to develop under clean, wholesome, healthful conditions. In declaring this right, this Society undertakes to use its influence to the end that children everywhere, through proper legislation, both local and general, and through proper supervision and protection, may grow to manhood and womanhood free from crippling conditions caused by insufficient nourishment, improper food, or unsanitary environment, and free, so far as possible, from danger of accident, wounding or maiming.

III—Notwithstanding the rights of children to be well born and to be protected throughout childhood, it is recognized that in spite of all human precautions there will be, unfortunately, some crippled children. These we declare to have the right to the earliest possible examination, diagnosis and treatment, recognizing, as we do, the fact that many thousand cases of permanent crippling may be eliminated by early and effective care.

IV—Every crippled child has a right, not only to the earliest possible treatment, but to the most effective continuing care, treatment and nursing, including the use of such appliances as are best calculated to assist in remedying or ameliorating its condition.

V—Every crippled child has the right to an education. Without this, all other provisions, unless for the relief of actual suffering, are vain.

VI—Every crippled child has the right not only to care, treatment and education, but to such treatment as will fit him or her for self-support, either wholly or partially, as the conditions may dictate. Without such practical application education is likewise purposeless.

VII—Every crippled child has the right to vocational placement, for unless the child,—boy or girl—after having been given physical care and treatment, and after being educated and trained, is actually placed in a proper position in the life of the World, all that has gone before is of no avail.

VIII—Every crippled child has the right to considerate treatment, not only from those responsible for its being and for its care, treatment, education, training and placement, but from those with whom it is thrown into daily contact, and every possible influence should be exerted by this and affiliated organizations to secure this right, in order that, so far as possible, the crippled child may be spared the stinging jibe or the bitter taunt, or, worse still, the demoralizing pity of its associates.

IX—Every crippled child has the right to spiritual, as well as bodily development, and, without regard to particular religious or denominational belief, is entitled to have nourishment for soul-growth.

X—In brief, not only for its own sake, but for the benefit of Society as a whole, every crippled child has the right to the best body which modern science can help it to secure; the best mind which modern education can provide; the best training which modern vocational guidance can give; the best position in life which his physical condition, perfected as best it may be, will permit, and the best opportunity for spiritual development which its environment affords.

Source: The International Society for Crippled Children (1931). "The Crippled Child's Bill of Rights," *The Crippled Child* 9 (June 1931), p. 25.

Cognitive Disability
and Childhood

1. "Blind Tom"

The story of Thomas Wiggins provides a fascinating account of a musical prodigy, as well as insights into post–Civil War attitudes concerning race and disability. This announcement of his death in 1908 in the New York Times *provides an overview of the life and career of the gifted musician known as "Blind Tom."*

Blind Tom, Pianist, Dies of a Stroke
Old Negro with Strange Mastery of Music Ends His Days in Hoboken
A Child All His Life
Cared for In His Declining Years by the Daughter of His Old Master

Thomas Wiggins, the "Blind Tom" whose strange mastery of the piano without teaching or scientific knowledge of the instrument made thousands wonder, died on Saturday at the home of a daughter of his old master and one-time owner, Col. James N. Bethune of Georgia.

Mrs. Albert J. Lerche, who was Miss Eliza Bethune before her marriage, had cared for the old blind negro musician for many years past, keeping him happy and comfortable in her home, at 60 Twelfth Street, Hoboken. It was there that he died suddenly of apoplexy.

"Blind Tom" was twice erroneously reported dead, once in 1908, and prior to that a body was identified as his after the Johnstown flood, was buried as his, and a tombstone put over it, marked with his name.

This time, the famous old musician is really dead. His body lies in the Frank Campbell Company's funeral chapel, at 241 West Twenty-third Street, and today after the last services "Blind Tom's" funeral march, composed by himself and in a way said to be typical of his own life, will be played on the chapel organ.

In this composition, which many musicians have declared to be of uncommon merit, a passage of great sonority is immediately followed by a passage of such lightness and gayety that the effect produced is one of pathos. The negro, weakminded all through his life, was as much of a child in middle age as at 7, and his pleasures were those of a child.

He applauded himself after the performance of every number, laughed lightly and with little provocation, and always needed a guardian. The sadness of a blind life and the gayety of a child's nature are shown in the funeral march which was played publicly at the funeral of his old master a number of years ago.

The fear of death was strong in Blind Tom in his later years. If he felt the wind blowing against him he would exclaim: "Tom's in a draft. He may catch cold and die. Wouldn't that be terrible!" But he was spared the agony of the fear of surely approaching death, the stroke of apoplexy striking him unconscious, and the end following in a very short time.

When Col. Bethune bought Charity Wiggins she had in her arms a pickaninny, blind, feeble, and not considered valuable as a slave asset. So Tom was "thrown in" by his mother's former master. He was a very small boy when he discovered that for the loss of his sight and the blight upon his mind his Creator had endowed him with a gift so strange and yet so productive of happiness to him that he has, in a way, been a living subject for marvel during the last half century.

The boy began by repeating words that he heard about him, mimicking every one and trying to imitate all sounds that fell on his ear. When he first heard a piano played every note of the music was stamped in his mind, and, groping to the instrument, he found that he could reproduce the music he had heard.

With the instrument he could imitate the tinkling of water in a fountain, the fall of rain, and the noises of the storm. His own composition, which gave him the most delight, he called "What the Wind and the Waves Told Tom."

The fame of the blind negro boy spread quickly, and during the twenty years and more that he performed in public here and abroad he made a great deal of money. A son of his old master toured him until about fifteen years ago, when he retired and went to live in New Jersey. Mrs. Lerche was appointed his guardian twenty years ago, and has since looked after him. The old negro's last days were spent with his piano or playing in the Lerche home, frequently holding imaginary receptions.

Up to ten years ago the old mother of the freak pianist was still alive in Georgia, very aged. Tom was in his sixtieth year. In his reproductions of the performances of masterpieces on the piano he was said to play with a conception of music that was as great as his skill. His technique came as naturally as did his musical emotions.

Source: New York Times (1857–Current file); June 15, 1908; ProQuest Historical Newspapers, the *New York Times* (1851–2001) p. 7.

2. "Provision for Idiotic and Feeble-Minded Children"

Isaac N. Kerlin, M.D., superintendent of the Elwyn School in Media, Pennsylvania, was among the most respected leaders in the field of mental retardation when he gave this important address. After describing the "degrees and grades of idiocy," Kerlin called for states to assume greater responsibility for funding institutional care. The complete address was published in the Proceedings of the National Conference of Charities and Corrections at the Eleventh Annual Session, *held in St. Louis, October 12–17, 1884.*

Excitable idiots are not so common as the apathetic. They usually die early from exhaustion or, less happily, sink into apathetic forms; but there is a group in every large asylum of this class, taxing the ingenuity of their present care-takers, after wasting the best life of their families.

The temptation for their extinction rises to the lips of the careless, forgetful how far such practice would be from all moral or judicial right, how revolting to every religious sentiment and contradictory to every logical principle.

So we have them with us, although so little of us. Annie F., the saddest type, aged eight years, mute, wild, and vicious, biting any one whom she can reach, with a nervousness in the act that suggests its irresponsibility; darting to an open window to throw herself headlong below, her glittering eyes, tensely drawn lips, and sudden pallors indicating the pain and commotion of her poor and worried brain. How fittingly and terribly does this disturbed life project itself from its ante-natal unrest,—an unwilling and unhappy conception, for the destruction of which the mother's stormiest passions had unceasingly but unavailingly contended! And there are a few others as sad, exciting wonder why they continue to live, and greater wonder how the home and the neighborhood tolerated for years their cries, discordant noises, and uncouthness.

Advanced beyond these apathetic and excitable idiots, we find an intermediate group, the idio-imbeciles. Many have the facial appearance, the deformed heads, the dwarfishness of body, the narrow buccal arches, the imperfect teeth of very imperfect creatures; but there is dawning intelligence. Taken from their isolation, they feebly grasp, through their shyness and sensitiveness, for the better things about them. Expecting them to do little or nothing, the trainer is daily sustained by successes, and goes on hopefully introducing most of them to a higher grade,—that of the lowest forms of imbecility; and here we discover the strongest individuality, so that it is quite impossible to select a type. T.T., age twelve, will illustrate as well as any. He is a microcephalic paralytic imbecile of low grade: articulation quite imperfect; sense of sight and hearing good; hand well formed; imitation above the grade in which he is placed; cruel in his disposition; showing discrimination, analysis, and candor, when he says he "likes to wear heavy boots,—good to kick boys with." He is the better of two similarly malformed and imbecile brothers now living. In this lowest plane of imbecility will be found many mutes who are yet possessed of perfect hearing, ready appreciation of language, and often dexterous finger and hand capacity. Under special training in articulation and the inspiring effect of concert recitation and song, they come to the partial possession of speech. They rarely become perfect in speech. As their capacity is gradually developed, they are carried forward into the higher ranks, to become our most interesting children. The idiocy or imbecility displayed by them is, as often as not, the effect of their isolation.

Source: Editor, Isabel C. Barrows, Boston: George H. Ellis, 1885, pp. 248–263.

3. "The How, The Why, and The Wherefore of The Training of Feeble-Minded Children"

Martin W. Barr both emphasized the positive benefits for persons with mental retardation to engage in productive work and stressed the need for lifelong institutionalization, separation of the sexes, and even sterilization. His address to the National Educational Association, in Washington, D.C., July 13, 1899, is excerpted here, is a call for understanding, a message of pessimism, and a dire warning. Reflecting the growing interest in classifying mental defect by level and type, Barr nonetheless endorses institutionalization for all.

Indeed we must take the child as he is without attempting to make him over again; direct the destructive activities into constructive channels. . . . [Here, Dr. Barr gives a lengthy account of a patient teacher channeling a child's destructive behavior into learning a modest but satisfying new skill.] You see she was wise enough to utilize the natural activities of the child and direct evil propensities into a healthful channel. . . . Now just what this shows is to be found in varying results throughout all the grades of trainable defectives or *imbeciles.* The *idiot* or unimprovable class and the *idio-imbecile,* the direction of whose feeble powers so far as to aid in the care of himself or his weaker brother can hardly be dignified by the term training, we will not discuss here, although they are unfortunately found in the custodial departments of all training schools in this country. It is the imbecile or trainable class which is here presented in the four different grades which experience has dictated and proven. . . .

Here we have the low-grade who can never learn to read or write, trainable only in the simplest acts of house or farm service, who can know nothing beyond a life of drudgery, but will on the whole be content therein. This grade generally presents two types—one good, docile, obedient, having little or no will power; such a one in the world becomes the ready tool or the victim of the designing or the vicious, and thus innocently helps to fill our prison ward. The other obstinate, perverse and indolent, needs always a strong hand to keep him at constant occupation, which is all that preserves him from a lapse into idiocy. He would be the tyrant of a household—the terror of a community.

The middle grade, trainable in varied degree in the useful and mechanical arts, may or may not as an aid in his development be taught to read and write, but will never use the knowledge practically in his work as a good servant or a fairly good mechanic.

The high grade, capable, in intellectual capacity, of advancement as far as the first intermediate, can never, without danger of breakdown, attempt all the studies of that course. His life work must therefore be sought in the various trades and handicrafts to which his development by means of manual training, from the kindergarten up, has always been directed, and life happiness, possibly as a skilled artisan, for him be assured.

Lastly, the moral imbecile found in all three grades, often abnormally bright, may vary intellectually from a brute to a genius, but the moral sense is absolutely wanting. It is from this class that the criminal ranks in all lands are largely recruited. His permanent segregation under close custodial care, with as many ameliorations as possible, is absolutely essential to the safety of himself and of society. . . .

And wherefore all this for imbeciles! Is it worth it? many may ask.

Ah! between that question and answer lies a hundred years of experience, and the working out by scientists and philosophers of a basis for the coming century to build upon.

Work among mental defectives, having its birth with the nineteenth century, has . . . so modified that its character and aims are alike changed. What in the beginning was a philanthropic purpose, *pure* and *simple*, having for its object the most needy, and therefore naturally directed toward paupers and idiots, now assumes the proportions of a socialistic reform as a matter of self-preservation, a necessity to preserve the nation from the encroachments of imbecility, of crime, and all the fateful consequences of a highly nervous age.

Source: The address can be accessed at http://www.disabilitymuseum.org/lib/docs/1392.htm, paragraphs 4–10, 17, and 18, Disability History Museum, www.disabilitymuseum.org (January 14, 2005).

4. "Fifteen Years a Prisoner as Feeble-Minded . . ."

Mary Lake's story described in this news article no doubt shocked readers. The article not only implies arbitrariness and fallibility of diagnosis, especially if there is "familial taint"; it also indicates what the consequences could be for persons labeled "feeble-minded" who make trouble for authorities. Many children and youth, as well as adults, have had such experiences.

Detained for 15 Years as "Feeble-minded"
Girl Then Pronounced Insane is Declared to be of Sound Mind
Now Under Commissioner Feeny's Protection—Tells a Story of
Ill-Treatment at Newark (N.Y.) Asylum

Fifteen years a prisoner as feeble-minded while not only not insane or even feeble-minded, has apparently been the lot of Mary Lake, now an inmate of the Richmond Borough Almshouse, but about to be set at liberty. Commissioner of Charities James Feeney of Richmond Borough is largely responsible for justice being done the girl even now.

The young woman is a daughter of George Lake of New Dorp. Lake, on Dec. 5, 1883, was sentenced for a serious offense to ten years in State prison. Lake's children were committed to the County Almshouse, and the records show that on Sept. 10, 1886, Mary, twelve years old, was committed to the State Institution for Feebleminded Children at Syracuse. She remained at that institution until she became of age on Jan. 4, 1896, when she was transferred to the New York Custodial Asylum for Feeble-Minded Women, at Newark, N.Y.

Commissioner Feeny on Sept. 10 last received a letter from C. W. Winspear, the Superintendent of that institution, stating that Mary Lake had become insane, and demanding that she be removed. The Commissioner found that she must be brought back to Richmond County, and proceedings were taken to have her legally declared insane before she could be committed to an insane asylum. Some correspondence ensued between Commissioner Feeny and Superintendent Winspear, and under date of Oct. 1 the latter sent a certificate made by the attending physician at the institution, which follows:

> Mary Lake has had a number of attacks of excitement, but none so severe as the present attack, nor did they last as long. Has been very much worse the last two weeks. I have no doubt of her insanity.
>
> N.E. Lando

Upon the receipt of this the Commissioner sent Superintendent of Alms-house Pierce with a nurse, and armed with straightjackets and other para-phernalia to bring the supposed insane and violent girl to her home county, and the Superintendent was surprised to have placed in his custody an attractive-looking young woman entirely docile, well-educated, bright, and intelligent. Miss Lake was brought to the almshouse on Oct. 2, and since that time she has undergone several severe examinations at the hands of Dr. Isaac L. Millspaugh and Dr. John T. Sprague, who finally certified to Commissioner Feeny that the young woman is not now insane, and perhaps never has been; that there is no evidence that she has ever been even feeble-minded, and, on the contrary, she is intelligent, well-educated, is willing to work, and is most competent in every respect. . . .

Miss Lake, when seen at the almshouse, talked freely of her life in the institutions, and told stories of ill-treatment at the hands of some of the assistants at the Newark Institution. She says there are others at the insti-tution who are sound-minded, and who desire to be and should be dis-charged from the asylum.

She claims the reason she was declared insane and sent back to Rich-mond is that she was charged with being the originator of a plan to appeal to Gov. Odell upon the occasion of his visit to the institution during his recent tour of the State institutions. The plan was not carried out by the inmates. While she was among the number who agreed to speak to the Governor, she was not, she says, the leader or the originator of the plan. She declared her determination to leave, however, and fearing that she would make some trouble, the authorities at the institution, she says, took the above-mentioned method to get rid of her.

Source: New York Times (1857–Current file); October 26, 1901; ProQuest Historical Newspapers, the New York Times (1851–2001), p. 1.

5. "The Burden of Feeble-Mindedness"

W. E. Fernald was one of the most widely respected leaders at the time he made the address that is excerpted here. This address to the Massachusetts Medical Society was an abbreviated version of one he had given at the annual meeting of the American Association for the Study of the Feeble-Minded, in June, 1912, titled "The Burden of Feeble-Mindedness," published in that organization's Journal of Psycho-Asthenics (1912, vol. 17, pp. 87–111). His dire warnings illustrate how the grow-ing eugenics movement was linked to increasingly negative beliefs about mental retardation. Fernald and other leaders (such as Goddard, whom he cites) would later change their views of persons with mental retardation as a "social menace," and the need for lifelong institutionalization.

The past few years have witnessed a striking awakening of professionals and popular consciousness of the widespread prevalence of feeblemindedness and its influence as a source of wretchedness to the patient himself and to his family, and as a causative factor in the production of crime, prostitution, pauperism, illegitimacy, intemperance and other complex social diseases. . . .

The hereditary cases are the most numerous. The recent intensive study of the family histories of large numbers of the feeble-minded by Goddard, Davenport, and Tredgold show that, in at least eighty per cent. of these cases, the mental defect had been preceded by other cases of defect in the immediate family line. Goddard finds that sixty-five per cent. of his institution cases had one or both parents actually feeble-minded. It is believed that this hereditary defect is the result of protoplasmic defect in the germ plasm of the family stock.

There is no doubt as to the potency and certainty of this hereditary tendency. Often the feeble-minded child represents a feeble-minded family. Davenport believes that aside from the Mongolian type, probably no imbecile is born except of parents who, if not mentally defective themselves, both carry mental defect in their germ plasm. . . .

There is a popular belief that feeble-mindedness is greatly on the increase. We do not know, and are not likely to know, whether or not there is now relatively more feeble-mindedness than there was fifty or one hundred or five hundred years ago. There is some reason for the belief that the remarkable shift of population from rural to urban conditions in the last half-century, with the resulting industrial and social stress, and a greater liability to syphilis, tuberculosis and alcoholism, has increased the ratio of defectives in the families with hereditary predisposition. It is certain that the feeble-minded girl or woman in the city rarely escapes the sexual experiences that too often result in the birth of more defectives and degenerates. At the same time the steady withdrawal of the more sturdy and virile individuals from the country to the towns leaves the ineffective and defective men and women in the country to marry and beget offspring even less efficient than themselves. Recent study of certain isolated rural communities in Massachusetts where the more vigorous families have migrated for several generations, shows a marked deterioration in the quality of the population, with a large number of the feeble-minded and a notable amount of immorality, intemperance and shiftlessness. The defective persons in these communities are very apt to be attracted to each other, and to marry or to intermarry, thus intensifying the degenerative process. The members of this society are only too familiar with these rural foci of feeblemindedness, immorality, crime and destitution.

The social and economic burdens of uncomplicated feeble-mindedness are only too well known. The feeble-minded are a parasitic, predatory class, never capable of self-support or of managing their own affairs. The great

majority ultimately become public charges in some form. They cause un-
utterable sorrow at home and are a menace and danger to the community.
Feeble-minded women are almost invariably immoral, and if at large usually
become carriers of venereal disease or give birth to children who are as
defective as themselves. The feeble-minded woman who marries is twice as
prolific as the normal woman.

We have only begun to understand the importance of feeble-mindedness
as a factor in the causation of pauperism, crime and other social problems.
Hereditary pauperism, or pauperism of two or more generations of the
same family, generally means hereditary feeblemindedness. In Massachusetts there are families who have been paupers for many generations. Some
of the members were born or even conceived in the poorhouse.

Every feeble-minded person, especially the high-grade imbecile, is a potential criminal, needing only the proper environment and opportunity for
the development and expression of his criminal tendencies. The unrecog-
nized imbecile is a most dangerous element in the community. There are
many crimes committed by imbeciles for every one committed by an insane
person. The term "defective delinquent" is applied to this special class of
defectives where the mental lack is relatively slight, though unmistakable,
and the criminal tendencies are marked and constant.

At least twenty-five per cent. of the inmates of our penal institutions are
mentally defective and belong either to the feeble-minded or to the defective delinquent class. Nearly fifty per cent. of the girls at the Lancaster
reformatory are mentally defective. The class of defective delinquents of
both sexes is well known in every police court, jail, reformatory and prison.
There is a close analogy between the defective delinquent and the instinc-
tive criminals who form a large proportion of the prison rounder type.
Under present conditions these irresponsible persons are discharged at the
expiration of their sentences to lay tribute on the community, to reproduce
their own kind, to be returned to prison again and again.

Source: The address can be accessed at http://www.disabilitymuseum.org/lib/
docs/1208.htm, paragraphs 3, 7, 8, and 13–17, Disability History Museum, http://
www.disabilitymuseum.org (January 14, 2005).

6. "The Deficient Child"

*A presentation by Dr. F. J. Russell, superintendent of the School for Feeble-Minded
at Brandon, Vermont, "The Deficient Child," is included in the* Proceedings of
the Second Annual Vermont Conference of Charities and Corrections, *January 24, 1917 (pp. 31–33). Russell's warning of the "menace of the moron," or
"high-grade feeble-minded" person, reflects the pessimism of the times, calling for
institutional segregation to prevent hereditary proliferation of "degenerate" stock.*

It is gratifying to report that the people in Vermont are beginning to take a marked interest in the study of feeble-mindedness and its baneful and increasing effects on the population of the state and that with a better understanding of the conditions which exist there will be a tendency to view the handling of the question in a more practical and common sense manner. The burden of feeble-mindedness is felt by the entire public and every intelligent person who has considered the subject realizes that this blight on mankind is increasing at an alarming rate and unless some heroic measures are adopted to stop the influences which tend to increase its growth, it will only be a matter of time before the resulting pauperism and criminality will be a bear.

Most common of all causes is heredity and in the great majority of cases either drunkenness, idiocy, epilepsy or other evidences of degeneracy are found in the parents or their immediate relatives. Goddard, Davenport and others making a study of the family histories of large numbers of the feeble-minded find that at least 75% of these cases have been preceded by other cases of mental defect in the immediate family line. We know that hereditarily feeble-minded parents produce feebleminded children and the feeble-minded families tend to be larger than the average normal families.

The greatest danger in the problem of the feeble-minded comes from the moron or high grade feeble-minded person. We do not have to be told how to recognize the low grade, their inability to care for themselves and their limitations make them easily recognized and for this reason they do not constitute a serious problem, but the morons on the other hand can in a measure care for themselves and may present no physical evidences of deficiency, but they lack in whole or in part the sense of values, the will power, the ability to withstand temptation, foresight and the fear of physical consequences and this is the class that makes for us our social and eco-nomic problems. Their resemblance to the normal person makes it difficult for many to believe that they cannot be developed into a law-abiding per-son. This is the type of individual person that charitable and correctional agencies have labored with for years, trying to reclaim them, but only to see nearly every effort prove fruitless, and the sooner that we realize that these defective persons cannot be made into normal ones the sooner will the prosperity and moral tone of the community be assured. At large the moron is always in danger of becoming a pauper, alcoholic, thief, prostitute or graver criminal.

A certain number of the boys and girls committed to the industrial school at Vergennes are feeble-minded and this institution has attempted to correct and train them and return them to society as law abiding indi-viduals. Now in the case of normal children who get into trouble through vicious influences and bad environment, this is sound doctrine and the industrial school has done meritorious work in reclaiming these boys and girls, but on the other hand feeble-minded children cannot be reclaimed in this manner and institutional training only covers their defect and can bring such children up to the normal. To give the feeble-minded training and then set them free into society is a moral as well as an economic mistake, yet up till now the industrial school had had no other alternative but to admit and discharge these defectives.

We have not realized that the moron is not a normal person mentally and that he can never be made normal, he has been misunderstood and has been credited with a degree of responsibility he does not and cannot possess. The remedy for this moral blunder lies in a mental and bio-sociological examination of each juvenile delinquent, with a view of determining what disposition of the case is best for the child and best for society.

In a rational and progressive policy for dealing with this great problem it is essential that we should recognize this condition in childhood; that there be some form of guardianship from infancy; that the backward children in the public schools be studied individually; that their physical defects be diagnosed and remedied, and those who are definitely feeble-minded be removed to special institutions. A central medical authority should be established to which every case of feeble-mindedness must be reported and which would have oversight of all mental defectives in the community.

If the state is to protect itself in its future citizens more attention must be paid to the causes of feeble-mindedness and methods of prevention. There is an increasing and insistent demand that society be protected from the evils to which it is exposed by allowing feeble-mindedness to develop and increase without any restrictions whatsoever.

Source: Special Collections, Bailey/Howe Library, University of Vermont, Burlington, VT 05405, http://cit.uvm.edu:6336/dynaweb/eugenics/orfrvcs012417(January 13, 2005).

7. Sterilization Laws

Although Vermont's governor vetoed the bill from which the following is excerpted after its passage by the Senate in 1912, within the next two decades most of the United States would have adopted sterilization laws with language such as is reflected in these paragraphs from the earlier Vermont bill. This sterilization "movement," which encompassed relatives as well as the "defectives" themselves, anticipated and helped to inspire the sterilization campaign in Nazi Germany, under Hitler. The bill is included in Legislative Records of the Sterilization Laws: Vermont. Eugenical Sterilization in the United States, maintained by Harry H. Laughlin (1922, pp. 43–45).

AN ACT to authorize and provide for the sterilization of imbeciles, feeble-minded and insane persons, rapists, confirmed criminals and other defectives.
Section 1. A board of examiners of feeble-minded, criminals and other

defectives is hereby created; and forthwith after the passage of this act, and biennially thereafter the governor shall appoint one neurologist, one surgeon and one practitioner of medicine, each with at least six years' experience in the actual practice of his profession, for the term of two years . . . who shall be sworn to a faithful discharge of their duties. The members of said board shall be paid ten dollars for each day actually spent in the performance of their duties, and their actual and necessary traveling expenses. . . .

Section 2. Said board shall examine into the mental and physical condition and the record and family history of the insane, feeble-minded, epileptic, criminal and other defective initiates confined in the hospitals for the insane, state prison, reformatories, and charitable and penal institutions in the state; and if it appears to said board that procreation by any such person would produce children with an inherited tendency to crime, insanity, feeble-mindedness, epilepsy, idiocy, or imbecility, said board shall appoint a time and place for hearing thereon within the town where such person is confined, and shall deliver to such person a notice in writing of such hearing, which shall plainly state the time, place and purpose thereof, and shall be delivered to him by some member of said board not less than six nor more than thirty days before the day of said hearing. Said board shall be present at the time and place appointed for such hearing, and shall make such further examination and investigation with respect to such person as shall seem to said board necessary, and shall hear such person in his defense if he appears and requests a hearing.

Section 3. If, in the judgment of all members of said board, after said examination and hearing, procreation by such person would produce children with an inherited tendency to crime, insanity, feeble-mindedness, epilepsy, idiocy, or imbecility, and if there is no probability that the condition of such person will improve to such an extent as to render procreation by such person advisable, or if, in the judgment of said board, the physical or mental condition of such person will be substantially improved thereby, and said board shall unanimously so find, said board shall order such an operation to be performed on such person for the prevention of procreation as shall be decided by said board to be safe and most effective, and shall appoint some member of said board to perform such operation, who shall perform it.

Source: The document can be accessed by contacting Eugenics Survey of Vermont Papers: Pamphlet Library, Vermont Public Records Division, Middlesex, VT, or online at http://cit.uvm.edu:6336/dynaweb/eugenics/ogact79123012 (January 13, 2005).

8. "All the pupils have improved . . ."

By the late nineteenth century, attitudes about mental retardation were entering a period of pessimism, in contrast to earlier reports such as the one excerpted here, which foreshadows today's "best practices."

The Legislature of 1853 is therefore to determine whether the Institution shall be continued or abandoned; and if continued, whether its capacity shall be enlarged to meet the urgent demand for its advantages to the most helpless of our race.

A recurrence to our first report will show with what caution, not to say doubt, the trustees entered upon the discharge of their duties. The popular and current opinion that this class of afflicted humanity were incapable of any essential improvement, had not been entirely changed by the imperfect information we possessed of the efforts made in other countries. Still, enough had been ascertained to justify an experiment on a moderate scale. It had been discovered that the term "idiot" very inaccurately described the different conditions of imbecility of intellect; that there were grades and degrees at great distances from each other; that the effects of bodily injuries had been confounded with original organization; that ill treatment and neglect had obscured minds naturally healthy, and finally that by proper discrimination and training, adapted to each case, in many instances the intellect had been aroused or developed, and new creatures born into the world. Fearing to trust too much to the sympathies and glowing hopes which such facts were calculated to excite, the trustees determined to test the experiment which the Legislature had authorized, by the same rigid rule which they would apply to any new theory in physics, viz: to see for themselves how it worked; to compare the condition of the pupils when admitted, with their condition at subsequent periods.

They have done so; and they now say, as the results of their observations, of their comparisons and of their deliberate convictions, that the experiment has entirely and fully succeeded. *All* the pupils have improved, some in a greater and others in a less degree. But the single fact of some improvement settles the question; for all experience shows that if a lodgment in the mind can once be made, it furnishes a foundation upon which further ideas, facts and combinations can be erected. This first, lodgment is the turning point, and when it is accomplished, every thing follows with more or less rapidity, according to circumstances. We have witnessed this rapidity in some instances with surprise, not to say astonishment. The process is as curious as it is interesting, and the manner of it, by commencing with efforts to teach what many animals are capable of learning, and advancing gradually and carefully, from step to step in the scale of intelligence, is admirably described in the appendix to the report from the superintendent which accompanies this paper, and which will be found exceedingly interesting.

The trustees therefore repeat and confirm absolutely what they intimated as their belief in their first report; that in almost all cases, and with very few, if any exceptions, those usually called idiots, under the age of 12 or 15, may be so trained and instructed as to engage in agriculture. Their minds and souls can be developed so that they may become responsible beings, acquainted with their relations to their Creator and a future state, and their obligations to obey the laws and respect the rights of their fellow citizens. In all cases, we believe, for we have seen what has been accomplished in apparently desperate cases, they can be made cleanly and neat in their personal habits, and enabled to enjoy the bounties of Providence and the comforts of life, and to cease being incumbrances and annoyances to the families in which they reside.

Source: New York State Asylum for Idiots, Second Annual Report of the Trustees, February 10, 1853. (Steve Taylor Collection) http://www.disabilitymuseum.org/lib/docs/ 1353.htm, paragraphs 7–10, Disability History Museum, www.disabilitymuseum. org (January 5, 2004).

Troubled, Troubling, and Troublesome Children

1. First Report of the Superintendent of the Lunatic Hospital at Worcester

This report, dated November 30, 1833, showed that 164 patients had been treated during the hospital's first year, only 4 of whom were younger than 21. However, 17 had reportedly incurred mental illness as children or teens. The sometimes mysterious "supposed causes" (e.g., menstrual dysfunction, physical illness, "fanaticism," etc.) illustrate alienists' thinking in the 1830s concerning causes of insanity.

Number	Age	Sex	Supposed Cause	Duration of Disease before Admittance	By whom committed to the Hospital
12	34	Male	Intemperance	14 years	By Court
20	23	Male	Excessive Venereal Indulgence	5 years	By Court
39	32	Male	Abuse of Parent	11 years	By Court
54	34	Male	Result of Measles	14 years	By Court
59	33	Female	Unknown	13 years	By Court
60	24	Female	Ill Health	5 years	By Court
72	23	Male	Masturbation	6 years	By Court
82	26	Female	Ill Health	7 years	By Court
84	30	Male	Masturbation	20 years	By Court
89	21	Female	Unknown	3 years	By Friends
92	30	Male	Wound in the Head	26 years	By Friends

97	28	Female	Fanaticism	8 years	By Friends
132	23	Male	Followed Fever	7 years	By Court
138	50	Male	Disappointed Affection	32 years	By Friends
152	19	Female	Repelled Eruption	4 weeks	By Court
154	16	Female	Amenorrhoea	3 months	By Friends
155	19	Female	Amenorrhoea	3 weeks	By Town

Source: The report was included in *Reports and Other Documents Relating to the State Lunatic Hospital at Worcester, Massachusetts* (Boston: Dutton and Wentworth), http://www.disabilitymuseum.org/lib/docs/1982.htm, Disability History Museum, www.disabilitymuseum.org (January 20, 2005).

2. *"A dreadful thing to be a maniac"*

The story of "Crazy Ann," from The Boy's Story Book, *by Francis Channing Woodworth (publisher: Clark, Astin & Co., 1851) illustrates use of children's literature to promote qualities of character, in this case an understanding of mental illness. It also indicates how mentally ill persons had been provided for before asylum care became more common. It is maintained by the American Antiquarian Society.*

"Father," said Margaret Standish, a merry little girl of my acquaintance; "father, what has become of Crazy Ann? I have not seen her for a long time. I wish she would come here again. She used to make a good deal of fun for us. What a woman she is to talk! Don't you remember that last time she was here, how she made us all laugh? She had a white dress on, and said she was going to be married to a spirit. How funny!"

"Yes, I remember all about Ann's last visit here," said Mr. Standish. "I have thought of it a great many times since."

"And, father," little Margaret went on, "brother Edward said he was flying his kite, with some other boys, last summer, and Ann came along, with another woman, as crazy as she was. They called themselves angels, and said they were going to have some wings pretty soon, and then they meant to fly back again to heaven, where they came from. I wonder if they ever got their wings."

And the merry girl laughed until she was red in the face.

Mr. Standish did not speak for some moments. He seemed to be thinking of something that made him sad.

"My dear," said he, after a while, "I did not feel at all like laughing, when I saw Ann that day, with the white dress on; and when I heard her talk so strangely, I felt more like weeping than I did like laughing. Poor woman! I pitied her with all my heart."

"I don't see why, I am sure," said Margaret.

"I will tell you why, my dear child," replied her father. "When Ann was in her right mind, she was as sensible as anybody. She was very good and kind, too. All the people in the neighborhood loved her. Don't you remember having heard your mother tell about the girl who was so kind to your uncle Joseph, when he was very sick with the rheumatism, and for weeks we thought he would never get well?"

"Oh, yes, sir," replied Margaret. "But she was a little girl. That was not Crazy Ann."

"It is true," said her father, "that is was a little girl, and it is equally true that it was Ann Bristol, the same person that you now call *Crazy Ann*. That was a good while ago, my dear. It was before you were born. Ann was quite small, when your uncle was so sick; but she used to come every day, and sit by his bed, and give him his medicine, and read to him." . . .

Margaret thought it was strange enough that Crazy Ann could ever have been an angel of mercy, or at all like one. "Father," said she, after a pause, "what makes people crazy? If they were good at one time, what makes them bad?"

"I can't answer all these questions in one breath," replied Mr. Standish. "They make quite a catechism. Some people lose their reason from one cause, and some from another. Sickness brings on insanity sometimes. Grief, disappointment, sudden fright, also produce it. You speak as if a good person becomes bad, when they are crazy. It is not so; that is, it is not certain that a person is any more wicked than anybody else, because she has lost her reason. People who are crazy, may be very wicked or they may not. They can't help being crazy."

"Can't help it! Could not Crazy Ann help acting so like a witch?"

"Did she act like a witch? How do witches act? Did you ever see a witch?"

"Isn't that something of a 'catechism', father? No, sir; I never saw a witch, and I don't know exactly how they act. But they act as bad as they can I suppose; and I am sure Ann acted as bad as she could."

"Ann Bristol could not help being crazy, any more than you could help having the scarlet-fever last summer."

"Why, what made her crazy, father?"

"When she was quite a young lady, she loved a man who went to sea. This man loved her, and they were engaged to be married. John Layton, the young sailor that Ann loved, was a very excellent man.

"I knew him well, and I always thought he would be a good husband for Ann. He made two or three voyages, and the captain of the ship in which he sailed, said he was one of the best sailors on board, always ready to do his duty, and always foremost in danger. He was a right merry fellow, too. Captain Holton told me he had known John to go aloft to take in the rigging, when a furious storm was raging, and after he had done the work, while he was hanging to the mast or the shrouds with one hand, he would take off his cap with the other, and swing it round his head, and give three cheers for his country.

"John left home for a long voyage to the East Indies, in the same year, I believe, that your brother George was born. Ann wept a great deal, when he went away. So did his father and mother. He had never been away from home before for so long a time as it took to make a voyage to the East Indies.

"The ship sailed. She made a good voyage. They had taken their cargo on board, and had left for home. They arrived near the coast of their own beloved land. All on board were hoping soon to see their dear friends again.

"But, alas! How terrible was their disappointment! A gale arose; the wind blew toward the land. Though every effort was made to get the ship out to sea again, when they found they could not enter the harbor, she struck the beach. The waves dashed furiously over her. She was soon a wreck, and nearly all on board were drowned. John Layton was among the lost.

"When Ann heard the tidings of the loss of that dear friend, whom she loved more than any one else in the world, she uttered a frightful shriek, and fainted. When she recovered, she was a raving maniac. Her reason had fled.

"For months after that sad wreck, almost every day, a woman might be seen on the seashore, walking back and forth near the spot where the vessel was dashed against the rocks. People said she seemed to be talking to the waves.

"Poor woman! You asked what had become of her. When she was here last, at the time you said she talked about her being a spirit, I saw she was so crazy that it would not do to let her walk the streets any more. She was worse then than I had ever seen her before. I had her taken to the alms-house, and told the keeper that he must take good care of her, and be very kind to her. Poor woman! She soon become so much deranged, that it was necessary to confine her in her cell, and to bind her with chains to keep her from taking her life.

"She did not live long after she went to the alms-house. She died, raving about the cruel ocean that destroyed her sailor-boy. I visited her cell while she was confined there to see if she was as comfortable as anybody could make her; and I saw on the walls of her room the picture of a ship. The keeper said she had drawn this vessel with her own hand, and that she used often to look at it, and talk as if she saw a man on board of it. Poor Ann! She will suffer no more in this world. She has left us, for a better land."

"Dear father," said Margaret after she had heard the story, "I shall never laugh and make fun of a crazy person any more."

"That's a dear child," said Mr. Standish.

"And I will go right up stairs, and find Eddy, and tell him how Ann became crazy and he will tell all the boys at school; and I don't think any of them will make sport of crazy folks again."

"I hope not," said her father. "It is very wrong, as well as foolish, to do so. People who have lost their reason deserve our pity. They cannot help what they say and what they do. It is a dreadful thing to be a maniac."

Source: Accessed at http://www.disabilitymuseum.org/lib/docs/789.htm, Disability History Museum, http://www.disabilitymuseum.org (January 18, 2005).

3. Dorothea Dix's Petition

The greatest nineteenth-century advocate for humane treatment of mentally ill persons was Dorothea Dix, who traveled the country ascertaining conditions, then presenting her findings to state legislatures and finally the U.S. Congress. Since a woman herself could not address Congress, her "memorials" were delivered for her by like-minded gentlemen, such as Samuel Gridley Howe. Her successful petition for a grant of public land "for the establishment of an asylum for the indigent curable and incurable in the United States," presented by "Mr. Pearce," described the horrible conditions she had observed, traveling over 60,000 miles during "eight years of sad, patient, deliberate investigation."

I have myself seen *more than nine thousand idiots, epileptics, and insane in these United States, destitute of appropriate care and protection;* and of this vast and most miserable company, sought out in *jails,* in *poorhouses,* and in *private dwellings,* there have been hundreds, nay, rather thousands, bound with galling chains, bowed beneath fetters and heavy iron balls, attached to drag-chains, lacerated with ropes, scourged with rod, and terrified beneath storms of profane execrations and cruel blows; now subject to gibes and scorn, and torturing tricks, now abandoned to the most loathsome necessities or subject to the vilest and most outrageous violations. These are strong terms, but language fails to convey the astounding truths. . . .

I pass by without detail nearly *one hundred* examples of insane men and women, in *filthy cells, chained and hobbled,* together with many idiots and epileptics wandering abroad. Some were confined in low, damp, dark cellars; some wasted their wretched existence in dreary dungeons, deserted and neglected. It would be fruitless to attempt describing the sufferings of these unhappy beings for a day even. What must be the accumulation of the pains and woes of years, consigned to prisons and poor-houses, to cells and dungeons, enduring every variety of privation—helpless, deserted of kindred, tortured by fearful delusions, and suffering indescribable pains and abuses. These are no tales of fiction. I believe that there is no imaginable form or severity, of cruelty, of neglect, of every sort of ill management for mind and body, to which I have not seen the insane subject in all our country, excepting the three sections already defined [i.e., North Carolina, Florida, and Texas, the only states she hadn't yet visited]. As a general rule, *ignorance* procures the largest measure of these shocking results; but, while of late years much is accomplished, and more is proposed, by far the largest part of those who suffer remain unrelieved, and must do so, except the General Government unites to assist the several states in this work.

Source: Publication source: *The Congressional Globe,* June 25, 1850, Library of Congress, accessible at http://www.disabilitymuseum.org/lib/docs/1219.htm, paragraphs 4, 5, and 7, Disability History Museum, www.disabilitymuseum.org (January 18, 2005).

4. Public Lands for the Indigent Insane

The cause led by Dorothea Dix gained public support, as the extent of need was made known.

The Insane and Idiotic

The bill now in the hands of the President, donating public lands for the support of the Indigent Insane, and whose fate at his hands has been much speculated about, concerns more people of these States than is generally supposed. According to the late Census there were in the United States 15,768 insane and 15,706 idiotic, total 31,474. How many of these are indigent we cannot guess—doubtless a large portion of them, however. New York had 2,580 insane and 1,739 idiotic; Massachusetts, 1,647 insane and 1,791 idiotic; Pennsylvania, 1,891 insane and 1,448 idiotic; Ohio, 1,352 insane and 1,399 idiotic; Virginia, 1,026 insane and 1,285 idiotic; Indiana, 579 insane and 919 idiotic. The looseness with which these terms are used, however, being held convertible in many quarters, renders the comparative numbers returned as "crazed" and "idiots" entirely untrustworthy. And the unwillingness of fond friends to admit to the Census-taker any member of their family or household under either class, would very greatly diminish the number as returned by the Marshals, from the actual number.

And yet faulty as the tables doubtless are, the insane and idiotic in our country, as returned by the Census, is little short of the whole population of the City of Lowell, only a third less than the population of Washington, a half more than that of Williamsburg, and nearly as great as that of Columbus and Cleveland united. Multiply their number by three, and you have more than the population of California.

As to their distribution among the States, though the populations of

Maine and Maryland are nearly alike, in the former the number of insane and idiotic is ten per cent. more than in the latter. The population of Massachusetts in 1850 was 994,000, of Georgia 906,000; but the insane and idiotic of Massachusetts numbered 2,438, of Georgia only 883. Who will expound the reason? One, however, is patent enough. In Massachusetts great pains are taken to gather such into asylums for their relief, and in these asylums none are omitted by the recording Marshalls. In another State where most of this unfortunate class are scattered among their friends—not even so generally gathered into poor-houses—many must be overlooked in the registration.

Whatever shall be the fate of the bill before alluded to, and which now for five years that indefatigable friend of these unfortunates, Miss Dix, has most faithfully labored with Congress to make a law, their large number and evident wants forbid us to leave them uncared for. Almost every State,—thanks to the philanthropy which she more than any score of others has directed and developed,—has its asylum for their relief. It is barbarously cruel to treat them as they *were* treated, like felons, chained in dungeons and confined in jails;—it deprives them of all expectation of care, gathering them into poor-houses—the feeble-minded, the imbecile, the raving, the broken-down debauchee, and the honestly, soberly poor, in common rooms on a common fare, and treated, sick and sound, able and weak, alike. The Insane need asylums apart from all others, where they may be classified as the nature of their malady demands. The idiotic need to be gathered into refuges where faithful instruction may shed such light as is possible over their dull paths. What humanity demands for their relief, the comfort and safety of the sane and the sound are equally clamorous for.

Source: Article 4—No Title, *New York Times (1851–1857);* April 25, 1854; ProQuest Historical Newspapers the *New York Times* (1851–2001) p. 4.

5. "On the Causes of Insanity"

Dr. Pliny Earle reported an analysis of 1,186 patients, summarized in "On the Causes of Insanity, published in American Journal of Insanity *(January 1848). The most frequent causes found were "pecuniary difficulties" (133), "intemperance" (117)—both much more frequent in males—"religious excitement, &c," parturition (childbirth-related; 66) and "domestic trouble" (65). Along with masturbation (37, all male), "death of relatives" (43), and "disappointed affection" (38), Dr. Earle also reported a few cases caused by "novel reading," "dealing in lottery tickets," and "ungoverned passions" among the 63 "physical" and 24 "moral" causes of insanity.*

During the prevalence of an epidemic, the fatality of the disease is greatly augmented by the panic which seizes upon the mass of the community, the depressing influence of which upon the energies, both physical and mental, prepares the way for an easy invasion of the disease. This influence may also affect the healthy action of the mind. Thus, of the nineteen cases alleged to have been produced by the cause in question, two are attributed to fear of the Asiatic cholera.

. . . if a proper equilibrium be maintained between the physical powers and the intellectual faculties, the development and energies of other portions of the body being so promoted and sustained by exercise, that they may preserve their due relations with an enlarging brain, there need be no fear that mental alienation will result from application to study, but unless this precaution be taken, the midnight oil consumed by the student as a beacon light to guide him towards the temple of fame, may become an ignis fatuus leading his mind into the labyrinth of insanity. Even in persons of strong constitution, and of great physical strength, severe and prolonged study exhausts the nervous energy and impairs the functions of the brain. How much greater must be these effects in a frame naturally delicate, and how much more alarming still if the body be debilitated by want of exercise!

In the table of causes, thirty cases are set down as supposed to have been induced by mental application.

Of the two cases placed against the term, "mental shock," one is represented to have been produced by the hearing of good news.

Domestic trouble ranks high among the moral causes. It includes forty-two men, and twenty-three women; a total of sixty-five.

Under the general and somewhat indefinite term "anxiety," there are twenty-two cases, twelve of men, and ten of women. In two of the men the anxiety was on account of a false accusation of seduction, and in five others it was in reference to annoying lawsuits in which they were engaged.

Eight cases are attributed to faulty education and parental indulgence. These are subjects which, during the past few years, have been fully discussed by several able writers on insanity, and hence require no extended comments on the present occasion. Sympathising deeply as we do in the feelings of the young, and entertaining a pleasing and affectionate emotion for all that cross our path who as yet treat but the vestibule of the temple of life, and ardently wishing to promote, by every judicious measure, their welfare, yet we must, and even for those very reasons, subscribe to the doctrine of the prophet of olden time, "It is good for a man that he bear the yoke in his youth." Let not that yoke, however, be placed upon them with despotic hands, but with that prudent combination of kindness and firmness which will render its burden light.

Three cases are attributed to undue indulgence in the reading of novels. Inasmuch as this subject has heretofore often claimed, and undoubtedly will continue to receive the attention of men who "stand in wisdom's sacred stole," we dismiss it without comment.

Source: The document can be accessed at http://disabilitymuseum.org/lib/docs/ 1368.htm, paragraphs 38–40 and 88–96, Disability History Museum, www.dis abilitymuseum.org (January 20, 2005).

6. *Life at the Texas State Lunatic Asylum*

The following paragraph is taken from a publisher's website announcing the publication of Life at the Texas State Lunatic Asylum, 1857–1997, *by Sarah C. Sitton.*

For more than a century, the asylum community resembled a self-sufficient village complete with its own blacksmith shop, icehouse, movie theater, brass band, baseball team, and undertakers. Beautifully landscaped ground and gravel lanes attracted locals for Sunday carriage drives. Patients tended livestock, tilled gardens, helped prepare meals, and cleaned wards. Their routines might include weekly dances and religious services, as well as cold tubs, paraldehyde, and electroshock. Employees, from the superintendent on down, lived on the grounds, and their children grew up "with inmates for playmates." While the superintendent exercised almost feudal power, deciding if staff could date or marry, a multigenerational "clan" of several interlinked families controlled its day-to-day operation for decades.

Source: Number Eighty-two: The Centennial Series of the Association of Former Students, Texas A&M University (Texas A&M University Press), http://www.tamu.edu/ upress/BOOKS/1999/sitton.htm (January 14, 2004).

7. *". . . there is something radically wrong about the system"*

At the Annual Conference of Charities and Corrections in 1884, P. H. Laverty, "Principal Keeper New Jersey State Prison," addressed "The Management of Reformatories." He described the undesirability of intermixing young offenders with hardened criminals, as well as the problem of recidivism when juveniles receive easy treatment in reformatories. His proposed solutions to this perennial problem were harsh.

The present arrangements of allowing inmates of jails to associate unrestrainedly, without regard to age, sex, or class, is demoralizing in the extreme. Separate apartments should be provided for women and children. Strict discipline should always be enforced. Three or six months of solitary confinement behind grated doors would destroy the social charm that the jail now possesses for the youthful criminal. I have seen from one to two hundred men and boys, ranging from ten to sixty years of age, allowed to spend the entire day outside of their cells, ostensibly for exercise, but virtually to enjoy themselves as they saw fit: card playing, telling obscene stories, learning and singing ribald songs, unrestricted intercourse of old men steeped in vice and crime with youth taking their first lessons in a life of vice and sin.

Where does the remedy lie? In a separation of these criminals. Confine them to their cells. Permit them to exercise, but under restraint. Teach them that criminal life is not a pleasant one. Separate the old criminals from the young. Throw every influence possible around the young, to induce them to become honorable and useful members of society. . . .

. . . what reason is there for any person to speak disparagingly of these reformatories? . . . In my capacity of sheriff, I have handled boys whom I have known from infancy. Through some slight infringement of the law, they were incarcerated in jail. After a residence there of several days, during which time they sipped heavy draughts from the cup of "happiness" which I have described as surrounding the jails, they were released. They looked up their companions, and regaled them with the "wit and wisdom" they learned during their short sojourn in the jail, and presently became the hero of a large aggregation of boys; and, because of the distinction of having been in the "lock-up," they led the "gang" in any mischief upon which they were bent. Within a short time, they were again in jail. As sheriff, I took many such boys to the Reform School. On my assuming charge of the New Jersey State prison, I was astonished, while personally interviewing the convicts, to find so many who were acquainted with me. . . .

The total number of former inmates of the New Jersey Reform School now serving their time in the New Jersey State prison is sixty-three; formerly in the House of Refuge, Philadelphia, eleven; formerly at the Elmira Reformatory, five; formerly in Baltimore Industrial School, two; formerly on Randall's Island House of Correction, New York, two; and three from other reformatories. . . . Now, when we consider that the percentage of convict graduates of the reformatories is more than ten per cent. of the entire population of a prison, we are forced to admit that there is something radically wrong about the system.

Then shall we advocate the abolition of reformatories? No: conduct them on a different principle. Instead of treating the inmates as inhabitants of a charitable institution, compel them to observe rules established on the basis of a penal institution. With vigorous treatment, they are more apt to learn the benefits that will accrue from following the path of rectitude; and the experience that will be theirs, should they continue in their downward career, will be similar to that which they there endure.

Source: Proceedings, "Reformatories and Houses of Refuge" (pp. 87–91).

8. Report for the Vermont State Board of Charities

Many states commissioned surveys to ascertain the extent and nature of needs for services to dependent children. The following excerpts are taken from a report by W. H. Jeffery for the Vermont State Board of Charities.

A dependent or neglected child is a child who needs food, clothing, shelter, kindly treatment; in short, a home, whose only offense is that it is not living in proper surroundings and tender conditions calculated to give it a fair chance. The delinquent child is that child, who either from neglect or heredity, has committed an offense against the law, a child who is incorrigible, who steals, who breaks into buildings, destroys property, or in any way commits an offense, is upon being found guilty adjudged by the juvenile court a delinquent child. . . .

The following is a brief summary of the child care work of the board during its first year:

Children placed in temporary or permanent home   61

Children sent to State Industrial School at Vergennes   25

Homes investigated involving children   279

Children in homes investigated   1,395

Children committed to Board of Charities and Probation   32

Sent to State School for Feeble-Minded   8

Survey made of all poor in all cities and towns in Vermont:

Children sent to hospitals   21

Defective, dependent child cases investigated   65

Dependent boys sent to Vail School   2

Poorhouses inspected   68

Children placed on probation   5

Children removed from three homes where parents were infected with venereal disease   5

"Baby Farms" found and investigated   2

Orphanage involving 60 children investigated

During the last few months many additional cases of defective children have been investigated and treated. . . .

How shall Vermont care for its dependent, defective, defective dependent, feeble-minded, and delinquent children? Nature has decreed that the child should live in the home of its father and mother, where it can have individualized care; where its peculiarities can be studied; its wants ministered to and trained into normal citizenship. When the child, either by death,

misfortune or other cause, is deprived of its natural home, then it should
be cared for as nearly like the home as is possible, namely in the foster
home. A home that has been selected, inspected and licensed by this board;
a home that is under supervision and inspection at all hours of the day or
night, by the visitors of this board. This, I believe, is the best solution for
the normal dependent child. The defective dependent child, whether that
defect be mental or physical must, so far as possible, be treated for that
defect. If incurable, it and the delinquent child must be cared for institu-
tionally. . . .

Mr. Van Patten inquired: Can we not prevent the sending of dependent
children to the Vergennes Industrial School which was established as a
school for delinquents?

Mr. Jeffrey stated that in the average case the court does not distinguish
carefully between delinquents and dependents; that he knows of numerous
instances in which dependent or neglected children have been committed
as delinquents.

C. W. Wilson, Superintendent of the Vermont Industrial School replied: I
do not believe in sending the dependent child to Vergennes. But it should
be known that the children committed to us are largely recruited from
delinquent families. So our "dependents" are about the same type as our
"delinquents." This, however, is not necessarily true of dependent children
at large in the state.

Source: The original document, published in the *Proceedings of the Fourth Annual
Vermont Conference of Social Work*, January 15–16, 1919, pp. 7–12, is located at University of Vermont, Special Collections, http://chipmunk.uvm.edu:6336/dyna
web/eugenics/orwjvcs011519.

9. "The Report of the Committee on Admitting and Placing Children"

*This report on the children of Beech Brook (formerly the Cleveland Protestant Orphan
Asylum) in 1919 reflects some of the effects of war on children and families, and
reveals optimism concerning "difficult" children, several of whom were reported as
successful married adults, some serving in the military service.*

The War has created conditions never before thought possible and daily
brings to our attention the conversion of the domestic mother from home
duties to the highly remunerative industrial positions.

   . . . The need must indeed be imperative before we sanction the breaking up of the home with the consequent placement of the children in the
asylum and the household goods in storage, and we know from experience,
that once separated they are difficult of reestablishment.

   During the past year we have cared for two hundred and ninety-six children. Of these eighty-five have been placed in foster homes, one hundred and thirty-two returned to friends, and seventy-nine were with us at the beginning of the new year. Of those two hundred and ninety-six much could be written. From little Robert, who was left on our doorstep when five weeks of age, to the eleven year old girl deserted by a heartless father, their histories rival the most imaginative tales of fiction. Some come to us in the happy innocence of childhood; others enter our door with an intimate knowledge of all that is degrading, but when their confidence is gained and the errors of their ways kindly but firmly corrected, they invariably respond mentally and physically. Of course, there are children whose mental caliber is so low as to make perilous their mingling with others, and this class compels special arrangements for their care.

The average person thinks little about the problems of childhood. People imagine that the child's life is care free and a perfect elysium of delight. Their own childhood is forgotten in the strenuous business of making a living, and altho they are cognizant of their own troubles, they regard the child's problems as immaterial and something to laugh about. They do not seriously consider their offspring's protests against this and that condition and the child ofttimes attains his midteens before his parents realize they greatly misunderstood him, and their egoism slumps in proportion to their degree of awakening. The work of the Juvenile Court is largely augmented by misunderstood children and unthinking parents.

Every child placed under our care is studied. Sometimes we are saved much time and work by having the true history and character of the child made known to us at the time of his admission, but generally it is left to us to discover any extraordinary traits of personality, and the more unusual they are the less inclination there is on the part of the one who is responsible for him, to faithfully describe his faults before we take him under our care. There are no set rules for the government of all children. There are no dispositions alike and that means individual methods. We think that we know a child perfectly, then some trait will assert itself and cause a change in the training. . . .

All organizations that have the responsibility of caring for children come in contact with what might be termed the difficult or unusual child. We also have the feeble minded, but they are understood because we know what is in the future for them, but the difficult child we do not know, and it takes patience and perseverance, both spelled with a capital, to guide these children as they grow older. We never know when they are going to fall from grace, and for that reason a constant vigilance is required in such cases. Our experience with the majority of these so called difficult children is, if they are carried over a certain period, they become our best men and women and the results are most encouraging. . . .

The dependent difficult child has imagination, a disregard for rule and convention, and excess of spirit and is generally capable of a certain amount of leadership and influence. Because he is more or less of a disturber he is passed from one organization to another until someone with vision sees his possibilities. The world is full of him. In later years his individuality marks him as extraordinary and his name is given prominence in the list of good citizens or on the police blotters, the status, in large measure, being established by the thoroughness of his early training. For him there seems to be no middle course.

Source: Ms. Collection No. 4544, Beech Brook, Western Reserve Historical Society, 10825 East Blvd., Cleveland, OH 44106.

III Bibliography and Resources for Inquiry

I. A SAMPLING OF SELF-NARRATIVES BY PERSONS WITH DISABILITIES

Beers, C. W. (1908). *A Mind That Found Itself: An Autobiography.* New York: Doubleday.

Brown, C. (1955). *My Left Foot.* New York: Simon & Schuster.

Cutsforth, T. D. (1933). *The Blind in School and Society: A Psychological Study.* New York and London: D. Appleton and Company. (The author frames this scholarly treatment in part in terms of his own experiences as a graduate of a residential school for the blind.)

Grandin, T. (1990). Needs of High Functioning Teenagers and Adults with Autism. *Focus on Autistic Behavior* 5(1), 1–16.

———. (1992). An Inside View of Autism. In E. Schopler and G. B. Mesibov, eds., *High-functioning Individuals with Autism* (pp. 105–126). New York: Plenum Press.

———, & Scariano, M. (1986). *Emergence: Labeled Autistic.* Novato, CA: Arena Press.

Irwin, Robert B. (1955). *As I Saw It.* New York: American Foundation for the Blind.

Kaysen, S. (1993). *Girl, Interrupted.* New York: Random House/Vintage Books.

Keller, H. (1955). *Teacher: Anne Sullivan Macy.* New York: Pyramid.

———. (1974). *My Religion.* New York: Pyramid.

———. (1976). *The Story of My Life.* New York: Andor.

Kingsley, J., & Levitz, M. (1994). *Count Us In: Growing Up with Down Syndrome.* New York: Harcourt Brace Jovanovich.

Scott, R. A. (1969). *The Making of Blind Men: A Study of Adult Socialization.* New York: Russell Sage Foundation.

Williams, D. (1992). *Nobody Nowhere: The Extraordinary Biography of An Autistic.* New York: Avon Books.

———. (1994). *Somebody Somewhere: Breaking Free from the World of Autism.* New York: Random House/Times Books.

II. A SAMPLING OF NARRATIVES ABOUT PERSONS WITH DISABILITIES

Biklen, D., & Duchan, J. F. (1994). "I Am Intelligent": The Social Construction of Mental Retardation. *Journal of the Association for Persons with Severe Handicaps* 19(3), 173–184.

Bogdan, R., & Taylor, S. (1976). The Judged, Not the Judges: An Insider's View of Mental Retardation. *American Psychologist* 31, 47–52.

Bogdan, R., & Taylor, S. J. (1994). *The Social Meaning of Mental Retardation: Two Life Stories.* New York: Teachers College Press.

Buck, P. S. (1950). *The Child Who Never Grew.* New York: The John Day Company.

Curtiss, S. (1977). *Genie: A Psycholinguistic Study of a Modern-day "Wild Child."* New York: Academic Press.

Dorris, M. (1989). *The Broken Cord.* New York: Harper & Row.

Ferguson, P. M., Ferguson, D. L., & Taylor, S. J., eds. (1992). *Interpreting Disability: A Qualitative Reader*. New York: Teachers College Press.

Fischer, R., & Lane, H., eds. (1993). *Looking Back: A Reader on the History of Deaf Communities and Their Sign Languages*. (International Studies on Sign Language and Communication of the Deaf, Volume 20.) Hamburg, Germany: Signum.

Freeberg, E. (2001). *The Education of Laura Bridgman: The First Deaf and Blind Person to Learn Language*. Cambridge, MA: Harvard University Press.

Goode, D. (1994). *A World Without Words: The Social Construction of Children Born Deaf and Blind*. Philadelphia: Temple University Press.

Greenfeld, J. (1986). *A Client Called Noah*. New York: Henry Holt and Company. (Greenfeld had written two previous accounts of the experiences of a family with a child with severe developmental disabilities: *A child called Noah* and *A place for Noah*.)

Groce, N. E. (1992). "The Town Fool": An Oral History of a Mentally Retarded Individual in Small Town Society. In P. M. Ferguson, D. L. Ferguson, & S. J. Taylor, eds., *Interpreting Disability: A Qualitative Reader* (pp. 175–196). New York: Teachers College Press.

Howe, M., & Hall, F. H. (1903). *Laura Bridgman—Dr. Howe's Famous Pupil and What He Taught Her*. Boston: Little, Brown.

Lamson, M. S. (1881). *Life and Education of Laura Dewey Bridgman: The Deaf, Dumb, and Blind Girl*. Boston: New England Publishing.

Lane, H. (1976). *The Wild Boy of Aveyron*. Cambridge, MA: Harvard University Press.

———, ed. (1984b). *The Deaf Experience: Classics in Language and Education*. Trans. F. Philips. Cambridge, MA: Harvard University Press.

Langness, L. L., & Levine, H. G., eds. (1986). *Culture and Retardation: Life Histories of Mildly Mentally Retarded Persons in American Society*. Boston: D. F. Reidel.

Lash, J. P. (1980). *Helen and Teacher: The Story of Helen Keller and Anne Sullivan Macy*. New York: Dell.

Longmore, P. K., & Umansky, L., eds. (2001). *The New Disability History: American Perspectives*. New York and London: New York University Press.

Massie, R., & Massie, S. (1975). *Journey*. New York: Alfred A. Knopf.

Matson, V. F. (1974). *A School for Peter*. Carol Stream, IL: Creation House.

Rymer, R. (1992). *Genie: An Abused Child's Flight from Silence*. New York: Harper-Collins.

Sacks, O. (1995). *An Anthropologist on Mars: Seven Paradoxical Tales*. New York: Alfred A. Knopf. (The title of this collection of accounts of gifted individuals with significant disabilities was suggested by a phrase used by Temple Grandin, Ph.D., a renowned scientist who has autism, to describe her social perceptions.)

Waite, H. E. (1961). *Make a Joyful Sound: The Romance of Mabel Hubbard and Alexander Graham Bell*. Philadelphia: Macrae Smith Company.

III. A SAMPLING OF LITERARY SOURCES CONCERNING PERSONS WITH DISABILITIES

Bower, E. M., ed. (1980). *The Handicapped in Literature: A Psychosocial Perspective.* Denver and London: Love Publishing.

Greenberg, J. (1964). *I Never Promised You a Rose Garden.* New York: Alfred A. Knopf.

Keyes, D. (1966). *Flowers for Algernon.* New York: Harcourt, Brace and World.

Landau, E. D., Epstein, S. L., & Stone, A. P., eds. (1978). *The Exceptional Child Through Literature.* Englewood Cliffs, NJ: Prentice-Hall.

Long, N., Morse, W., & Newman, R. (1971). *Conflict in the Classroom* (2nd ed.). Part I: How It Feels to Be Emotionally Disturbed (pp. 3–126). Belmont, CA: Wadsworth.

Mann, T. (1927). *The Magic Mountain.* Trans. H. T. Lowe-Porter. Garden City, NY: International Collectors Library.

Maugham, W. S. (1915). *Of Human Bondage.* New York: G. H. Doran.

McCullers, C. (1940). *The Heart Is a Lonely Hunter.* New York: Houghton Mifflin.

Rubin, T. I. (1961). *David and Lisa.* London: Macmillan.

Sheed, W. (1973). *People Will Always Be Kind.* New York: Farrar, Straus & Giroux.

Thurer, S. (1980). Disability and Monstrosity: A Look at Literary Distortions of Handicapping Conditions. *Rehabilitation Literature* 41, 12–15.

Wells, H. G. (1910). *The Country of the Blind.* London: Nelson.

IV. NARRATIVES ABOUT NONDISABLED AMERICANS IMPORTANT IN THE HISTORY OF PERSONS WITH DISABILITIES

Adams, M. E. (1927). Sarah Fuller. *American Annals of the Deaf* 72, 432–436.

Ball, T. S. (1971). *Itard, Seguin, and Kephart: Sensory Education—A Learning Interpretation.* Columbus, OH: Merrill.

Berry, M. F. (1965). Historical Vignettes of Leadership in Speech and Hearing: III. Stuttering. *Journal of the American Speech and Hearing Association* 7(3), 78–79.

Boatner, M. T. (1959). *Voice of the Deaf: A Biography of Edward Miner Gallaudet.* Washington, DC: Public Affairs Press.

Breunig, H. L. (1990). The Legacy of Dr. Bell. *Volta Review* 92(4), 84–96.

Bruce, R. V. (1973). *Alexander Graham Bell and the Conquest of Solitude.* Boston: Little, Brown.

Coss, C., ed. (1989). *Lillian D. Wald: Progressive Activist.* New York: Feminist Press at The City University of New York.

Davis, A. F. (1973). *American Heroine: The Life and Legend of Jane Addams.* New York: Oxford University Press.

Fennimore, K. J. (1988). *Faith Made Visible: The History of Floyd Starr & His School.* Albion, MI: Starr Commonwealth.

Frazier, J. (1974). America's "Turbulent Spirit": Dr. Benjamin Rush. *American History* 9(7), 20–31.

Gallaudet, E. M. (1888). *Life of Thomas Hopkins Gallaudet.* New York: Henry Holt.

Gardiner, R. A. (1958). Alfred A. Strauss, 1897–1957. *Exceptional Children* 24, 373–375.

Gibson, W. (1957). *The Miracle Worker: A Play for Television.* New York: Knopf.

Hawke, D. (1971). *Benjamin Rush.* New York: Bobbs-Merrill.

Kramer, R. (1976). *Maria Montessori: A Biography.* New York: G. P. Putnam's Sons.

Mackenzie, C. (1928). *Alexander Graham Bell: The Man Who Contracted Space.* New York: Grosset & Dunlap.

Marshall, H. E. (1937). *Dorothea Dix, Forgotten Samaritan.* Chapel Hill: University of North Carolina Press.

Meltzer, M. (1964). *A Light in the Dark: The Life of Samuel Gridley Howe.* New York: Crowell.

Richards, L. E. (1909). *Letters and Journals of Samuel Gridley Howe, the Servant of Humanity* (2 vols.). Boston: Dana Estes.

———. (1935). *Samuel Gridley Howe.* New York: Appleton-Century.

Schwartz, H. (1956). *Samuel Gridley Howe, Social Reformer 1801–1876.* Cambridge, MA: Harvard University Press.

Stickney, W., ed. (1872). *Autobiography of Amos Kendall.* Boston: Lee & Shepard.

Talbot, M. E. (1964). *Edouard Seguin: A Study of an Educational Approach to the Treatment of Mentally Defective Children.* New York: Teachers College Press.

Taylor, H. (1933). Caroline Ardelia Yale. *Volta Review* 35, 415–417.

Wilson, D. C. (1975). *Stranger and Traveler: The Story of Dorothea Dix, American Reformer.* Boston and Toronto: Little, Brown.

Zimmerman, D. P. (1991). The Clinical Thought of Bruno Bettelheim: A Critical Historical Review. *Psychoanalysis and Contemporary Thought* 14(4), 685–721.

V. SOURCES OF HISTORICAL INFORMATION ABOUT CHILDREN WITH DISABILITIES IN AMERICA

General: A Sampling of Historical Issues Affecting American Children with Disabilities

Aiello, B. (1972). *Exceptional Child Education at the Bicentennial: A Parade of Progress.* Reston, VA: Council for Exceptional Children.

Black, E. (2003). *War Against the Weak: Eugenics and America's Campaign to Create a Master Race.* New York: Thunder's Mouth Press.

Bogdan, R., & Knoll, J. (1988). The Sociology of Disability. In E. L. Meyen & T. M. Skrtic, eds., *Exceptional Children and Youth: An Introduction* (pp. 449–477). Denver: Love Publishing.

Connor, F. P. (1976). The Past Is Prologue: Teacher Preparation in Special Education. *Exceptional Children* 42, 366–378.

Dybwad, G., & Bersani, H., Jr., eds. (1996). *New Voices: Self-advocacy by People with Disabilities.* Cambridge, MA: Brookline Books.

Frampton, M. E., & Powell, H. G. (1938). *Education of the Handicapped, v. I: History.* Yonkers-on-Hudson, NY: World Book Company.

Gallagher, J. J., & Vietze, P. M. (1986). *Families of Handicapped Persons: Research, Programs, and Policy Issues.* Baltimore: Paul H. Brookes.

Goffman, E. (1963). *Stigma: Notes on the Management of Spoiled Identity.* Englewood Cliffs, NJ: Prentice-Hall, Inc.

Gould, S. J. (1981). *The Mismeasure of Man.* New York: W. W. Norton.

Guralnick, M. J., ed. (1997). *The Effectiveness of Early Intervention.* Baltimore: Paul H. Brookes.

Hobbs, N., ed. (1975). *Issues in the Classification of Children* (vols. I and II). San Francisco: Jossey-Bass.

Jordan, D. S. (1908). Report of the Committee on Eugenics. *American Breeders Association* 4, 201–208.

Kevles, D. J. (1984). Annals of Eugenics (I–IV) *New Yorker* 60, October 8 (51–52), 15 (52–54ff.), 22 (92–110ff.), 29 (51–52ff.).

———. (1985). *In the Name of Eugenics: Genetics and the Uses of Human Heredity.* New York: Alfred A. Knopf.

Lipsky, D. K., & Gartner, A. (1997). *Inclusion and School Reform.* Baltimore: Paul H. Brookes.

Martens, E. H. (1932). Parents' Problems with Exceptional Children. Office of Education, Pamphlet no. 14. Washington, DC: U.S. Government Printing Office.

———. (1934). Teachers' Problems with Exceptional Children, III: Mentally Retarded Children. Office of Education, Pamphlet no. 49. Washington, DC: U.S. Government Printing Office.

Powell, T. H., Aiken, J. M., & Smylie, M. A. (1982). Treatment of Involuntary Euthanasia for Severely Handicapped Newborns: Issues of Philosophy and Public Policy. *Journal of the Association for Persons with Severe Handicaps* 6, 3–10.

Remedial and Special Education (Special Issue: History of Special Education) 19(4) (July–August).

Reynolds, M. C., Wang, M., & Walberg, H. (1987). The Necessary Restructuring of Special and Regular Education. *Exceptional Children* 53, 391–398.

Rogers, L. J., & Swadener, B. B., eds. (2001). *Semiotics and Disability: Interrogating Categories of Difference.* Albany, NY: State University of New York Press.

Safford, P. L., & Safford, E. J. (1996). *A History of Childhood and Disability.* New York: Teachers College Press.

Shonkoff, J. P., & Meisels, S. J., eds. (2000). *Handbook of Early Childhood Intervention* (2nd ed.). Cambridge, UK: Cambridge University Press.

Skirtic, T. M. (1991). *Behind Special Education: A Critical Analysis of Professional Culture and School Organization.* Denver: Love Publishing.

Stainback, W., & Stainback, S. (1996). *Controversial Issues Confronting Special Education: Divergent Perspectives* (2nd ed.). Boston: Allyn and Bacon.

Turnbull, H. R., & Turnbull, A. P. (1985). *Parents Speak Out: Then and Now*. Columbus, OH: Merrill.

Wallin, J.E.W. (1924). *The Education of Handicapped Children*. Boston: Houghton Mifflin.

———. (1955). *Education of Mentally Handicapped Children*. New York: Harper & Brothers.

Warner, M. L. (1944). Founders of the International Council for Exceptional Children. *Journal of Exceptional Children* 10, 217–223.

Washington Research Project (1974). *Children Out of School in America*. Washington, DC: Children's Defense Fund.

Winzer, M. A. (1993). *The History of Special Education: From Isolation to Integration*. Washington, DC: Gallaudet University Press.

Ysseldyke, J., & Algozzine, B. (1982). *Critical Issues in Special and Remedial Education*. Boston: Houghton Mifflin.

Deafness and Deaf Culture

Baynton, D. (1996). *Forbidden Signs: American Culture and the Campaign Against Sign Language*. Chicago: University of Chicago Press.

Bell, A. G. (1883). *Memoir Upon the Formation of a Deaf Variety of the Human Race*. New Haven, CT: National Academy of Science.

Bender, R. (1970). *The Conquest of Deafness: A History of the Long Struggle to Make Normal Living Possible for Those Handicapped By Lack of Normal Hearing*. Cleveland, OH: Case Western Reserve University Press.

Brill, R. G. (1984). *International Congresses on Education of the Deaf: An Analytical History, 1878–1980*. Washington, DC: Gallaudet College Press.

Burch, S. (2002). *Signs of Resistance: American Deaf Cultural History, 1900 to 1942*. New York: New York University Press.

Connor, L. P. (1992). *The History of the Lexington School for the Deaf (1864–1985)*. New York: Lexington School for the Deaf.

Crouch, B. A. (1986). Alienation and the Mid-nineteenth Century American Deaf Community: A Response. *American Annals of the Deaf* 131(5), 322–324.

Fay, E. A. (1898). *Marriages of the Deaf in America*. Washington, DC: Gibson Brothers.

———, ed. (1893). *Histories of American Schools for the Deaf*. Washington, DC: Volta Bureau.

Gallaudet, E. M. (1883). *History of the College for the Deaf, 1857–1907*. Washington, DC: Gallaudet College Press.

Gallaudet, T. H. (1817). A Sermon Delivered at the Opening of the Connecticut Asylum for the Education and Instruction of Deaf and Dumb Persons. Hartford, CT: pp. 6–8.

Gannon, J. R. (1981). *Deaf Heritage: A Narrative History of Deaf America*. Silver Spring, MD: National Association of the Deaf.

Groce, N. E. (1985). *Everyone Here Spoke Sign Language: Hereditary Deafness on Martha's Vineyard*. Cambridge, MA: Harvard University Press.

Hairston, E., & Smith, L. (1983). *Black and Deaf in America: Are We That Different?* Silver Springs, MD: TJ Publishers.

Jordan, I., & Karchmer, M. (1986). Patterns of Sign Use Among Hearing-impaired Students. In A. Schildroth & M. Karchmer, eds., *Deaf Children in America* (pp. 125–138). Boston: Little, Brown.

Lane, H. (1984a). *When the Mind Hears: A History of the Deaf.* New York: Random House.

———. (1992). *The Mask of Benevolence: Disabling the Deaf Community.* New York: Alfred A. Knopf.

Padden, C., & Humphries, T. (1988). *Deaf in America: Voices from a Culture.* Cambridge, MA: Harvard University Press.

Reagan, T. (1985). The Deaf as a Linguistic Minority: Educational Considerations. *Harvard Educational Review* 55(3), 265–277.

Sacks, O. (1989). *Seeing Voices: A Journey into the World of the Deaf.* Berkeley: University of California Press.

Stokoe, W. C. (1980). Sign Language Structure. *Annual Review of Anthropology* 9, 365–390.

Van Cleve, J. V., ed. (1993). *Deaf History Unveiled: Interpretations from the New Scholarship.* Washington, DC: Gallaudet University Press.

Van Cleve, J., & Crouch, B. (1989). *A Place of Their Own.* Washington, DC: Gallaudet University Press.

Wright, M. (1999). *Sounds Like Home: Growing up Black and Deaf in the South.* Washington, DC: Gallaudet University Press.

Visual Disability

Anagnos (Anagnostopoulos), M. (1882). *Education of the Blind: Historical Sketch of Its Origin, Rise, and Progress.* Boston: Rand, Avery.

Best, H. (1934). *Blindness and the Blind in the United States.* New York: Macmillan.

Carroll, T. J. (1981). *Blindness: What It Is, What It Does, and How to Live With It.* Boston and Toronto: Little, Brown.

Chevigny, H., & Braverman, S. (1950). *The Adjustment of the Blind.* New Haven: Yale University Press.

Farrell, G. (1956). *The Story of Blindness.* Cambridge, MA: Harvard University Press.

Fraiberg, S. (1977). *Insights from the Blind: Developmental Studies of Blind Children.* New York: Basic Books.

Frampton, M. E. (1940). *Education of the Blind: A Study of Methods of Teaching the Blind.* Yonkers-on-Hudson, NY: The New York Institute for the Education of the Blind.

Frampton, M. E., & Kerney, E. (1953). *The Residential School: Its History, Continuation, and Future.* New York: The New York Institute for the Education of the Blind.

French, R. S. (1932). *From Homer to Helen Keller: A Social and Educational Study of the Blind.* New York: American Foundation for the Blind.

Howe, S. G. (1840). *Eighth Annual Report of the Trustees of the Perkins Institution and Massachusetts Asylum for the Blind.* Boston: John H. Eastburn.

———. (1871). *Proceedings of the Second Convention of American Instructors of the Blind.* Indianapolis: Indianapolis Printing and Publishing House.

Koestler, F. (1976). *The Unseen Minority: A Social History of Blindness in the United States.* New York: David McKay.

Lende, H., ed. (1938). *What of the Blind? A Survey of the Development and Scope of Present-day Work with the Blind.* New York: American Foundation for the Blind.

Lowenfeld, B. (1975). *The Changing Status of the Blind: From Separation to Integration.* Springfield: Charles C. Thomas.

Matson, F. L. (1990). *Walking Alone and Marching Together: A History of the Organized Blind Movement in the United States, 1940–1990.* New York: National Association of the Blind.

Megivern, J. J., & Megivern, M. L. (2003). *People of Vision: A History of the American Council of the Blind.* Bloomington, IN: American Council of the Blind.

Merry, R. V. (1933). *Problems in the Education of Visually Handicapped Children.* Cambridge, MA: Harvard University Press.

Roberts, F. K. (1986). Education for the Visually Handicapped: A Social and Educational History. In G. T. Scholl, ed., *Foundations of Education for Blind and Visually Handicapped Children and Youth: Theory and Practice* (pp. 1–18). New York: American Foundation for the Blind.

Ross, I. (1951). *Journey into Light: The Story of the Education of the Blind.* New York: Appleton-Century-Crofts.

Physical Disabilities and Medical History

Ablon, J. (1984). *The Little People in America: The Social Dimensions of Dwarfism.* New York: Praeger.

Abt, H. E., ed. (1924). *The Care, Cure, and Education of the Crippled Child.* Elyria, OH: The International Society for Crippled Children.

Abt, I. (1965). *Abt-Garrison History of Pediatrics.* Philadelphia and London: W. B. Saunders.

Bates, B. (1992). *Bargaining for Life: A Social History of Tuberculosis, 1876–1938.* Philadelphia: University of Pennsylvania Press.

Bogdan, R. (1988). *Freak Show: Exhibiting Human Oddities for Amusement and Profit.* Chicago: University of Chicago Press.

Cummins, S. L. (1949). *Tuberculosis in History.* Baltimore: Williams & Wilkins.

Dubos, R., & Dubos, H. (1954). *The White Plague: Tuberculosis, Man and Society.* Boston: Little, Brown.

Eberle, L. (1914–1922). The Maimed, the Halt, and the Race. *Hospital Social Service* 6, 59–63.

Holt, L. E., & McIntosh, R. (1933). *Holt's Diseases of Infancy and Childhood* (10th ed.). New York: Appleton-Century.

Kenney, E. (1941). *The Treatment of Infantile Paralysis in the Acute Stage.* Minneapolis: Bruce.

Oliver, M. (1990). *The Politics of Disablement: A Sociological Perspective.* New York: St. Martin's Press.

Paul, J. R. (1971). *A History of Poliomyelitis.* New Haven and London: Yale University Press.

Plank, E. (1962). *Working with Children in Hospitals.* Cleveland, OH: Case Western Reserve University Press.

Reeves, E. (1914). *Care and Education of Crippled Children in the United States.* New York: Russell Sage Foundation.

Rosenberg, C. E. (1987). *The Care of Strangers: The Rise of America's Hospital System.* New York: Basic Books.

Scott, D. (1973). *About Epilepsy.* New York: International Universities Press.

Sontag, S. (1978). *Illness as Metaphor.* New York: Farrar, Straus & Giroux.

Sullivan, J. F. (1921a). Who Are the Unfit? *The Hospital School Journal* 9 (May–June), 3.

———. (1921b). There Should Be No Crippled Beggars. *The Hospital School Journal* 9 (May–June), 11–12.

Teller, M. E. (1988). *The Tuberculosis Movement: A Public Health Campaign in the Progressive Era.* New York: Greenwood Press.

Cognitive Disability

Anderson, M. (1917). *Education of Defectives in the Public Schools.* New York: World Book Co. Press.

Barr, M. W. (1910). *Mental Defectives: Their History, Treatment and Training.* Philadelphia: P. Blackstone's Son & Co.

Binet, A., & Simon, T. (1916). *The Development of Intelligence in Children.* Trans. E. S. Kite. Baltimore: Williams & Wilkins.

Blatt, B. (1981). *In and Out of Mental Retardation: Essays on Educability, Disability, and Human Policy.* Baltimore: University Park Press.

Blatt, B., & Kaplan, F. (1974). *Christmas in Purgatory: A Photographic Essay on Mental Retardation.* Syracuse, NY: Human Policy Press.

Blatt, B., Ozolins, A., & McNally, J. (1979). *The Family Papers: A Return to Purgatory.* New York: Longman.

Doll, E. A. (1962). A Historical Survey of Research and Management of Mental Retardation in the United States. In E. P. Trapp & P. Himmelstein, eds., *Readings on the Exceptional Child: Research and Theory.* New York: Appleton-Century-Crofts.

Dugdale, R. (1877). *The Jukes: A Study in Crime, Pauperism, Disease, and Heredity.* New York: G. P. Putnam.

Dunn, L. M. (1968). Special Education for the Mildly Retarded: Is Much of It Justifiable? *Exceptional Children* 35, 5–22.

Edgerton, R. B. (1967). *The Cloak of Competence: Stigma in the Lives of the Mentally Retarded.* Berkeley: University of California Press.

Estabrook, A. H. (1916). *The Jukes in 1915*. Washington, DC: Carnegie Institute.

Esten, R. A. (1900). Backward Children in Public Schools. *Journal of Psycho-Asthenics* 5, 40–45.

Farrell, E. K. (1908–09). Special Classes in the New York City Schools. *Journal of Psycho-Asthenics* 13, 91–96.

Goddard, H. H. (1912). *The Kallikak Family: A Study of the Heredity of Feeblemindedness*. New York: Macmillan.

Howe, S. G. (1848). Report of Commission to Inquire into the Conditions of Idiots of the Commonwealth of Massachusetts. Boston: Senate Document no. 51.

Kanner, L. (1964). *History of the Care and Treatment of the Mentally Retarded*. Springfield, IL: Charles C. Thomas.

Kerlin, I. N. (1885). Provision for Idiotic and Feeble-minded Children. In I. C. Barrows, ed., *Proceedings of the National Conference of Charities and Corrections at the Eleventh Annual Session* (pp. 246–263). Boston: Georgett Ellis.

———. (1891). *The Manual of Elwyn*. Philadelphia: J. B. Lippincott Co.

Mercer, J. (1973). *Labeling the Mentally Retarded: Clinical and Social System Perspectives on Mental Retardation*. Berkeley: University of California Press.

Noll, S., & Trent, J. W. (2004). *Mental Retardation in America: A Historical Reader*. New York: New York University Press.

Rosen, M., Clark, G. R., & Kivitz, M. S. (1976). *The History of Mental Retardation: Collected Papers*. Baltimore: University Park Press.

Sarason, S. B. (1959). *Psychological Problems in Mental Deficiency* (3rd ed.). New York: Harper & Row.

Sarason, S. B., & Doris, J. (1969). *Psychological Problems in Mental Deficiency* (4th ed.). New York: Harper & Row.

Scheerenberger, R. C. (1983). *A History of Mental Retardation*. Baltimore, MD: Paul H. Brookes.

———. (1987). *A History of Mental Retardation: A Quarter Century of Progress*. Baltimore, MD: Paul H. Brookes.

Seguin, E. (1866–1907). *Idiocy and Its Treatment by the Physiological Method*. New York: Albany-Brandon Printing.

Skeels, H. M. (1941). A Study of the Effects of Differential Stimulation on Mentally Retarded Children: A Follow-up Report. *American Journal of Mental Deficiency* 46, 340–350.

———. (1966). Status of Children with Contrasting Early Life Experiences. *Monographs of the Society for Research in Child Development* 31 (Whole no. 105).

Sloan, W., & Stevens, H. A., eds. (1976). *A Century of Concern: A History of the American Association on Mental Deficiency, 1876–1976*. Washington, DC: AAMD.

Talbot, M. E. (1964). *Edouard Seguin: A Study of an Educational Approach to the Treatment of Mentally Defective Children*. New York: Teachers College Press.

Trent, J. W. (1994). *Inventing the Feeble Mind: A History of Mental Retardation in the United States*. Berkeley: University of California Press.

Tyor, P. L., & Bell, L. V. (1984). *Caring for the Retarded in America: A History*. Westport, CT: Greenwood Press.

White, W. D., & Wolfensberger, W. (1969). The evolution of dehumanization in our institutions. *Mental Retardation* 7, 5–9.

Wolfensberger, W. (1972). *The Principle of Normalization in Human Services.* Toronto: National Institute on Mental Retardation.

———. (1975). *The Origins and Nature of Our Institutional Models.* Syracuse, NY: Human Policy Press.

Speech and Language Impairments

Moore, P., & Kester, D. G. (1958). Historical notes on speech correction in the pre-Association era. *Journal of Speech and Hearing Disorders* 23(1), 48–53.

Newby, H. A. (1965). "Reflections" on Becoming Forty: Presidential Address—1964 national convention. *American Speech and Hearing Association* 7(1), 3–7.

O'Neill, Y. V. (1980). *Speech and Speech Disorders in Western Thought Before 1600.* Westport, CT: Greenwood Press.

Schiefelbusch, R. L. (1984). The Odyssey of a Speech Clinician. In B. Blatt & R. J. Morris, eds., *Perspectives in Special Education: Personal Orientations* (pp. 233–262). Glenview, IL: Scott, Foresman.

Scripture, E. W. (1912). *Stuttering and Lisping.* New York: Macmillan.

West, R. W. (1960). The Association in Historical Perspective. *Journal of the American Speech and Hearing Association* 2(1), 8–11.

Autism Spectrum Disorder

Berkell, D. E., ed. (2002). *Autism: Identification, Education, and Treatment* (2nd ed.). Hillsdale, NJ: Lawrence Erlbaum.

Bettelheim, B. (1967). *The Empty Fortress.* New York: Free Press.

Cohen, D. J., & Volkmar, F. (1997). *Handbook of Autism and Pervasive Developmental Disorders* (2nd ed.). New York: John Wiley & Sons.

Kanner, L. (1943). Autistic Deviations of Affective Contact. *Nervous Child* 2, 217–250.

Rimland, B. (1964). *Infantile Autism.* New York: Appleton-Century-Crofts.

Ritvo, E. R., ed. (1976). *Autism: Diagnosis, Current Research, and Management.* New York: Spectrum.

Sacks, O. (1994). A Neurologist's Notebook: An Anthropologist on Mars. *The New Yorker* 44, 106–125.

Neurological Disabilities and Specific Learning Disabilities

Barkley, R. A. (1990). *Attention Deficit Hyperactivity Disorder: A Handbook for Diagnosis and Treatment.* New York and London: Guilford Press.

Boake, C. (1991). History of Cognitive Rehabilitation Following Head Injury. In J. Kreutzer & P. Wehman, eds., *Cognitive Rehabilitation.* Baltimore: Paul H. Brookes.

Carrier, J. G. (1986). *Learning Disability: Social Class and the Construction of Inequality in American Education*. Westport, CT: Greenwood Press.

Cruickshank, W. M., Bentzen, F., Ratzeberg, F., & Tannhauser, M. A. (1961). *A Teaching Method for Brain-injured and Hyperactive Children*. Syracuse, NY: Syracuse University Press.

Goldstein, K. (1939–1942). *Aftereffects of Brain Injuries in War*. New York: Grune & Stratton.

Kephart, N. C. (1971). *The Slow Learner in the Classroom* (2nd ed.). Columbus, OH: Charles Merrill.

Kessler, J. W. (1980). History of Minimal Brain Dysfunction. In H. Rie & E. Rie, eds., *Handbook of Minimal Brain Dysfunctions: A Critical View* (pp. 18–52). New York: Wiley.

Lipson, M. Y., & Wixson, K. K. (1986). Reading Disability Research: An Interactionist Perspective. *Review of Educational Research* 56(1), 111–136.

Mann, L. (1979). *On the Trail of Process: A Historical Perspective on Cognitive Processes and Their Training*. New York: Grune & Stratton.

Mercer, C. D. (1979). *Children and Adolescents with Learning Disabilities*. Columbus, OH: Charles Merrill.

Monroe, M. (1932). *Children Who Cannot Read*. Chicago: University of Chicago Press.

Morgan, B. S. (1914). *The Backward Child: A Study of the Psychology and Treatment of Backwardness—A Practical Manual for Teachers*. New York and London: G. P. Putnam's Sons.

Orton, T. (1925). Word-blindness in School Children. *Archives of Neurology and Psychiatry* 14, 582–615.

Russell, R. W. (1973). History of ACLD. Unpublished paper, Association for Children with Learning Disabilities.

Schrag, P., & Divoky, D. (1975). *The Myth of the Hyperactive Child*. New York: Pantheon.

Schwartz, K. B. (1992). Occupational Therapy and Education: A Shared Vision. *American Journal of Occupational Therapy* 46(1), 12–18.

Strauss, A. A., & Kephart, N. C. (1955). *Psychopathology and Education of the Brain-injured Child*, vol. 2. New York: Grune & Stratton.

Strauss, A. A., & Lehtinen, L. E. (1947). *Psychopathology and Education of the Brain-injured Child*, vol. 1. New York: Grune & Stratton.

Wiederholt, J. L. (1974). Historical Perspectives on the Education of the Learning Disabled. In L. Mann & D. A. Sabatino, eds., *The Second Review of Special Education* (pp. 103–152). New York: Grune & Stratton.

Mental Illness and the Emotionally Disturbed Child

Aichhorn, A. (1951). *Wayward Youth* (10th ed., orig. pub. 1925). New York: Viking Press.

Alexander, F. G., & Selesnick, S. T. (1966). *The History of Psychiatry: An Evaluation of Psychiatric Thought and Practice from Prehistoric Times to the Present.* New York: Harper & Row.

Altshule, M. D. (1957). *Roots of modern psychiatry.* New York: Grune & Stratton.

Axline, V. M. (1947). *Play Therapy.* Boston: Houghton Mifflin.

Barton, W. E. (1987). *The History and Influence of the American Psychiatric Association.* Washington, DC: American Psychiatric Association Press.

Berkowitz, P. H., & Rothman, E. P. (1960). *The Disturbed Child: Recognition and Psychoeducational Therapy in the Classroom.* New York: New York University Press.

Bower, E. M. (1960). *Early Identification of Emotionally Disturbed Children.* Springfield, IL: Charles C. Thomas.

Bowlby, J. (1945). *Maternal Care and Mental Health,* (2nd ed.), Monograph Series no. 2. Geneva, Switzerland: World Health Organization.

Brigham, A. (1833). Remarks on the Influence of Mental Cultivation and Mental Excitement upon Health. Boston: Marsh, Cappen, & Lyon. In *The Beginnings of Mental Hygiene in America: Three Selected Essays, 1833–1850.* New York: Arno Press, 1973.

———. (1845). Schools in Lunatic Asylums. *American Journal of Insanity* 1, 326–340.

Carlson, E., & Dain, N. (1988). The Psychotherapy That Was Moral Treatment. *American Journal of Psychiatry* 117, 519–524.

Despert, J. L. (1965). *The Emotionally Disturbed Child: Then and Now.* New York: Robert Brunner.

Deutsch, A. (1949). *The Mentally Ill in America: A History of Their Care and Treatment from Colonial Times* (2nd ed.). New York: Columbia University Press.

———. (1950). *Our Rejected Children.* New York: Little, Brown.

Devereux, G. (1956). *Therapeutic Education: Its Theoretical Bases and Practice.* New York: Harper & Brothers.

Dix, D. (1843). *Memorial to the Legislature of Massachusetts.* Boston: Munroe and Frances.

Dwyer, E. (1987). *Homes for the Mad: Life Inside Two Nineteenth-century Asylums.* New Brunswick: Rutgers University Press.

Freud, A. (1964). Psychoanalytic Knowledge and Its Application to Children's Services. *The Writings of Anna Freud, Vol. V: Research at the Hampstead Clinic and Other Papers* (pp. 460–469). New York: International Universities Press.

Furman, R. A., & Katan, A. (1969). *A Therapeutic Nursery School.* New York: International Universities Press.

Galt, J. M. (1846). *The Treatment of Insanity.* New York: Harper & Brothers.

Goffman, E. (1961). *Asylums: Essays on the Social Situation of Mental Patients and Other Inmates.* Garden City, NY: Doubleday/Anchor Books.

Grob, G. N. (1965). *The State and Mentally Ill.* Chapel Hill: University of North Carolina Press.

Grosenick, J. K., George, M. P., & George, N. L. (1987). A Profile of School Programs for the Behaviorally Disordered: Twenty Years after Morse, Cutler, and Fink. *Behavioral Disorders* 12, 159–168.

Hale, N. G. (1971). *Freud and the Americans: The Beginnings of Psychoanalysis in the United States, 1876–1917.* New York: Oxford University Press.

Hildreth, G. H. (1930). *Psychological Services for School Problems.* Yonkers-on-Hudson, NY: World Book Co.

Hiner, N. R., & Hawes, J. M. (1985). *Growing up in America; Children in Historical Perspective.* Chicago: University of Illinois Press.

Hobbs, N. (1964) Mental health's third revolution. *American Journal of Orthopsychiatry* (34) 5, 822–833.

———. (1982). *The Troubled and Troubling Child.* San Francisco: Jossey-Bass.

Holl, J. M. (1971). *Juvenile Reform in the Progressive Era: William R. George and the Junior Republic Movement.* Ithaca: Cornell University Press.

Joint Commission on Mental Health of Children. (1970). *Crisis in Child Mental Health: Challenge for the 1970s.* New York: Harper & Row.

Jones, K. W. (1999). *Taming the Troublesome Child: American Families, Child Guidance, and the Limits of Psychiatric Authority.* Cambridge, MA: Harvard University Press.

Kanner, L. (1944). The Origins and Growth of Child Psychiatry. *American Journal of Psychiatry* 100, 139.

———. (1957). *Child Psychiatry.* Springfield, IL: Charles C. Thomas.

———. (1960). Child Psychiatry: Retrospect and Prospect. *American Journal of Psychiatry* 117, 15–22.

———. (1962). Emotionally Disturbed Children: A Historical Review. *Child Development* 33, 97–102.

Katz, M. (1986). Child Saving. *History of Education Quarterly* 26, 413–424.

Kaufman, J. (1993). *Characteristics of Emotional and Behavioral Disorders of Children and Youth* (5th ed.). New York: Merrill/Macmillan.

Kessler, J. W. (1966). *Psychopathology of Childhood.* Englewood Cliffs, NJ: Prentice Hall, Inc.

Kratochwill, T. R., & Morris, R. J. (1991). *The Practice of Child Therapy* (2nd ed.). Elmsford, NY: Pergamon Press.

Linton, T. E. (1971). The Educateur Model: A Theoretical Monograph. *Journal of Special Education* 5(2), 155–190.

Long, N. J., Morse, W. C., & Newman, R. G., eds. (1971). *Conflict in the Classroom: The Education of Children with Problems* (2nd ed.). Belmont, CA: Wadsworth.

Morse, W. C., Cutler, R. L., & Fink, A. H. (1964). *Public School Classes for the Emotionally Handicapped: A Research Analysis.* Washington, DC: Council for Exceptional Children.

Moustakas, C. E. (1953). *Children in Play Therapy.* New York: McGraw-Hill.

Pearson, G.H.J. (1954). *Psychoanalysis and the Education of the Child.* New York: W. W. Norton.

Polsky, H. N. (1962). *Cottage Six.* New York: Russell Sage Foundation.

Redl, F. (1959). The Concept of a Therapeutic Milieu. *American Journal of Orthopsychiatry* 29, 1–18.

Redl, F., & Wineman, D. (1957). *The Aggressive Child.* (Contains *Children who hate* and *Controls from within.*) Glencoe, IL: The Free Press.

Rosen, G. (1968). *Madness in Society: Chapters in the Historical Sociology of Mental Illness.* Chicago: University of Chicago Press.

Rothman, D. (1971). *The Discovery of the Asylum: Social Order and Disorder in the New Republic.* Boston: Little, Brown.

Rush, B. (1812–1962). *Medical Inquiries and Observations Upon the Diseases of the Mind.* New York: Hafner (Facsim., 1962). New York: Harper.

Szasz, T. S. (1970). *The Manufacture of Madness: A Comparative Study of the Inquisition and the Mental Health Movement.* New York: Harper & Row.

Wallin, J.E.W. (1914). *The Mental Health of the School Child: The Psychoeducational Clinic in Relation to Child Welfare.* New Haven, CT: Yale University Press.

Zilboorg, G., & Henry, G. W. (1941). *A History of Medical Psychology.* New York: W. W. Norton.

VI. A SAMPLING OF REFERENCES ON THE HISTORY OF CHILDHOOD

Addams, J. (1911). *Twenty Years at Hull House.* Chautauqua, NY: Chautauqua Press.

Ames, L. B. (1989). *Arnold Gesell—Themes of His Work.* New York: Plenum/Human Sciences.

Aries, P. (1962). *Centuries of Childhood: A Social History of Family Life.* New York: Knopf.

Bremner, R. H., ed. (1971). *Children and Youth in America: A Documentary History, Vol. 1, 1600–1865; Vol. II, 1866–1932.* Cambridge, MA: Harvard University Press.

deMause, L., ed. (1974). *The History of Childhood.* New York: The Psycho-history Press.

Demos, J. (1970). *A Little Commonwealth: Family Life in Plymouth Colony.* New York: Oxford University Press.

Elkind, D. (1981). *The Hurried Child.* Reading, MA: Addison-Wesley.

Fass, P. S., editor in chief. (2004). *Encyclopedia of Children and Childhood in History and Society* (3 vols.). New York: Macmillan Reference USA.

Frazier, T. R., ed. (1971). *The Underside of American History.* New York: Harcourt Brace Jovanovich.

Gesell, A. (1930). A Decade of Progress in the Mental Hygiene of the Preschool Child. *Annals of the American Academy of Political and Social Sciences* 151, 143–148.

———. (1948). *Studies in Child Development.* New York: Harper.

———. (1949). Human Infancy and the Ontogenesis of Behavior. *American Scientist* 37, 529–553.

Goldstein, J., Freud, A., & Solnit, A. J. (1973). *Beyond the Best Interests of the Child.* New York: Macmillan.

Greenleaf, B. K. (1978). *Children Through The Ages: A History of Childhood.* New York: McGraw-Hill.

Hall, G. S. (1904). *Adolescence.* New York: D. Appleton.

Handlin, O., & Handlin, M. F. (1971). *Facing Life: Youth and the Family in American History.* Boston: Little, Brown.

Hawes, J. M., & Hiner, N. R., eds. (1985). *American Childhood: A Research Guide and Historical Handbook.* Westport, CT: Greenwood.

History of Childhood Quarterly.

Hulbert, A. (2003). *Raising America: Experts, Parents, and a Century of Advice About Children.* New York: Knopf.

Mead, M., & Wolfenstein, M., eds. (1954). *Childhood in Contemporary Cultures.* Chicago: University of Chicago Press.

Mintz, S. (2004). *Huck's Raft: A History of American Childhood.* Cambridge, MA: Belknap Press of Harvard University Press.

Montessori, M. (1914–1964). *Dr. Montessori's Own Handbook.* Cambridge, MA: Robert Bentley.

———. (1917–1965). *Spontaneous Activity in Education.* New York: Schocken Books.

Payne, G. H. (1916). *The Child in Human Progress.* New York: G. P. Putnam's Sons.

Schwartz, M. J. (2000). *Born in Bondage.* Cambridge, MA: Harvard University Press.

Vandewalker, N. C. (1917). *The Kindergarten in American Education.* New York: Macmillan.

Watson, J. B. (1928). *Psychological Care of Infant and Child.* New York: Norton.

Weber, L. (1969). *The Kindergarten: Its Encounter with Educational Thought.* New York: Teachers College Press.

White House Conference on the Care of Dependent Children. (1909). *Proceedings of the Conference on the Care of Dependent Children.* Washington, DC: U.S. Government Printing Office.

Wishy, B. W. (1968). *The Child and The Republic: The Dawn of Modern American Child Nurture.* Philadelphia: University of Pennsylvania Press.

VII. RESOURCES ON THE WORLD WIDE WEB

Disability Studies: Historical Resources

Center on Human Policy, Syracuse University: Disability Studies for Teachers http://disabilitystudiesforteachers.org/.

Disability History Museum http://www.disabilitymuseum.org.

Disability Social History Project. http://www.disabilityhistory.org.

Disability Studies: Annotated Bibliography on Community Integration, Third Edition http://thechp.syr.edu/abdisstu.htm.

Disability Studies in the Humanities. http://www.georgetown.edu/crossroads/interests/ds-hum/.

Journal of Deaf Studies and Deaf Education http://deafed.oupjournals.org/.

Gallaudet University Archives http://archives.gallaudet.edu/lefttool.html.

Laurent Clerc National Deaf Education Center, Gallaudet University: History-related Web Pages http://clerccenter.gallaudet/edu/InfoToGo/history-info.html.

Overbrook School for the Blind: Library Web Page http://www.obs.org/library/library_web_page-overbrook_school.htm.

Perkins School for the Blind: Museum http://www.perkins.org/section.php?id=211.

The Review of Disability Studies: An International Journal http://www.rds.hawaii.edu/.

Selected Annotated Bibliography: Disability Studies and Mental Retardation (Compiled by Steve Taylor and Perri Harris); reprinted from *Disability Studies Quarterly*, 16(3), 4–13. http://soeweb.syr.edu/thechp/dsbiblio.htm.

Society for Disability Studies and *Disability Studies Quarterly* journal http://www.uic.edu/orgs/sds/.

Children's Literature and Disability

Resources You Can Use: Children's Literature & Disability. A publication of the National Dissemination Center for Children with Disabilities, Resource List 5 (BIB5). 2nd Edition, June 2001 http://www.nichcy.org/pubs/bibliog/bib5txt.htm.

Other Resources for and about Persons with Disabilities

Many of the web pages listed here have links to information of historical interest concerning children with disabilities in America.

Alexander Graham Bell Association for the Deaf and Hard of Hearing http://www.agbell.org/DesktopDefault.aspx.

American Association on Mental Retardation http://www.aamr.org/.

American Council of the Blind http://www.acb.org.

American Occupational Therapy Association, Inc. http://www.aota.org/.

American Orthopsychiatric Association http://www.amerortho.org/home.htm.

American Physical Therapy Association http://www.apta.org/.

American Psychiatric Association http://www.psych.org/.

American Psychological Association http://www.apa.org/.

American Speech-Language-Hearing Association (ASHA) http://www.asha.org/default.htm.

The ARC of the United States http://www.thearc.org.

Autism Society of America http://www.autism-society.org/site/PageServer.

Children's Defense Fund http://www.childrensdefense.org/data/default.aspx.

Council for Exceptional Children http://www.cec.sped.org/.

Disability Directory: Resource Links to Disability Related Websites http://disabilitydirectory.lovebyrd.com/.

Epilepsy Foundation http://www.epilepsyfoundation.org.

Individuals with Disabilities Education Act Amendments and Regulations of 1997 http://www.cec.sped.org/law_res/doc/law/index.php.

Information Center on Disabilities and Gifted Education, Council for Exceptional Children http://ericec.org/digests/e583.html.

Learning Disabilities Association of America http://www.ldaamerica.org.

National Association of Social Workers http://www.socialworkers.org/.

National Resource Center on AD/HD http://www.help4adhd.org/en/about/what.

National Resources, A Publication of the National Dissemination Center for Children with Disabilities. http://nichcy.org/pubs/genresc/gr2.htm.

TASH: Equity, Opportunity, and Inclusion for People with Disabilities since 1975. http://www.tash.org/.

Tourette Syndrome Association, Inc. http://www.tsa-usa.org/news_events.html.

United Cerebral Palsy http://www.ucp.org/.

World Association for Infant Mental Health http://www.kaimh.org/video.htm.

Index

School exclusion policies, 105
Schools for blind and deaf students, 7,
  8, 37
Schools for the blind: curriculum of,
  36–37, 44; family-cottage system in,
  38; public funding of, 37; pupil
  demographics of, 37; technology in,
  38, 44–45
Schools for the deaf: public funding
  of, 8, 9; pupil demographics of, 8;
  religious influence in, 6–7
Schowalter, J. W., 102
Scullin, M. H., 67, 68
Searl, S. J., 68, 70
Section 504, Public Law, 93–112, Voca-
  tional Rehabilitation Act, 34
Seguin, Edouard, 72
Sellers, C., 53
Semba, R. D., 40
Seriously emotionally disturbed (SED),
  as special education classification,
  106
Settlement houses, 52
Shifflett, Dorothy, 23
Sight-saving classes, 39, 42–43. *See also*
  Low vision
Sigourney, Lydia, 116, 118–119
Singer, G.H.S., 65, 73
Sleeter, Christine E., 105
Smith, A., 66, 67, 69
Smith, J. D., 67
Smith, L., 16
Snow, K., 69
Social Darwinism, 11
Social isolation: and blind children, 44–
  45; and deaf children, 19–21
Social maladjustment, and serious
  emotional disturbance, 106
Society for the Instruction and Mainte-
  nance of the Indigent Deaf and
  Dumb and Blind, 8
Society for the Prevention of Delin-
  quency, 95
Sonia Shankman Orthogenic School,
  99
Southard School, Menninger Founda-
  tion, 99

Specific learning disabilities, 100, 105,
  106, 107
Standford, Rev. John, 5, 8
Stanford-Binet Intelligence Scale, 68
Starr, P., 54
Stein, G., 55
Sterilization, involuntary, of persons
  with disabilities, 32, 74, 76, 151–152
Stiker, H., 67
Stokoe, W., 23
Story of a Bad Boy, The (Aldrich), 92
Stough, L. M., 32
Stout, Judy Cummings, 19
Sullivan, Anne, 32, 128–129
Sullivan, Joseph F., 49–52, 57, 59
Supalla, S., 19, 22

TASH, 80
Taylor, S. J., 68, 70
Tay-Sachs Disease, 32
Telecommunication Devices for the
  Deaf (TDD), 21
Texas School for the Deaf (Texas Deaf
  and Dumb Asylum), 15
Texas State Lunatic Asylum, 163
Thom, D. A., 101
Thomas, S. B., 33
Thorndike, Augustus, 55, 59
Thoryk, R., 22
Thurston, H., 95
Tierney, D., 44, 45
Total Communication, and deaf educa-
  tion, 23
Trachoma epidemic, in reservation
  schools for Native Americans, 40–41
Tracy, M. L., 106
Traumatic brain injury (TBI), 106, 107
Trent, J., 54
Trent, J. W., 68, 79
Tuberculosis, 40
Tuke, William, 88, 93
Turner, W., 9
Twain, Mark (Samuel Clemens), 73, 91–
  93

U.S. Children's Bureau, 102
Umansky, L., 69

About the Editors and Contributors

PHILIP L. SAFFORD is Adjunct Professor of Psychology and Associate Director of Teacher Licensure at Case Western Reserve University. He is also Emeritus Professor of Special Education at Kent State University, where he chaired the special education program and directed federally funded projects preparing specialists in early intervention with young children with developmental delays or disabilities. Prior to earning his Ph.D. through the Combined Program in Education and Psychology at the University of Michigan, Phil had been a teacher and administrator in programs for children with serious emotional disturbance. His publications include *Human Diversity in Education: An Integrative Approach*, co-authored with Kenneth Cushner and Averil McClelland, now in its fifth edition (2006); *A History of Childhood and Disability*, co-authored with his daughter, Elizabeth J. Safford (1996); and several texts in early childhood/special education.

ELIZABETH J. SAFFORD, who previously collaborated with Philip L. Safford in writing *A History of Childhood and Disability*, earned her Master of Arts degree in history, with emphasis in historical editing, from Northeastern Unversity and her Master of Library Science degree from Kent State University. Currently Reference Librarian for the Nevins Library, in Methuen, Massachusetts, while also working as a freelance academic text editor, Beth has had prior experience as a research librarian, Donor Relations Administrator with Boston University, Data Processing Coordinator with the Schepens Eye Research Institute, and Editorial Assistant with *The Journal of Orthopaedic Research*, *The New England Quarterly*, and *World Almanac* publications.

ANGELA BATTISTONE-POTOSKY, who received the Cleveland YWCA Award for Woman of Professional Excellence in 2005, is a graduate of Franklin University. An instructor in American Sign Language (ASL) at Lakeland Community College, in Kirtland, Ohio, as well as an accountant in a Cleveland firm, Angie is a member of the Ohio and the National Associations of the Deaf, and has served as a member of the Board of Trustees of the Cleveland Signstage Theatre. She co-authored, with Robertta Thoryk and Patricia Roberts, "Both Emic and Etic: A View of the World through the Lens of the Ugly Duckling" in *Semiotics and Dis/Ability: Interrogating Categories of Difference* (2001).

ELIZABETH L. BRENNAN, whose Ph.D. in Special Education was earned at Kent State University, has been a faculty member at Saint Mary's College, in California, where she coordinated the special education program, and Research Coordinator for the Early Childhood Research Institute on Inclusion (ECRII) at San Francisco State University. Beth's clinical and administrative experience in agencies serving young children with disabilities and their families reflects her particular interests, which have also been the focus of her publications and professional presentations.

BRAD BYROM received his Ph.D. from the University of Iowa and is a tenured professor of history at MiraCosta College in Oceanside, California. His research interests focus on disability history and progressivism in the early twentieth century. Brad has previously published book chapters on the development of institutions for children with disabilities, including "A Pupil and a Patient: Hospital Schools in Progressive America" in *The New Disability History: American Perspectives* (2001), and the life of Joseph F. Sullivan.

CAROL LINSENMEIER, who recently completed her Ph.D. at Kent State University in Special Education, has extensive experience as a teacher of students with disabilities and as a program administrator. As Music Chair of The Fine Arts Association, in northeast Ohio, Carol oversaw a music curriculum that has a strong focus on inclusion of children and adults with disabilities. Carol is also Adjunct Professor of Violin and Viola at Lake Erie College, in Painesville, Ohio.

JEFF MOYER, an often-honored and versatile advocate within the Disability Rights Movement, is well known as a composer, writer, concert performer, radio personality, and speaker, who has been called "The Troubadour of Inclusiion." Titles of Jeff's published musical productions for schools include *We're People First: A Celebration of Diversity* and *How Big Is Your Circle? A Musical Promoting Healing of Exclusion, Ridicule & Violence*. He composed and performed the music and lyrics for the TASH Silver Anniversary

Album, *See How Far We've Come.* Among his most recent releases is a two-CD set entitled *Lest We Forget,* an oral history based on his interviews with pesons who had lived in state institutions in Ohio.

FRED PALCHIK, who is a graduate of Gallaudet University with a major in Accounting, is currently a lecturer at Kent State University, where he teaches all levels of American Sign Language, monitors and updates ASL instruction for Kent's ASL major, and promotes and implements inclusion of hearing ASL students in area activities of the Deaf community. Fred is also President/CEO of the Greater Akron (Ohio) Deaf Services. His main goal is to achieve greater public awareness and understanding of Deaf persons, especially children.

ROBERTTA THORYK, who has extensive professional experience in schools and in clinical settings, received her clinical training in child psychology and in school psychology at Cleveland State University and her Ph.D. in Special Education at Kent State University. A frequent speaker on Deaf Culture and instructor of American Sign Language (ASL) in northeast Ohio colleges and universities, currently at Lakeland Community College in Kirtland, Ohio, Robbie co-chaired a state task force that pressed successfully for Ohio legislation recognizing AOL's legitimacy for educational credit as a foreign language. Her presentations and publications, including *Exploring the Interface between Two Cultures* (T. A. Sebeck Monograph Series, *International Journal of Applied Semiotics,* v.2, 1998), have focused on Deaf Culture identity and empowerment issues.